D0793698

Guilt and Extenuation in Tragedy

Faux Titre

ÉTUDES DE LANGUE ET LITTÉRATURE FRANÇAISES

Sous la direction de / Series Editors

Keith Busby
Sjef Houppermans
Paul Pelckmans
Emma Cayley
Alexander Roose

VOLUME 445

The titles published in this series are listed at *brill.com/faux*

Guilt and Extenuation in Tragedy

Variations on Racinian Excuses

By

Edward Forman

BRILL

RODOPI

LEIDEN | BOSTON

Cover illustration: Sarah Bernhardt as Phèdre in Racine's *Phèdre* by Nadar. Negative about 1874; print and mount 1880s, albumen silver print, 14.6 × 11.4 cm (5 3/4 × 4 1/2 in.), 87.XA.71.8. The J. Paul Getty Museum, Los Angeles. Digital image courtesy of the Getty's Open Content Program.

The Library of Congress Cataloging-in-Publication Data is available online at http://catalog.loc.gov
LC record available at http://lccn.loc.gov/2020040608

Typeface for the Latin, Greek, and Cyrillic scripts: "Brill". See and download: brill.com/brill-typeface.

ISSN 0167-9392
ISBN 978-90-04-44277-1 (hardback)
ISBN 978-90-04-44278-8 (e-book)

Copyright 2021 by Koninklijke Brill NV, Leiden, The Netherlands.
Koninklijke Brill NV incorporates the imprints Brill, Brill Hes & De Graaf, Brill Nijhoff, Brill Rodopi, Brill Sense, Hotei Publishing, mentis Verlag, Verlag Ferdinand Schöningh and Wilhelm Fink Verlag.
All rights reserved. No part of this publication may be reproduced, translated, stored in a retrieval system, or transmitted in any form or by any means, electronic, mechanical, photocopying, recording or otherwise, without prior written permission from the publisher. Requests for re-use and/or translations must be addressed to Koninklijke Brill NV via brill.com.

This book is printed on acid-free paper and produced in a sustainable manner.

For Debbie, of course
with apologies that it took so long
(*it's just been one thing after another ...*)

∴

Contents

Preface   IX

Introduction   1
1 Approaches to Guilt in Tragedy and Life   2
2 Performance   10
3 Words   14
4 *Phèdre*   17

1 **Helplessness**   22
  1 Fatalism in Racine   25
  2 Agamemnon   30
  3 The Seventeenth Century   35
  4 Divine Authority   40
  5 Genetic Determinism   42
  6 The Sense of the Inevitable   46

2 **Flaws, Errors and Excuses: Theories of Hamartia**   49
  1 Aristotle   52
  2 Flaw versus Error   56
  3 Renaissance and Pre-Classical   61
  4 Racine   64
  5 Hamartia Re-Assessed   79

3 **Ignorance**   81
  1 Theories   82
  2 Oedipus at Thebes and at Colonus   86
  3 Deianeira   89
  4 Hercules, Agave and Others   96
  5 Credulity – Macbeth and Others   99
  6 *Phèdre*   101
  7 Oedipus Revisited   102

4 **Diminished Responsibility: Medea and the *Crime passionnel***   108
  1 Euripides   111
  2 Early-Modern and Modern Medeas   116
  3 Corneille   119

5 **Provocation: The Defence of Clytemnestra** 130
   1 Racine 135
   2 Twentieth-century France: Giraudoux and Sartre 138
   3 Marguerite Yourcenar 142
   4 Jean Anouilh 146
   5 Jean-Jacques Varoujean, Jean-Pierre Giraudoux 149

6 **Saul, King of Israel, as Tragic Hero in French Drama** 155
   1 Jean de la Taille 159
   2 Pierre du Ryer 163
   3 Augustin Nadal 168
   4 Voltaire 175
   5 Alphonse de Lamartine 177
   6 André Gide 180

7 **Scapegoats: Passing the Buck to Snakes, Partners, Parents and Others** 184
   1 Parents 186
   2 Teachers, Advisors, Counsellors 195
   3 Spouses and Other Partners 201
   4 Devils and Demons 208

   Bibliography 217
   Index of Names and Subjects 226
   Index of Plays 228

Preface

Our ethical culture is rightly tolerant and compassionate. Our ethos is responsive to exceptions, excuses and justifications. As a result, we have become clever at concocting imagined grounds for exoneration. Some people seem to believe somewhere out there lies a good excuse that can redeem them. We run from blame, even when the choices we have made are clearly wrong. That bad habit is threatening to turn America into a culture of cheaters. We must shake the habit of overreliance on exceptions, excuses and justifications.

Ethical behaviour is not simply a matter of 'fessing up' after you get caught. [...] It is certainly admirable to take the blame after getting caught, but it is even better not to cave in to the rationalizations that lead to unethical conduct in the first place.[1]

∴

This diagnosis is by no means confined to America, and the extract and the attitudes which it both charts and challenges provide the framework for the discussions in this book. One symptom of the condition diagnosed is a move to re-interpret dramatic stories from classical mythology in such a way as to explore, on behalf of the protagonists, excuses which they might not previously have thought of. Such defensive re-appraisals of shameful characters abound: even such apparent monsters as the child-slayer Medea or the husband-killer Clytemnestra are portrayed in ways that seek to understand, explain or even exonerate their crimes. If Macbeth – or Othello – has not yet been diagnosed as suffering from post-traumatic stress disorder, it seems only a matter of time – Jason certainly has. The biblical King Saul was given tragic dignity through his transformation by Gide into something approaching a gay icon, tortured by repressed feelings into a state of diminished responsibility. These and other test cases will be examined in the ensuing chapters as we explore the ways in which excuses are used within tragic drama to open debates about guilt and exoneration which are often central to the works' moral impact.

---

1 A.L. Allen, *The New Ethics: A Guided Tour of the 21st-century Moral Landscape* (New York: Hyperion, Miramax Books, 2004), p. 258.

This is a work of literary criticism rather than moral philosophy, but it draws on ethics (both old and new) as well as performance theory and reception theory to try to bring out how the study of classical tragedy – ancient, early modern French and twentieth-century adaptations – can inform debates on moral issues that continue to challenge society, however old they may appear. Central to the study is French seventeenth-century tragedy, the plays on ancient classical themes by Racine, Corneille and their contemporaries, for no better reason than that that is where my professional expertise lies. I have sought to explore their distinctiveness by comparing them to the ancient models and to modern adaptations, and I have not resisted the temptation to bring in comparative comments from other cultures, in particular Shakespeare, where they have seemed relevant to the argument or its illustration. What I bring to the discussion is over thirty-five years of interaction with undergraduate and postgraduate students on these matters at the University of Bristol. It is conventional at this point to thank them for what they have taught me, and I am grateful to each generation of them for the stimulation they provided. The commonest experience relevant to this study is this: seminars exploring responsibility and extenuation in a particular tragedy would usually take the form of some variant on the hardy standby of the mock trial, and I would generally allocate roles to individual students or small buzz groups by lot. The students did not always know in advance what other students (who would become their opponents in debate) were being asked to do. The surprising thing is how often a student who vocally wished they had not been given the task allocated them turned out a week later to be a most passionate advocate of that cause, indeed a committed convert to it! If anything can justify this book it is that: the plays I am studying, centuries after they were written, raise questions about moral choices, responsibilities and extenuations that continue to stimulate live debate in ever-changing new social environments.

I do acknowledge a greater debt still to those postgraduate doctoral students whom I have had the privilege to supervise in related fields. Véronique Desnain and Ramona Dana Lungu sparred with me patiently over many years on the plays and interpretations which form the substance of the book. In the context of a postgraduate supervision session, it really is impossible to determine which idea or expression originated in which mind, so I hope that if they think they instigated a train of thought that has ended up in these pages, they will accept this blanket acknowledgement. Neither I nor this book would be the same without my contacts with them, and Véro's existing and Dana's forthcoming publications deserve to remain on university reading lists.

I would like finally to record my gratitude to the editorial colleagues at Brill for their perceptiveness, patience and meticulous attention to detail: Christa Stevens, Paul Pelckmans and Carina van den Hoven.

Earlier versions of chapters 5 and 6 were previously published as follows:

'The Provoked Wife: The Defence of Clytemnestra in Twentieth-century French Drama', *Essays in French Literature*, 44, 2007, pp. 85–108 (ISSN 0071-139X)

'"Pour être donc humain j'éprouve sa colère!" Saul, King of Israel, as Tragic Hero in French Drama', *Modern Language Review*, 108, 2013, pp. 438-458 (ISSN 0026-7937)

We are grateful to the *Essays* and to MHRA for permission to republish them here.

There being a readily available translation into English blank verse of the plays dealt with in most detail, I spared myself the daunting task of providing my own. All translations from Racine are therefore taken from the relevant Penguin Classics translations by John Cairncross:

Racine, *Andromache, Britannicus, Berenice* (London: Penguin Books, 1967)

Racine, *Iphigenia, Phaedra, Athalia* (London: Penguin Books, 1963)

On the rare occasions when I have suggested alternative renderings of individual words, this is not to imply that Professor Cairncross could have done better within the constraints of his commission to provide accurate but performable texts. I have sometimes merely pointed out small nuances or resonances, most often associated with the use of tenses or modal verbs, that his version could not quite convey. All other translations from French texts are my own.

Introduction

'Natcherly we're punks!' The Jets in *West Side Story* present a riotous fantasy about their day in court, in which they mockingly take on the roles of authority figures who use the justice system to find excuses for scoundrels.

> Dear kindly Sergeant Krupke,
> You gotta understand,
> It's just our bringin' upke
> That gets us out of hand.

Poor parenting and an absence of healthy role models: the hoodlum unwittingly gives himself the helpless status of an Orestes or a Hippolytos.

> Our mothers all are junkies,
> Our fathers all are drunks.
> Golly Moses, natcherly we're punks!

Genetic determinism within dysfunctional families: they are as doomed as Racine's Phèdre or Néron to be helplessly overwhelmed by shameful instincts.

> My parents treat me rough.
> They didn't wanna have me,
> But somehow I was had.
> Leapin' lizards, that's why I'm so bad!

Environmental determinism, too: they claim just as much right as Electra or Agamemnon to feel trapped in situations of helplessness.

> The trouble is he's crazy.
> The trouble is he drinks.
> The trouble is he's lazy.
> The trouble is he stinks.

Mad or bad, ignorant or misled, their responsibility is diminished in a comparable way to that of a Medea or an Oedipus.

> My Daddy beats my Mommy
> My Mommy clobbers me
> My Grandpa is a Commie

© KONINKLIJKE BRILL NV, LEIDEN, 2021 | DOI:10.1163/9789004442788_002

My Grandma pushes tea
My sister wears a mustache
My brother wears a dress
Goodness Gracious, that's why I'm a mess!

Again, genetic determinism linked to ingrained abnormality, coupled with provocation: the Jets in this caricatural view have no more hope than the Atrides of escaping a cycle of violence and retribution, more especially since all this arises within a gang culture informed by strong peer pressure to resist the norms of conventional society, to conform only to non-conformist attitudes, and to respond with violence (akin to what in other cultures might be called 'honour killing') to any perceived external threat. Their analysis of the underlying causes of (or excuses for) their own delinquency even brings them close to articulating an awareness of the sort of moral ambiguity that characterizes Aristotle's ethical standpoint:

We ain't no delinquents
We're misunderstood
Deep down inside us there is good!

The hoodlum presumes to see himself as an exemplification of the theory of hamartia, an essentially virtuous figure who falls short as a result of forces that are not always under his own control.

Genetic predisposition, inadequate education or unhealthy role models, environmental pressures, a quest for scapegoats or others to blame, ignorance, any of which factors can be interpreted as leading to a general sense of diminished responsibility: almost all the excuses for deviant behaviour that are adduced in our own day by liberal social workers are here raised and mocked by the very delinquents those social workers are seeking to understand and defend. Sarcasm and a quest for someone else to blame provide a promising refuge for the scoundrel: 'Hey, I'm depraved on account I'm deprived!'

1   Approaches to Guilt in Tragedy and Life

Sociologist Anthony Walsh cited this song with the comment: 'Pundits on both the political left and right would agree with them. The left blames criminal behaviour on financial poverty, and the right moral poverty.'[1] Here, indeed, is one

---

1 A. Walsh, *Love: The Biology behind the Heart* (New Brunswick, NJ: Transaction Publishers, 2016), p. 89.

expression of the frustration of religious orthodoxy in the face of a tendency to identify and cling to excuses in extenuation of personal decision-making:[2]

> In the area of freedom and responsibility, the discoveries of psychology about subconscious motivation and the influence of heredity and environment tend to lessen people's sense of guilt and consequently their admission of sin. It is frequently believed that because a motive for an action can be identified, the action was not fully free, and so the evils in the world can be attributed to outside forces and circumstances beyond our control.

Drawing a balance between extenuation and evasion in the analysis of excuses is certainly delicate. This study looks at excuses, with reference not to sarcastic delinquents and caricatures, but to the serious cases raised by the characters of tragedy. What characterizes tragedy is the exploration of areas of moral or ethical ambiguity, where responsibility, guilt and shame are felt by the protagonists, but where they, or their family and friends, or more detached observers, are made aware of sufficient extenuating factors to raise awkward and deep questions about the justice of a universe in which their misdemeanours, miscalculations or errors of judgment are followed by apparently disproportionate retribution. Setting guilty actions against potentially extenuating circumstances is as much part of the study of tragedy as it is of the investigation of crime, and the mock trial remains a popular and fruitful vehicle for seminars on tragic plays. If 'the legal system is in the business of asking for and evaluating the merits of the excuses provided by defence attorneys',[3] much the same might be said of tragic drama. My hope here is that the interaction of ancient stories with modern attitudes, setting the deadly serious against the cynical, the defensive and the legalistic, will indeed enable us to negotiate that borderline both in life and art with greater certainty.

At the centre of the study will be the classical tragedies of seventeenth-century France. These have been the central focus of my attention throughout my professional life, so there is no need to apologize for that priority, but I do think that the characters of Racine, like those of Classical Greek tragedy from which many of their stories are taken, have a tendency to convey their helplessness more hauntingly than those from other tragic traditions. Although I did not set out explicitly to produce a history of extenuation, some suggestive patterns have emerged, underpinning if not necessarily justifying my central focus on

---

2 S. Fagan, S.M., *Has Sin Changed?: A Book on Forgiveness* (Dublin: Gill & Macmillan, 1977), p. 4.
3 C.R. Snyder, R.L. Higgins and R.J. Stucky, *Excuses: Masquerades in Search of Grace* (New York: Wiley, 1983), p. 300.

three periods of literary history. Tragedians in the ancient world reflected the view that malevolent gods or depersonalized fate controlled the behaviour of helpless humans. A thread of belief and art in seventeenth-century France (directly or indirectly influenced by the transmission of such fatalism into Christianity by Saint Augustine of Hippo and/or Calvin) expressed a similar sense of impotence, coupled more explicitly with a sense of shame. And in the second half of the twentieth century, as we have just seen, serious consideration was given to re-evaluating the very nature of individual human responsibility, and adaptations or reworkings of myths from the ancient world were a common vehicle for fresh explorations of different forms of extenuation. The following chapters will therefore for the most part examine the presentation in tragedies from those three periods – classical antiquity, seventeenth-century France and the late twentieth century up to the present time – of key figures whose fate illuminates attitudes towards responsibility, guilt and extenuation of various sorts. Agamemnon and the biblical figure of King Saul demonstrate a general sense of helplessness in the face of uncontrollable external forces, Oedipus the excuse of ignorance, Medea the plea of diminished responsibility and Clytemnestra the more technical variant of the latter, provocation.

I would not wish to exaggerate a claim that the seventeenth century was a turning-point in the history of extenuation or excuse-seeking, but there does seem to be a haunting preoccupation with guilt, shame and human worthlessness in the plays of Racine and some of his contemporaries. At the risk of over-simplification, we might feel that tragedies in the Shakespearean tradition seek to explain human failings whilst continuing to uphold humanist values and celebrate the human spirit, whereas those of Racine point towards a disintegration of that human spirit and are more likely to seek refuge in excuses. Projects like *Shakespeare Behind Bars*[4] have claimed considerable success in aiding the rehabilitation of offenders through engagement with Shakespeare, but I would be very cautious about introducing Racine's tragedies to such troubled souls. Is it not likely that violent criminals would embrace the excuses for weakness or sin put forward by or on behalf of such as Néron, Oreste, Clytemnestre or Agamemnon, and be sucked by their example into an attitude of 'There you are, that's what I'm like, I couldn't help who I was or what I did'?[5]

It is Racine's *Phèdre* that for me most powerfully exemplifies an excruciating balance between blame and extenuation, and it is for that reason that

---

4   http://www.shakespearebehindbars.org/.
5   There is a whimsical but haunting exploration of this mind-set in Natalie Haynes's novel, *The Amber Fury* (London: Corvus, 2014).

I consider it one of the most powerful tragedies ever written. In practice, everyone involved contributes substantially to the tragic outcome, yet in each individual case a defence counsel would have, if not an easier task than the prosecution, at least a solid list of extenuating circumstances to draw on. The play, in short, is a study in excuses. If we summarize the actions of the play in tabular form, it is not hard to see how the events can be spun in several ways: here, the left hand column puts the responsibility for the terrible outcome squarely on Phèdre's shoulders, the second articulates her potential excuses and blames others, whilst the third explores a further set of excuses on behalf of those potential scapegoats.

King Thésée of Athens, departing on a journey, leaves his wife Phèdre, former princess of Crete, in the care of his son Hippolyte. Feelings of lust which she has long harboured towards the latter, and which she has controlled only by feigning enmity and having him exiled, re-emerge, and – with active encouragement from her nurse and confident Œnone – she approaches Hippolyte and blurts out the nature of her desire for him. He rejects her with disdain: the idea of relations with his father's wife fills him with horror, and in any case he has a reputation to live up to, for chastity and the pursuit of manly virtue. In the face of his scorn, she begs him to kill her,	Phèdre, having been married to Thésée for dynastic reasons, finds herself abandoned by him with no explanation. Having hitherto successfully combated the temptation posed by her stepson – closer in age to her than her husband is – she is now forced to live in proximity to the young prince. She feels herself to be in the grip of an uncontrollable passion, but her urge to commit suicide is resisted by her nurse who uses emotional blackmail to force her to admit the cause of her distress. At that moment, the news of Thésée's death is apparently confirmed, and Œnone persuades Phèdre to approach Hippolyte to safeguard the political interests of	Œnone encourages her beloved princess to reveal the cause of her distress, only so that she can support her and save her from the pernicious effects of depression, anorexia and sleeplessness.

Once Thésée's death is confirmed, Œnone realizes that Phèdre's feelings for Hippolyte are neither adulterous nor incestuous. It is only to |

clutching his own sword to attempt suicide, but is hustled off by Œnone.

Phèdre's sons by Thésée. In Hippolyte's presence, however, her irresistible feelings overcome her and she reveals them to him. At once, however, she regrets this and again is prevented from suicide only by Œnone's intervention.

talk about the political consequences of the power vacuum that Œnone encourages her to see Hippolyte. She could not predict Phèdre's inability to control her tongue.

Thésée, reports of whose death had been reaching Trézène, now returns unexpectedly, and Phèdre is filled with shame over her feelings and actions. To save her mistress from public humiliation and certain death, Œnone suggests and (with Phèdre's encouragement) implements a scheme to convince Thésée that Hippolyte had attempted to rape Phèdre – his sword, which they still have in their possession, supports this accusation. Thésée believes Œnone and calls down on Hippolyte a curse which his tutelary god Neptune has promised to grant him. As a result, Hippolyte is killed when his horses stampede, frightened by a sea monster.

At this point, to Phèdre's further shame and horror, it is revealed that Thésée is not dead, but has returned. In despair and shame she is too weak to resist Œnone's persistent suggestions that they accuse Hippolyte of violence towards her.

On overhearing Thésée's frenzied anger, Phèdre does make one further effort to tell him the truth, but is reduced to even greater depths of despair on learning that Hippolyte is actually in love with someone else, the Greek princess Aricie.

Œnone assumes that Thésée's love for Hippolyte is too great for him to envisage killing his son, and they are both unaware of his special relationship with Neptune. When they slander Hippolyte, therefore, they believe that they are weighing certain death for Phèdre against the relative discomfort of exile for Hippolyte.

The circumstantial evidence of the sword provokes Thésée to uncontrollable rage.

By this time, Phèdre
in shame and despair
has taken poison, but
lives long enough to
confess to Thésée both
her lust for her stepson
and her acquiescence
in Œnone's slander.
The king is left alone to
lament the death of his
innocent son.

Having taken poison,
Phèdre takes steps to
clear Hippolyte's name
before she dies, although
Thésée's promptness in
calling for his death
means that she is not in
time to save his life.

Diminished responsibility, provocation, genetic predisposition, inadequate education or unhealthy role models, scapegoats, environmental pressures, ignorance of pertinent factors: many of the excuses for deviant behaviour that we identified in analysing the Sergeant Krubke song are raised and explored, at least in embryo, by Racine, most penetratingly in *Phèdre*. His perspective, influenced by his deep study of Greek fatalism (whereas his predecessors had focussed more on Latin models such as Seneca) and by the Jansenist slant on the Christian concept of original sin and predestination,[6] may make him a special case, and *Phèdre* may be the extreme example of that individual perspective, but it is by no means isolated in the history of tragic drama. Examples abound from all periods. Would a modern Medea or Clytemnestra get away with 'manslaughter on the grounds of diminished responsibility', or the more precisely defined grounds of 'provocation'? Was Macbeth suffering from post-traumatic stress disorder? What does the human genome project tell us about Hamlet's feelings of helpless insecurity? Should Oedipus at Thebes have made more of his defence of ignorance, as would the shamed and ashamed Communists scathingly described in Kundera's *The Unbearable Lightness of Being*? Could Willie Loman or Stanley Kowalski have done anything, or at least more than they did, to escape from the peer pressure that led them inexorably from the American dream into the American nightmare? By investigating these potential excuses for shameful action, in law, in ethics and through the worked examples provided by tragedy, we hope to be led both towards new insights into the nature of human responsibility, and also towards a re-evaluation of the power of performance art to help us assess human behaviour with justice and compassion.

---

6 See G. Brereton, *Principles of Tragedy* (London: RKP/Florida: University of Miami Press, 1968), p. 225. These contexts will be discussed more fully below.

Tragedy opens up a sliding scale of checks and balances, suggesting parallels that are worth exploring between its ethical judgments and those made routinely within a legal framework by juries reaching verdicts and judges passing sentence. If the agent in a tragedy is obviously guilty, we see his suffering as a just punishment for wrongdoing and are unsympathetic; if he is not guilty enough, we are outraged rather than healthily cleansed by the spectacle of unjust suffering.[7] Ancient Greek fatalism has *something* in common with genetic or environmental determinism, so characters in tragedy who consider themselves to be in the grip of forces that control their feelings and thoughts, and who use this perception, with varying degrees of defiance and self-justification, as an excuse for actions which others condemn, might expect modern expert witnesses to support their pleas in extenuation. Tragedy often charts the descent of an authoritative figure into madness, so the legal notion of *mens rea* may be helpful in charting the degree of responsibility and control exercised by the character as he contemplates and takes actions that lead to catastrophe. Revenge tragedies explore the limits of justice, so that Judith Butler, in her analysis of responses to 11 September 2001, was right to urge the American leadership 'to remember the lessons of Aeschylus' in refusing a 'cycle of revenge in the name of justice'.[8] The relationship between concept and illustration can fruitfully be approached from each end: the study of Racine, Euripides and Shakespeare invites us to keep our notions of justice under review, while modern concepts of individuality and responsibility lead to a constant reassessment of classical literature and the archetypes on which it is based.

The ways in which humans feel guilty, the ways in which they are made to feel guilty, and the ways in which they sometimes resent their own feelings of guilt and shame, are the source of widespread uncertainty and unhappiness in modern societies. Contemporary developments in psychoanalysis and recent shifts in the perception of gender relationships impinge on the experience of guilt in relation to political, religious and legal structures in the west, and perhaps even more strongly as western society is regarded from a worldwide perspective. Legal and political problems do of course need legal and political solutions, but all forms of creative art can still illuminate contemporary human experience in ways which go far beyond what their creators could have envisaged. The creation in 2018 of a Chair in Law and the Arts at UCL suggests that this can be seen as a fruitful two-way collaboration.[9] In particular, those

---

7 This is the essence of the theory of hamartia, which will be explored more fully in chapter 2.
8 *Precarious Life* (London/New York: Verso, 2004), p. 17.
9 See https://www.ucl.ac.uk/laws/news/2017/jan/professor-anthony-julius-joins-ucl-first-chair -law-and-arts.

dramatic works to which the label 'tragic' has most consistently been applied explore, fruitfully and constructively for all the pain they generate, precisely the moments at which the human experience of helplessness, shame and guilt becomes problematic. The presentation and exploration of such feelings, in tragedy and in other contexts, involve assumptions about the nature of the self – the mind, the will, the soul, and how all of these relate to the body. All discussion of these assumptions has been influenced by Ancient Greek fatalism and by Senecan Stoicism; Racine's world was further informed by Jansenism; our own response to both modern and ancient dramatizations of these issues is affected by twentieth-century concepts of the psyche and by shifts in perception about the nature of individual autonomy and responsibility.

If guilt leads to shame and a sense of worthlessness, it is at best an unhelpful strategy, at worst – as tragedy often demonstrates – the trigger for moral disintegration and suicide. It is better, healthier and more fruitful to concentrate on cultivating the inner policeman that is a sense of virtue than to hold ourselves in thrall to an external controlling system based on a sense of vice. Ancient Egyptian and ancient Indian moral systems both gave restitution priority over retribution, and hence allowed for reconciliation, a fresh start and a clean slate; and modern social services have rediscovered that reward mechanisms are more likely than punishment to lead to restored relationships. In practice, Christian churches in history have frequently crushed individuals with a sense of guilt rather than liberating them with a sense of responsibility. If humanity possesses any innate sense of right and wrong, of fairness and justice, this all too easily becomes a neurotic burden. An idealistic aspiration to do ever better drives an increasing sense of frustrated failure, and any public shortcoming, however trivial, is damned as hypocrisy, as though it were preferable to have no ideals at all than to fail even marginally to live up to those that one professes. In their weekly attempts to reconcile themselves with what is presented to them as God's loving purpose, Anglican Christians, for the several hundred years during which the *Book of Common Prayer* was standard in their churches, were indoctrinated into a weekly self-imposition of the label 'miserable offenders'.

On the other hand, the healthy operation of conscience is no doubt a necessary check on excess and social deviance. The trouble is that in the world of tragedy, confession is almost always unhealthy – self-justificatory like that of Racine's Agrippine or Pyrrhus, or morbid like that of Lady Macbeth; while in the real world, in both criminological and ecclesiastical contexts, the confessional has tended to become a system of control and manipulation. The perceived reward for confessing, even to something one has not done, may be greater than the pain of continuing to be questioned, and atonement for a sinful thought may carry with it a disproportionate bonus which restores the sense of well-being of the sinner with no reference to notions of restitution or reconciliation towards those who have suffered harm.[10] What confessions replaced may indeed have been even worse – trial by ordeal, or the imposition of orthodoxy through fear of the inquisition – but the cost of escaping from those practices has been a privatization of conscience, where it is all but impossible to assess the relative costs and benefits of admitting to some excusable misdemeanour in order to avoid the risk of confronting a genuine source of shame. The artistic experience of tragic drama can surely be helpful in negotiating this balance.

2   Performance

The stories analysed here are mostly drawn from theatrical representations of human distress, and most if not all of the worked examples are open to an almost infinite range of interpretations. Statements such as 'Phèdre is wrong/ in the wrong/guilty/ashamed/helpless/defiant' are at best unhelpful, at worst meaningless, if they are divorced from the experience of a spectator witnessing a specific incarnation of the character by an actor in the context of a thought-through production of the play. When Diana Rigg portrayed Racine's Phèdre in an English translation on the London stage in 1998, the impact of her performance on any spectator was derived from at least six layers of input – Euripides, Seneca, Racine, Ted Hughes (translator), Jonathan Kent (director), Diana Rigg – and then interpreted in the light of each spectator's private preoccupations and perspectives.[11] If no two members of the audience saw it in quite the same way, this may be an uncomfortable fact for us, but it is also the point of the exercise. Phèdre's concluding speech contains the words:

> Le ciel mit dans mon sein une flamme funeste ;
> La détestable Œnone a conduit tout le reste.
>
> V, 7, 1625–26

---

10   See P. Brooks, *Troubling Confessions: Speaking Guilt in Law and Literature* (Chicago/ London: UCP, 2000).

11   The same principle applies to other notable interpretations on the London stage: Phèdre portrayed by Helen Mirren in a production by Nicholas Hytner of Ted Hughes' translation (National Theatre, 2009), or by Glenda Jackson in a production by Philip Prowse of Robert David MacDonald's translation (Old Vic and Aldwych, 1984).

[Heaven in my heart lit an ill-omened fire.
Detestable Œnone did the rest.][12]

We will return quite frequently to this couplet: does it constitute a confession, an evasion of responsibility, or a humble acknowledgment of her subservience to a higher power? The words may appear despicable and self-pitying in one production, defiant in another, serenely resigned in others, healthily self-protective or unhealthily shifty, and this effect will depend on the actors at that moment, and on the relationship they have built up with the audience throughout the production. 'Actors', because the impact of these lines depend not only on Phèdre, but also on the portrayal of Œnone, whom different productions have presented as a figure akin to Juliet's Nurse or Desdemona's Emilia, or more like a witch, Phèdre's evil genius. With all examples such as this, it is essential to remember that the implied message of drama is not fixed, even if the dramatist originally had a clear idea of the division of blame. While trying to avoid tortuous circumlocution, I will also be trying even harder to avoid saying that any given character in a play 'is' guilty or innocent, clinging as I shall to a belief that *any*, or almost any, interpretation of a play text is *possible*. Different productions will, can and should suggest different degrees of guilt, innocence, helplessness and extenuation in every dramatic situation, even the most apparently clear-cut, without necessarily betraying the text.

This interpretative ambiguity is explored by Aristotle who, in an uncharacteristically dogmatic statement, alleged that in a rather obscure play by Euripides, which survives only in fragmentary form, Alcmaeon's defence for his matricide was 'plainly ludicrous'.[13] It is an example given more current interest than it might otherwise be thought to have, because a modern reconstruction of it, incorporating some of the extant fragments, by Colin Teevan, was performed in Newcastle in 2004 under the title *Cock of the North*, and subsequently published as *Alcmaeon in Corinth*.[14]

Alcmaeon and his father Amphiaraus were relatively minor characters in the story of Polynices' assault on Thebes. Amphiaraus had been persuaded or bullied by his wife Eriphyle to join that expedition, although his prophetic powers enabled him to foresee that it would bring about his death and end in

---

12   The basic reference throughout the book is Racine, *Théâtre complet*, eds. J. Morel and A. Viala (Paris: Garnier, 1980). For translations see the Preface, above, p. XI. Note that in Cairncross's translation, Œnone has three syllables. In French it has two.

13   *Nicomachean Ethics* (3.1), edited by Sarah Broadie and Christopher Rowe (Oxford: Oxford University Press, 2002), p. 123.

14   London: Oberon Books, 2004.

disaster. Eriphyle accepted the truth of this prophecy, but had received bribes from Polynices to exert pressure on her husband, who before his departure formally charged his sons, Alcmaeon and Amphilocus, to avenge his death. When he grew up, Alcmaeon – with much reluctance and only after seeking further reassurance from the oracle – carried out this command, killing Eriphyle and (like Orestes) sinking into insanity as a result. On the face of it, this is just the sort of moral dilemma which Aeschylus and Euripides would have enjoyed teasing out, and it seems uncharacteristically insensitive of Aristotle to dismiss the defence of Alcmaeon so bluntly. Depending on how sorry he felt for the actor, he might have said either, 'Euripides doesn't give the character much to get his teeth into here', or 'In the performance I saw, the actor playing Alcmaeon totally failed to win my sympathy' – going on to consider whether this was a defect, and why the author, the actor or the director might have decided to present the play in that way. (Colin Teevan's reinterpretation of the fragments, acknowledging some advice from Edith Hall, moved the play in the direction of comedy, but it ends with 'something more bleak and profound'; Euripides' text was always referred to as a tragedy, and Aristotle lists his family, alongside those of Oedipus and Orestes, as one 'on which the best tragedies are founded'.)[15] Whatever the pros and cons in this case, we will seek, in analysing these and similar situations, to leave open the potential of any text, in the hands of real actors, to tilt the argument towards or away from sympathy. In an ideal performance, no doubt, the audience will always be made aware of the real *and* the alleged motives for any action, and will be encouraged to debate how far any extenuating circumstances are genuine, as opposed to evasive excuses.

In the case of Euripides' *Alcmaeon*, this is largely an abstract exercise since the play has survived only in fragmentary form – barely fifty lines remain, which may have come from two separate plays.[16] The fragments that have survived contain several hints that attempts were indeed made to defend, explain or excuse Alcmaeon's actions, and if the play was a successful tragedy, Aristotle should not have found it too difficult to take this defence seriously.[17] Alcmaeon's excuses include the claim that he was obeying his father's orders:

---

15   See *Alcmaeon in Corinth*, edn. cit., p. 12. Aristotle, *Poetics*, chapter 13, 1453a20.

16   See W.N. Bates, *Euripides: A Student of Human Nature* (New York: Russell and Russell, 1930, reissued 1969), pp. 207–211.

17   The fragments are edited in A. Nauck, *Tragicorum Græcorum Fragmenta* (Lipsiæ: Teubner, 1856), pp. 302–308; edited and translated into French in F. Jouan & H. van Looy (eds.), *Euripide : tome viii: Fragments, 1ᵉ Partie* (Paris: Les Belles Lettres, 1998), pp. 81–116; edited and translated into English in C. Collard & M. Cropp, *Euripides Fragments, Aegeus-Meleager* (Cambridge, MASS: Harvard University Press, 2008), pp. 79–99. The lines quoted below will be given as translated in the last of these sources.

'I was especially moved by my father's injunction [...]' (Collard, 69/Nauck, 70/ Jouan, 4). This might mean that he felt himself to be in a genuine dilemma, as shall be discussed in the next chapter: he must either kill his mother or endure his father's curse for not doing so – 'Either way, ruin', as Agamemnon will put it at Aulis. Alcmaeon further explains how difficult it is to escape from the influence of parental inheritance and example: 'How true then it has proved, that from noble fathers noble children are born, and from base ones children resembling their father's nature' (Collard 75/Nauck, 76/Jouan, 12, with a similar hint in Collard, 82/Nauck, 83/Jouan, 23 – 'the god pursues for punishment foul sins committed by or against fathers'). More broadly, he reminds the audience that the god Apollo lies behind his fate and actions as he had lain behind those of Oedipus: '[Apollo] destroyed Oedipus, as Oedipus destroyed me' (Collard 70/Nauck, 71/Jouan, 6). There is even a perplexing couplet (Nauck, 69/ Jouan, 3 – omitted by Collard who identifies it with *Bellerophon* fragment 304a) in which the possibility seems to be raised that Eriphyle had some complicity in her own death: 'Was the murderer willing or unwilling? Was the victim willing or unwilling?'[18] It was this exchange that was picked out by Edith Hall as pointing to a 'predominantly comic' treatment, but Aristotle's treatment of Alcmaeon's dilemma does not suggest that it was comic or parodic. The catalogue of excuses is not quite so impressive as that detected in *Phèdre*, but still covers diminished responsibility, provocation, genetic predisposition, inadequate education or unhealthy role models and scapegoats.

If this digressive analysis has seemed somewhat laboured, its point is important: I shall endeavour to avoid following Aristotle (in this instance) in dismissing any claimed excuse as 'plainly ludicrous', or indeed as self-evidently justified. Only if there is some room for manoeuvre, if the actor can win sympathy from some observers but be treated with suspicion by others, will we be in the realm of tragedy. 'Plainly ludicrous' excuses are put forward by pantomime villains, not tragic victims, and characters who are too obviously trapped, helpless or justified are liable to appear pathetic rather than dignified. The study will thus draw on performance analysis and reception theory alongside the resources of literary history and character analysis in the hope that it will trigger precisely the sorts of ethical debates that these plays were themselves designed to generate.

---

18   The line is quoted somewhat wryly by Aristotle in the *Nicomachean Ethics*, 5.9, p. 171.

3   Words

Much of the study will therefore depend on close textual analysis of key speeches in which the nature of responsibility, guilt and extenuation is explored. Since few of the texts studied were written in English, another issue immediately arises: shame, guilt, responsibility are not precisely the same as *aidos*, *Schande*, or *péché*. We are dealing with words as well as with concepts, and the interaction between the two is frequently itself a problem. Our response to what we see Phèdre doing may be coloured in advance by whether we have been invited to consider her behaviour as 'criminal' or 'sinful' or 'monstrous'. How can we be sure that the emotive loading of a translated term is identical to that of the original? In a poetic context this issue is especially acute, since many considerations other than purely lexical or semantic ones have entered into the choice of word both in the source and in the target language. If Phaedra applies the word *aidos* to one of her real or projected actions, it makes a significant difference (to the actor as well as the spectator) whether this is translated as 'shameful', 'sinful', 'disgusting' or 'monstrous'. It has been pointed out that the English word 'shame' is required to be the equivalent of several different words in each of a number of other languages: Greek *aischyne*, *aeikes*, *entrope*, *elencheie*, *aidos*; Latin *fœdus*, *mucula*, *pudor*, *turpitudo*, *vercundia*; French *honte*, *pudeur*; German *Scham*, *Schande*.[19] It would be equally valid to claim that the French word *honte* has to carry at least part of the weight of several English words – shame, disgrace, dishonour – each with its own subtly different set of religious or social overtones, which will themselves vary between native speakers. And *aidos* means 'modesty', presumably with a positive loading, as well as the more negative 'shame'.[20] Even within English there is no unanimity about the borderline, or the overlap, between 'shame' and 'guilt'.[21] It is certainly possible to feel a sense of shame without any tangible awareness of a specific improper action; and this is probably what most people really mean when they say 'I feel so guilty', a phrase which seems to invite the response,

19   C. Schneider, *Shame, Exposure and Privacy* (New York: W.W. Norton, 1987), pp. 18 and 145, quoted in S. Pattison, *Shame: Theory, Therapy, Theology* (Cambridge: CUP, 2000), p. 42; see also I. Iglesias, 'Vergüenza ajena', in R. Harré & G. Parrott (eds.), *The Emotions* (London: Sage, 1996), pp. 122–131.

20   For the specific issues surrounding Greek terminology, of particular reference to studies of ancient tragedies and of the theories underpinning this discussion, see Christina H. Tarnopolsky, *Prudes, Perverts, and Tyrants: Plato's Gorgias and the Politics of Shame* (Princeton, NJ: Princeton University Press, 2010), p. 11, which incorporates reference back to many other sources.

21   Pattison, *ibid.*, p. 43, and see also H.B. Lewis, *Shame and Guilt in Neurosis* (New York: International Universities Press, 1971), pp. 11, 38–9, and 42.

'Oh, you couldn't help it, you mustn't blame yourself'. *Qui s'accuse, s'excuse.* On the other hand, if someone clearly has performed a shameful action, but is too quick to seek excuses, the tendency is for observers to be less sympathetic: *qui s'excuse, s'accuse.*[22] When a character in a play protests helplessness, or alternatively admits responsibility, we must take into account the dramatist's skill in manipulating his audience by playing with this rather perverse tendency of observers to show sympathy in inverse proportion to a character's self-pity.

A distinction may helpfully be drawn between characters who are basically good but who have one flaw or commit one serious miscalculation – which will normally be easier to excuse on the basis of their perceived fundamental goodness – and characters who really are villainous, or commit a series of unpardonable miscalculations or careless actions, but for whom we might still instinctively wish to seek excuses, either because there clearly are extenuating circumstances (Oedipus), or because the author and/or actor succeeds in generating human sympathy for them (Medea, Phaedra), or – perhaps more exceptionally – simply because their villainy is of a scale or splendour to excite a degree of wonder, even a grudging admiration (Shakespeare's Richard III, Corneille's Cléopâtre).[23] These distinctions and examples inevitably recall the arguments of Aristotle's *Poetics* on the concept of hamartia, to which a later chapter is devoted, and the background in moral philosophy against which his analysis of tragic guilt should be interpreted, which is expounded in his *Nicomachean Ethics.* The discussion there brings out how different excuses may often interact, which will make our classification of them into separate categories problematic at times. The relationship between the *Nicomachean Ethics* and the *Poetics* points to very complex scales of blameworthiness in life as well as in drama, with variable degrees of intention, knowledge (of both principles and circumstances), duress and suffering caused. At one extreme may be the psychopath, who simply has no moral sense, and who therefore cannot be blamed for the consequences of his actions: restraining him will be a matter of treatment, not punishment (although the law is of course involved), but this is not suitable material for tragedy. At the other extreme may be the pantomime villain, deliberately and selfishly setting out to cause harm to a known victim; again, tragedy cannot be generated from this, and in practice the distinction

---

22   The latter expression was included by Gabriel Meurier in his *Trésor des sentences*, c. 1570, by which date it was presumably considered proverbial. It may be related to a comment by St Jerome, and it occurs (in italic) in Stendhal's *Le Rouge et le noir*, 11, 34 (Paris: Bordas, Classiques Garnier, 1989, p. 426).

23   See W.D. Howarth, '"A Hero like ourselves": A Theoretical Commonplace Re-examined', in U. Horstmann and W. Zach (eds.), *Kunstgriffe : Festschrift für Herbert Mainusch* (Frankfurt am Main: Peter Lang, n.d., c. 1990), pp. 152–162.

between this character and the psychopath may well be difficult to draw. An optimistic view of human nature suggests that anyone who commits the most serious crimes *must*, at least temporarily, have lost control. On the other hand, someone with even the most highly developed moral sense can also lose control, or take actions based on ignorance or on a miscalculation: in such cases, in life, in law and in drama, the degree of extenuation is a matter of judgment, and is likely to give rise to discussion, dispute or – in cases where the resultant suffering is extreme – even further violence. Agamemnon has excuses for his behaviour at Aulis and at Troy, but Clytemnestra rejects them; she therefore does have reasons for destroying Agamemnon, but Orestes and Elektra do not consider those to be valid extenuating circumstances. Further ambivalences arise as different excuses interact: ignorance may amount to negligence, so is not necessarily blame-free; drunkenness, as well as its consequences, can and should be avoided; minor miscalculations or lapses of care are more easily forgiven than major ones, so that '"I did it inadvertently" will do as an excuse for treading on a snail, but not for treading on a baby';[24] the spectator's or witness's response will also be affected by the degree of remorse shown when the full facts emerge, and by our sense of whether the perpetrator has perhaps been *too easily* swayed by threats, blackmail, bribes or other forms of duress.

It is often tempting to substitute and accept a lesser source of shame as an excuse for a major charge. One might be uncomfortable to be accused of clumsiness or tactlessness or thoughtlessness, but if these attributes are used in extenuation of accusations of murder, cruelty or theft, the perpetrator – and in some circumstances even the victim – may in the end obtain some relief. A violent man whose first defence is 'She was asking for it!' might fall back on his own upbringing and parental influence if that initial attitude is exposed as unacceptable.[25] It also turns out that some excuses, while letting you off the hook in a particular instance, give rise to wider causes for shame: 'if that's the sort of excuse you rely on for that action, then your overall standards are unacceptable'. It is no doubt a measure of the skill of a tragic dramatist that he can contrive situations around these interactions of shame, extenuation and evasion of responsibility in such a way as to maximize the potential for debate and thereby for tantalizing the spectators and holding their attention. The plays on which we shall concentrate are those where this has been achieved:

---

24   J.L. Austin, 'A plea for excuses', in J.L. Austin (ed. J.O. Urmson & G.J. Warnock), *Philosophical Papers* (Oxford: Clarendon Press, 1961, 3rd edition, 1979), pp. 175–204; quoted in J. Glover, *Responsibility* (London: Routledge and Keegan Paul, 1970), p. 20.

25   Austin, *ibid.*, p. 177.

versions of the stories of Phaedra, Agamemnon, Medea and Oedipus, *Macbeth*, and dramatizations of the Biblical story of Saul.

4   *Phèdre*

Do these preliminary considerations affect our reaction to the position of Racine's Phèdre, with which we began, and to which we will return with some regularity? At the start of the play, she feels deeply ashamed, although she has done nothing sinful, criminal or even socially unacceptable. The conscious decisions she makes in the course of the play – to explain to Œnone the basis of her suicidal feelings, to visit Hippolyte with the intention of discussing the political situation arising out of Thésée's reported death, to commit suicide when Hippolyte has rejected her and Thésée returns unexpectedly, to try to defuse Thésée's rage when it seems likely (against her prediction) to lead to Hippolyte's death – all seem at least defensible. Yet in that final speech, already quoted, sometimes referred to as her 'confession', she exonerates Hippolyte completely, but does not truly accept responsibility for what has happened:

> Le ciel mit dans mon sang une flamme funeste ;
> La détestable Œnone a conduit tout le reste.
>
>   v, 7, 1625–26

> [Heaven in my heart lit an ill-omened fire.
> Detestable Œnone did the rest.]

Phèdre firstly has a sense that her basic human motivation is imposed on her by a superior force that is sometimes, as here, depersonalized, but is more often referred to as a personal and vindictive being, the goddess Venus, who had been alienated by Phèdre's ancestor Apollo. Venus had earlier vented her vengeful fury on Apollo's daughter Pasiphaë, inflicting on her a monstrous lust for a bull, as a result of which the Minotaur, Phèdre's half-brother, was conceived. Thus Phèdre's sense of the shamefulness of her feelings for Hippolyte is doubly determined: she can't help it because it is inflicted on her by Venus, and she can't help it because as the daughter of Pasiphaë she is bound to suffer, like her mother, from unhealthy and uncontrollable lust. The sense that feelings, if not actions, are beyond human control can be interpreted and reinterpreted in the light of many ethical, religious and legal frameworks. The combination of Venus and Pasiphaë in Phèdre's background points predominantly but not exclusively to a genetic sense of causation, and Racine's Christian upbringing would leave him in no doubt at all that a sinful thought is just as shameful as a sinful action.[26]

In the event, the death of Hippolyte was brought about by Thésée's rage. We do not have to believe in mythical divine intervention to accept that the loss of confidence and self-esteem occasioned by his father's inexplicable outburst of violence, against a background of ethical confusion engendered by his upbringing, made it impossible for the young man to control his horses when they were frightened into stampeding, as he, defiantly but miserably, went in search of allies in a projected act of rebellion.[27] But Thésée could not help it: he was blinded well beyond the point of diminished responsibility by Œnone's lie, backed up as it was by the ambiguous words of Phèdre and Hippolyte (III, 4–5, particularly 915–928), and by the latter's sword in the nurse's possession. But Œnone was not entirely blameworthy: she was driven to make a snap decision by her suicidal and beloved mistress's brutal rejection of her initially sound advice (III, 3, particularly 825–838), and did not have the capacity, status or knowledge to anticipate Thésée's reaction. In any case, alternative scenarios would to her seem monstrously unfair: how could she allow her mistress to die in misery and dishonour for an affliction over which she had no control? Phèdre's passion for her stepson may appear to well up irresistibly from within her – 'Oh God, I'm just like my mother!' – or it may appear to be inflicted from without – Venus 'gripping her prey with all her might' (I, 3, 306) – but in either interpretation, both Phèdre and Œnone sense that it destroys her will-power and thus deprives her of genuine freedom. Nevertheless, she did resist it for many years, and she would never have approached Hippolyte if she had not been given the false news that Thésée's death had released her from a marriage to which she had remained loyal despite the serial infidelity of her absentee husband. The only link in this chain of causes and effects that could be considered fortuitous is the coincidence by which Thésée returned to Trézène only a few hours after the formal but false announcement of his death – an invention by Racine which brings about a significant reduction in Phèdre's responsibility.

---

26   See, e.g. *Matthew*, 5.28, and cf. R. Calder, '"La seule pensée du crime ...": the Question of Moral Rigour in *Phèdre*', *Seventeenth-century French Studies*, 20, 1998, pp. 45–56, with a sequel in the same journal, 21, 1999, pp. 113–122.

27   For a fuller study of Hippolyte, see L.-L. Naneix, *Phèdre l'incomprise* (Paris: La Pensée universelle, 1977); E.R.B. Forman, '"Je commence à rougir": Shame, Self-esteem and Guilt in the Presentation of Racine's Hippolyte', in K. Cameron & E. Woodrough (eds.), *Ethics and Politics in Seventeenth-century France* (University of Exeter Press, 1996), pp. 233–243; Y. Stalloni, 'Hippolyte ou la passion impossible', in P.L. Assoun (ed.), *Analyses et Réflexions sur Phèdre de Racine: La passion* (Paris: Marketing, Ellipses, 1983), pp. 72–76.

Determinism of a social sort is exemplified by the scapegoat character of Œnone. Œnone is so frequently branded as Phèdre's evil genius, on stage, in the study and in the undergraduate seminar, that a new effort at rehabilitation still seems necessary, although the case for her defence has been coherently argued.[28] It is clear that by the end of her life she, like Phèdre, *feels* guilty and ashamed: she accepts condemnation – 'Et j'en reçois ce prix? Je l'ai bien mérité' (IV, 6, 1328: 'But this is the reward I have deserved') – and implicitly admits her guilt, at least in the eyes of some, by committing suicide. But current legal orthodoxy casts considerable doubt on the value of a confession extracted by force or under emotional duress, and an objective analysis of Œnone's decisions and decision-making processes throughout the play reveals a great deal of reason, common sense and rectitude, which is generally rejected, often with frenzy, by Phèdre, who ought, after all, from her position of responsible authority, to be giving a moral lead to her servant, rather than seeking her advice on such difficult ethical issues. It is true that if we work backwards from the end, Œnone can appear to be the starting-point for many disastrous sequences of events. Most obviously, Hippolyte's death is a direct consequence of the false accusation against him, and that accusation was her idea. In persuading Phèdre to agree to this action, she even articulates a position of extreme moral irresponsibility:

> [...] Pour sauver votre honneur combattu,
> Il faut immoler tout, et même la vertu.
>> III, 3, 907–8

> [To safeguard your honour, everything,
> Yes, even virtue, must be sacrificed.]

Nevertheless, extenuating circumstances can be found for her position here and elsewhere in the play. She may miscalculate, but she does not callously condemn Hippolyte to death: her argument (III, 3, 899–902) that Thésée could not inflict on his beloved son any punishment more severe than exile may not totally convince even her, but it is not ludicrously implausible: it is what happened before, at the instigation of Phèdre herself when she was first married (cf. I, 3, 292–6). Furthermore, Œnone suggests this dire expedient only when she is driven to distraction and despair by Phèdre's brutal rejection of her initial, perfectly sound, advice:

---

28   L.-L. Naneix, pp. 165–175. We will return to this argument in more detail in our final chapter, on scapegoats, pp. 199–201. See also pp. 74–75.

Il faut d'un vain amour étouffer la pensée,
Madame. Rappelez votre vertu passée.

(III, 3, 825–6)

[Your love is vain and you must stifle it,
O Queen, and summon up your former strength.]

Driven mad by love for Phèdre, just as Phèdre is driven mad by love for Hippolyte, she is in no position to think through the consequences of her actions. If we apply to her position here the four aspects identified by Bernard Williams as constituting responsibility[29] – Cause, Intention, State and Response – then only two of the four conditions apply: Œnone does bring about a bad state of affairs (cause), and subsequently accepts a need for reparation (response), but she does not intend the actual outcome, and she is not in a normal state of mind when she makes her proposal. Whether any particular observer thinks of these excuses as genuine grounds for sympathy or as a wriggling form of casuistry will depend on many elements, some of them intangible and intuitive, in the relationship between the spectator and the actor.

It is, indeed, impossible to avoid a circular argument here. I incline towards an interpretation of the text which invites sympathy for Œnone, even if this is at Phèdre's expense, so I am more likely to respond enthusiastically to a performance which shares that perspective. But most of the changes which Racine introduced in his version of the story suggest, as he explains in his own *Préface* to the play, a desire on his part to elicit as much sympathy as possible for Phèdre herself, so another spectator might feel uncomfortable with an interpretation which does not follow that lead and portray Œnone uncompromisingly as an evil influence. The point for the moment is to stress that neither interpretation is impossible, and that neither is definitive: the play both influences and depends on the spectator's concept of responsibility, extenuation and blame, and any spectator is capable of being won over, contrary to his or her expectations, and even in defiance of his or her conscious wishes, by a performance of integrity and power which invites an interpretation different from his or her own.

The next two chapters will deal generally with my conception of the tragic, dealing respectively with the overwhelming feeling of helplessness that pervades the characters in the face of threats or dilemmas which they cannot escape from, and with the precarious balance between responsibility and extenuation which tragedy explores through the Aristotelian theory of hamartia.

---

29   B. Williams, *Shame and Necessity* (Berkeley, Los Angeles and Oxford: California UP, 1993), p. 55.

After this we will undertake more historical studies of three major areas of extenuation, namely ignorance (focussed significantly but not exclusively on the treatment of Oedipus), diminished responsibility (dealing mostly with Medea) and provocation (applying this more specialized excuse for violence somewhat anachronistically to the story of Clytemnestra). The perspective will then open out to include a character from the non-Classical tradition, the Biblical King Saul, who is seen to resemble characters from ancient tragedies in admitting shame for actions which he knows to be wrong, but allying this to a self-righteous tendency to claim excuses. The final chapter will bring together the arguments of the whole by exploring a general tendency on the part of tragic characters – or more often their audiences – to seek other individuals to blame. This tendency to scapegoat as a means of deflecting blame for our own actions has been seen as a pervasive attitude in late twentieth- and early twenty-first century culture, which no doubt contributed in part to the increasing desire on the part of theatres and directors to re-evaluate these ancient stories.

In all of this, as we have seen, we are seeking to explore the double and reciprocal reaction between the texts and the ideas – reinterpreting the texts in the light of modern attitudes to responsibility and using the stories to refine our attitudes to blame and extenuation. The great majority of the book was compiled over a number of years in the early decades of the twenty-first century when life appeared to be normal but often troubling in its blame and compensation culture. It is being pulled together for publication during the period of global lockdown following the word-wide outbreak of the Covid-19 virus which has led in turn to widespread re-evaluation of political and ethical attitudes. Such reconsideration, however, predated the Corona virus: what became known as the 'New Ethics' had already begun to call into question the selfish nationalisms and consumerism of the globalized world, in which, it was already beginning to be thought, 'What has mattered more has been the "my" not the "right or wrong".[30] I do not intend to rewrite the book to take account of the lockdown itself, but hope that in its unexpected new context the ethical issues it raises will have even greater relevance and resonance.

---

30   K. Booth, T. Dunne and M. Cox (eds.), *How Might We Live? Global Ethics in a New Century* (Cambridge: Cambridge University Press, 2001), p. 2.

CHAPTER 1

Helplessness

... to represent the pain of new kinds of impotence and choicelessness.[1]

⁘

Adrian Poole used these terms 'impotence' and 'choicelessness' to describe the challenge facing *modern* tragedy, which seeks to address issues of power and choice arising out of changes brought about in society by modern technology, particularly in relation to conception, birth, survival and death. However, as the title of his book – *Tragedy, Shakespeare and the Greek Example* – implies, this task may also be undertaken by contemporary enactments of the most ancient of tragedies, and *must* be undertaken by them if those works are to retain their impact and point. Classical tragedies were written at a time when (we may feel) human beings genuinely had less control over their lives, fates and fortunes than (we may feel) we have today, but the most confident of individuals sometimes experiences, or claims to experience, a sense of impotence and choicelessness such as tragedy reflects and conveys, and many individuals experience this for a distressing proportion of their lives.

Helplessness is a question of perspective rather than reality. It may be true that most normal lives are built on an essential contradiction – we assume that the laws of nature operate reliably (which implies that the universe is essentially determined), but nevertheless retain a faith in our own existence as autonomous decision-making beings (so do not feel our lives to be inescapably determined from outside)[2] – and the balance between those two perspectives shifts from experience to experience, even from moment to moment. Philosophical analysis of whether individuals are *really* able to exercise control over their decisions or actions do not in the end necessarily affect our literary

---

1   A. Poole, *Tragedy, Shakespeare and the Greek Example* (Oxford: Blackwell, 1988), p. 9.
2   Issues such as these are discussed by John Martin Fischer in *The Metaphysics of Free Will* (Oxford: Blackwell, 1994), particularly pp. 1–22. What he calls the 'internal tension within common sense' is defined on p. 13.

interpretation of works of tragic drama. If characters are portrayed who to a significantly greater extent than average *feel* helpless, and if they evoke a sympathetic response in public audiences, no amount of ratiocination will help them or their witnesses to escape from the feeling that they *are* helpless; and if members of an audience themselves feel helpless, a good performance of a dramatic tragedy reflecting that feeling may comfort and console them, or so it often seems, much more effectively than any intellectual proofs that their own feeling is illogical or unhealthy.

Hopeless expressions of impotence, of frustration, of an urge to sin without the strength to resist it, abound in tragedy. It is one of the commonest excuses for weakness, as our initial analysis of Racine's *Phèdre* has already shown. Characters may become convinced of an apparently irresistible inner compulsion to act in a particular way, or they may believe that external forces – higher authorities, other people, or impersonal configurations of circumstance – are exerting equally irresistible pressure. The interaction between genuine exoneration and excuse is complicated. For an action to be excused, entirely or partially, it is not essential for the agent to *be* helpless, provided observers accept that a reasonable person might *feel* similarly helpless under comparable circumstances. A character who genuinely is conditioned by genetics or upbringing to behave in a shameful way may in practice ascribe his or her behaviour to a different sort of compulsion – so that we do not have to believe in Venus to accept that Phèdre was in some sense trapped by her instincts. Often, the characters of tragedy are warned about the impact of their intended actions, but reject with some violence the moderation, resistance or control advocated by their wiser counsellors. Thus when Œnone assures Phèdre that her love for Hippolyte is hopeless, and encourages her to concentrate on political activity on behalf of her own son, the queen expresses her sense of helplessness in outraged terms:

> Moi, régner? Moi, ranger un Etat sous ma loi
> Quand ma faible raison ne règne plus sur moi ?
> [...]
> Enfin tous tes conseils ne sont plus de saison :
> Sers ma fureur, Œnone, et non point ma raison.
> III, 1, 759–792

> [*I* reign? *I* bring a State beneath my rule,
> When reason reigns no longer over me?
> In short, the time for good advice is past.
> Serve my wild heart, Œnone, not my head.]

Phèdre nevertheless goes on to blame Œnone when things turn out badly, as though the only, or even the first, advice the queen received from her servant was the later suggestion that they should lie to Thésée. Similarly, in a tragedy on the story of Lucretia by Racine's near-contemporary Pierre du Ryer (c1605–58),[3] Tarquin says to Brutus:

> Cher ami, je connais mon péché,
> Mais pour m'en dégager j'y suis trop attaché.
> > II, 2, 461–2

> [Dear friend, I recognize my sin,
> But it grips me so hard I cannot let it go.]

In a subsequent monologue Tarquin insists even more violently on his helpless inability to resist temptations and instincts (it is still the departing Brutus who is being addressed):

> Insensé, tes avis sont pour moi des injures,
> Et le rang où je suis déteste les censures.
> Lorsque mes passions consultent tes pareils,
> J'en attends des effets et non pas des conseils.
> > II, 3, 527–30

> [...]
> Tes généreux conseils ont pour lui [mon amour] des amorces,
> Ta folle résistance a confirmé ses forces [...]
> Je n'aime plus Lucrèce à cause qu'elle est belle,
> Mais parce que tu veux que je sois froid pour elle.
> > II, 3, 555–9

> [Mad counsellor, you wound where you should help me,
> My status does not welcome condemnation.
> When in my passion I turn to such as you,
> It's action I require and not advice.
> My love is but enflamed by your wise counsel,
> Made stronger still by your opposing madness.
> No longer for her beauty do I love Lucretia,
> But more through your resistance to her charms.]

---

3   1638. Eds. James F. Gaines and Perry Gethner (Genève: Droz, 1994).

Such a lucid articulation of Tarquin's position clearly implies awareness that this appeal to helplessness is an excuse rather than a truly mitigating circumstance. Even more blatantly, the biblical figure of King Saul, in the same playwright's tragedy on his fate, blusters:[4]

> Je reconnais mon mal, et ce qui m'en délivre,
> Bref, je sais mon devoir, mais je ne puis le suivre.
>   III, 2, 837–8

> [I know the evil in me and its cure:
> My duty's clear; I lack the strength to do it.]

These are lines which it must be quite hard to deliver without giving an almost comically pathetic impression. The Racinian characters Eriphile and Oreste (as well as Taxile in *Alexandre le Grand*, Xipharès in *Mithridate* and Antiochus in *Bérénice*) all claim that they are swept along by unstoppable forces, summed up in the word 'fate' (*sort/destin/destinée*).

1   Fatalism in Racine

Racine's first surviving play, *La Thébaïde*, contains an expression of this sort of helplessness, in the words of Oedipus's widow Jocasta, insisting that she cannot be blamed for her incestuous marriage to her son:[5]

> Et toutefois, ô dieux, un crime involontaire
> Devait-il attirer toute votre colère ?
> Le connaissais-je, hélas! ce fils infortuné ?
> Vous-mêmes dans mes bras vous l'avez amené.
> C'est vous dont la rigueur m'ouvrit ce précipice.
> Voilà de ces grands dieux la suprême justice !
> Jusques au bord du crime ils conduisent nos pas,
> Ils nous le font commettre, et ne l'excusent pas !
>   RACINE, *La Thébaïde*, III, 2, 603–610

---

4 Du Ryer, *Saül*, ed. Maria Miller (Toulouse: Société de littératures classiques, 1996).
5 The speech is discussed in connection with Racine's assumed affinity with Jansenism by John Sayer, *Jean Racine: Life and Legend* (Bern: Peter Lang, 2006), pp. 73–77, particularly p. 76: 'The play reveals in the author an ingrained acceptance of Augustinian doctrines and a protest at a universe so constituted.'

[And yet, o gods, is it just that an involuntary crime
Should have attracted all your unremitting blame?
Could I have known the name, alas, of my ill-fated son?
You yourselves drove him into my arms;
Yours was the stern will that led me to this abyss.
Such is the bountiful justice of the gods:
They lead our footsteps to the very edge of crime,
Require us to commit it, and then refuse to excuse it!]

Even within Racine's corpus, this total fatalism does not go unchallenged. Some of his more helpless characters do hint that they are putting this sort of attitude forward as an excuse rather than as the true reason for whatever it is they are ashamed of in their actions. Pat Short[6] has argued that fatalism expressed by a Racinian character is often an excuse rather than a perspective which Racine himself can be assumed to share (despite his association with the study of Greek tragedy and with Jansenism), or to wish his spectators to share. If Racine had really wanted to portray a universe dominated by Fate – an external force, whether personal or impersonal, that is indifferent to justice or to the suffering of man – he would have been less squeamish than he claimed to be about permitting innocent suffering, and more consistent in driving his bleak scenarios to their logical conclusion. As often as not, his characters' appeals to fate as the source of their woes amount to no more than formulaic expressions of despair:

> Avec quelle rigueur, destin, tu me poursuis !
>> *Phèdre*, IV, 1, 1003

[How harshly you pursue me, destiny.]

> [...] La fortune, obstinée à me nuire,
> Ressuscite un rival [...]
>> *Alexandre le Grand*, IV, 5, 1261–2

[Fortune, bent on my destruction,
Brings my rival back to life.]

---

6 J.P. Short, 'The Concept of Fate in the Tragedy of Racine', in J.C. Ireson et al. (eds.), *Studies in French Literature presented to H.W. Lawton* (Manchester/New York: Manchester UP, 1968), pp. 315-29.

Qu'ai-je donc fait, grands dieux? Quel cours infortuné
A ma funeste vie aviez-vous destiné ?
  Bérénice, V, 4, 1297–8

[What have I done, great gods! What ill-starred course
Have you assigned to my unhappy life?]

Je suis un malheureux que le destin poursuit.
  Mithridate, IV, 2, 1218

[By fortune harried, what a wretch am I.]

In these cases, no doubt, actors and directors may – and must – make a conscious decision as to how far the audience should accept the character's statement as an accurate reflection of helplessness. Eriphile's choice of words in a
similar context suggests a greater awareness that she is at least participating in
a decision-making process:

Au sort qui me traînait il fallut consentir.
  Iphigénie, II, 1, 515

[I yielded to the fate that drove me on.]⁷

She claims to have been powerless to prevent fate, but she fails to specify what
form of necessity she uses the word 'fallut' ('I had to') to evoke. Oreste is even
more honest: he feels that there is an impersonal external force controlling his
life, but he does not deny that his conscious will has embraced this:

Je me livre en aveugle au destin qui m'entraîne.
  Andromaque, I, 1, 98

[I follow blindly my impelling fate.]

Such feelings of helplessness do not necessarily trigger shameful action, which
means that when they do so, it is more difficult for the characters concerned
to argue with conviction that they have a valid excuse. In the case of Oreste,

---

7   John Cairncross's translation of the line, for reasons of metre, is unable to include the full
    force of the words 'il fallut'. A more literal translation would read 'I had no choice but to
    accept the fate that was dragging me on'.

Racine can even be accused of manipulating his spectators' responses to a certain extent by drawing on their awareness that this character was pursued by the Furies. The expressions of helpless fatalism which Racine ascribes to him are seldom more than conventional declarations of unhappiness: there is no mention at all in Racine's play of his murder of his mother Clytemnestra, which in Aeschylus, Euripides and Virgil was the real cause of his being hounded, yet Racine contrives to give the impression that Oreste feels doomed. Furthermore, it is only at a late stage in the author's life that he cements that overall impression in this particular quotation: in all editions of the play until 1687, the line reads 'Je me livre en aveugle au transport qui m'entraîne' ('I follow blindly my impelling passion' or more literally 'I give myself up, as though I was blind, to the passion that overwhelms me'), and the given reading, with the word 'destin', occurs first in the edition of 1697, shortly before Racine's death. It is indeed, as John Campbell put it, 'more noble to be swept away by fate than by passion', and he used that variant and observation tellingly as part of his intricate warning against too glib an acceptance of a close association between Racine's tragedies and the Jansenist attitudes towards human freedom and value.[8]

The origin and status of the characters quoted above vary considerably. Because Orestes is associated with fatalism in Ancient Greek literature, we tend to use his expressions of it in Racine as evidence that Racine shared this fatalistic attitude; but not to notice that other characters, like Antiochus and Xipharès, are given similar expressions by Racine, although they are not so widely recognized as exemplary figures of humanity buffeted by fate. Short concludes: 'That Racine should have chosen to present Oreste in this manner is not at all surprising, and it would be foolish to try and deduce from this that he had certain views about fate'.[9] For all these characters, the appeal to fate is as much a rationalization as an excuse: perplexed at their rejection by those they love, they use conventional expressions of fatalism to make this feeling of inadequacy and outrage bearable. A parallel from a different context may be drawn with the Chevalier des Grieux, the young hero or anti-hero of l'abbé

---

8 John Campbell, *Questioning Racinian Tragedy* (Chapel Hill: North Carolina Studies in the Romance Languages and Literatures, number 281, 2005), p. 28 and pp. 157–8. The argument against too close an association between Racinian tragedy and Jansenism had been foreshadowed in John Campbell's 'Racine and the Augustinian inheritance: the case of *Andromaque*', *French Studies*, 53, 1999, pp. 279–91, and was saluted, inter alia, by Nicholas Hammond in 'Educating Joas: The Power of Memory in *Athalie*', *Seventeenth-century French Studies*, 22, 2000, pp. 107–14 (p. 107).

9 J.P. Short, 'The Concept of Fate', p. 318.

Prévost's eighteenth-century novel *Manon Lescaut*.[10] There may indeed be some extenuating circumstances behind the succession of crimes which des Grieux commits (they include kidnapping, theft and murder, as well as many acts of swindling and deceit), but the constant appeals he makes to fate are clearly exposed by a careful reading of the novel as a deceitful excuse: he longs to be considered a tragic hero, so uses the language of a tragic hero – which for him of course is the language of Racine – to express his fatalism. Thus in describing (retrospectively) the moment at which he first fell under Manon Lescaut's spell, he does not consider for an instant the possibility that he made a decision:

> La douceur de ses regards, un air charmant de tristesse en prononçant ces paroles, ou plutôt l'ascendant de ma destinée qui m'entraînait à ma perte, ne me permirent pas de balancer un moment sur ma réponse.
>   p. 40

> [The sweetness of her glances, her sad, bewitching air in speaking thus, or rather the overwhelming force of destiny, driving me to destruction, prevented me from hesitating an instant before replying.]

Admittedly, Manon herself has encouraged such an attitude:

> Elle me dit [...] que c'était apparemment la volonté du ciel, puisqu'il ne lui laissait nul moyen de l'éviter.
>   p. 40

> [She told me that it was clearly the will of heaven since she was given no means to resist it.]

But it is des Grieux who returns to it most persistently:

> Je lis ma destinée dans tes beaux yeux !
>   p. 61

> [I read my fate in your bewitching eyes!]

---

10   In full, *L'Histoire du Chevalier des Grieux et de Manon Lescaut*. Page references are to the Garnier-Flammarion edition, edited by H. Coulet (Paris: Flammarion, 1967).

Hélas! oui, c'est mon devoir d'agir comme je raisonne! mais l'action est-elle en mon pouvoir? De quel secours n'aurais-je pas besoin pour oublier les charmes de Manon?

p. 98

[Indeed, alas, it is my duty to follow my reason – but have I the power to do so? What help shall I depend on to resist Manon's charms?]

When des Grieux utters those last words, his faithful if rather earnest friend Tiberge underlines the parallel with Racine, or with pseudo-Racinian posturing, by exclaiming reproachfully that these are 'Jansenist' views, clearly implying that he sees them as an evasion of responsibility rather than as a genuine or credible theological position. Nevertheless, significant numbers of readers, particularly those whose instincts lead them to be critical of Manon, are swayed by des Grieux's tendentious self-defence, and we shall see many other, more convincing, instances of the tragic exploration of such a sense of helplessness, allied to low self-esteem or the loss of personhood.

Racine does work hard to ensure that the misfortunes which dog his supposedly fatalistic characters are always explicable in rational human terms. In *La Thébaïde*, the sons of Oedipus may be fated to struggle, but their struggle is motivated by ambition and greed rather than imposed on them by some blind external force. One of the most explicit appeals to helplessness in that text – 'Triste et fatal effet d'un sang incestueux' ('Woeful, fateful effect of incestuous blood', IV, 1, 921) – turns out also to have been added by Racine in his late edition, thirty-three years after the original composition of the play, as though the ageing Racine deliberately wished to give greater emphasis to an aspect which he had – consciously or not, but clearly with a degree of deliberation – played down in his first stage work.

2   Agamemnon

Comparable feelings of helplessness may be generated by a genuine dilemma, under which a character is obliged to make a choice between actions, knowing that either of them will result in loss of esteem and/or self-esteem. Thus, Agamemnon:[11]

---

11   Aeschylus, *Agamemnon*, 204–216, trans. P. Vellacott, in Aeschylus, *The Oresteian Trilogy* (Harmondsworth: Penguin, 1965), p. 49.

> [...] What can I say?
> Disaster follows if I disobey;
> Surely yet worse disaster if I yield
> And slaughter my own child [...]
>   [...] Either way,
> Ruin! [...]
> Their chafing rage demands it – they are right!
> May good prevail, and justify my deed!

These words, according to Aeschylus, were spoken by Agamemnon at Aulis as he contemplated the necessity of sacrificing his daughter Iphigenia, the cost imposed by the gods for a favourable wind in the Greek expedition against Troy. Just before he returned home, years later, to the brutal reception prepared for him by his estranged wife Clytemnestra, the lines are quoted, with apparent sympathy, by the Chorus of Argive citizens, who go on to sum up the leader's position in the gnomic line:

> Then he put on
> The harness of Necessity.[12]

Agamemnon's speech and the Chorus's commentary on it constitute one of the most problematic and complex expressions of helplessness from Classical Antiquity, involving diminished responsibility as well as fatalism and the imposed choice between evils. Agamemnon publicly claims helplessness as an excuse for an action which is clearly a source of blame and shame: faced with a choice between two crimes, for either of which he knew he would have to incur punishment, he 'slipped his neck in the strap of Fate'.[13] All translations of this line pick up the image of the king as a helpless beast of burden, with a yoke or harness imposed by Fate, Compulsion, Necessity or (in Gilbert Murray's phrase) 'that which Must Be'.[14]

Paul Hammond has pointed out that this formula, however translated, combines an action and an imposition – Agamemnon put on whatever it was, but what it was was inescapable – and that this was 'typical of Greek thought [...]. Often Greek characters are represented as being taken over by some force

---

12   *Ibid.* (line 217), p. 49.
13   Aeschylus, *The Oresteia*, translated by Robert Fagles (London: Wildwood House, 1976), p. 100. Hugh Lloyd-Jones, *Agamemnon by Aeschylus* (Englewood Cliffs, NJ: Prentice-Hall, 1970), p. 28, refers to 'the yoke-strap of compulsion'.
14   Gilbert Murray, *The Complete Plays of Aeschylus* (London: George Allen & Unwin, 1952), p. 44: 'To that which Must Be he subdued him slowly'.

larger than themselves which is nevertheless part of them: anger, desire, pride, infatuation.'[15] Racine's Phèdre borrows this attitude by conceding that her irresistible passion wells up within her, but also claims that it is imposed on her from without by the personified Vénus. Sophocles' Oedipus, too, accepts the need for reparation for deeds that were 'his', yet still maintains:

> How could someone, judging such a fate,
> Not think me the plaything of a savage god?[16]

Here too, the translation can only be an interpretation of the sort of force which Oedipus envisages as acting upon or through him: and over two centuries, editors and translators have reinvented this 'savage god', Oedipus's 'demon', as 'fiend', 'malicious spirit', 'devil', 'divinity', or as a less personal force: 'some cruel power above man', or 'malignant stars'.[17]

Agamemnon's own words seem to encapsulate the slightly self-righteous sense of helpless outrage of a political leader forced to choose between personal sacrifice or the loss of prestige and power. Vellacott's use of the word 'justify' ('May good prevail, and justify my deed!') suggests that Agamemnon is expecting to be called to account for his action, legally, or at any rate legalistically; other translators have stressed the element of prayer, if not despair, in the words:

> O God, may the end be well![18]

> May all be for the best![19]

In yet other translations and adaptations, the text allows Agamemnon to sound more positive about his justification:

---

15   Paul Hammond, *The Strangeness of Tragedy* (Oxford: Oxford University Press, 2009), p. 46.

16   Sophocles, *Oedipus tyrannos*, 828–29 as given in *The Theban Plays*, translated and edited by Ruth Fainlight and Robert J. Littman (Baltimore: Johns Hopkins University Press, 2009), p. 35.

17   I hoped to trace some pattern through time, but translations from both 1841 and 2009 used the word 'god' here, while those of 1887 and 2008 gave the phrase respectively as 'some cruel power above man' and 'some crude, raw demonic force'. To list the detail of all these sources seems otiose.

18   Gilbert Murray, *ibid.*, p. 44.

19   Hugh Lloyd-Jones, p. 28.

Yes, it's *right*! –
Let all go well.[20]

They're asking for blood   it's right what they're asking
So be it then   daughter!   there's no other way[21]

Such a slant makes the Argive Chorus's later supporting statement seem more natural, since the inevitability of Agamemnon's suffering is confirmed, although it is still open to a production of the *Agamemnon* to convey a note of irony in reporting the king's confidence here, as all spectators are of course aware of his imminent fate. Tony Harrison seems most effectively to convey the ambiguity inherent in the situation, as Agamemnon utters words of confidence – 'it's right' – in a tone and context which nevertheless convey bleak resignation, picked up in the Chorus's visualization of the harness image:

Necessity   he kneels to it   neck into the yokestrap.

However expressed, the speech illustrates the interrelated questions about the nature of guilt, shame and responsibility that Agamemnon raises in the many dramatic works in which he appears. Almost all his actions and decisions have given rise to some controversy over whether he deserves censure or sympathetic understanding. Many different excuses are put forward, by him or on his behalf, in the course of his life and career, and any production of any play about him, his wife and their children, will be obliged to take up a position on his blameworthiness. Does his bleating indicate genuine grounds for exoneration, or an embarrassed attempt at self-justification? To what extent should audiences be swayed by the fact that his daughter does frequently seek to articulate excuses on his behalf, while his wife and his political allies condemn him and accuse him of evasion?

Agamemnon can certainly claim, with more justification than many who use the defence, that he is put into impossible situations by divine forces. He is instructed by Zeus to carry out the Trojan expedition, swears to do so, and is subsequently told that the cost of success in that divinely inspired mission is the sacrifice of his daughter Iphigenia. In Aeschylus' *Agamemnon*, the character is not given space to defend himself, and Clytemnestra rejects all his

---

20   Fagles translation, p. 99.
21   Tony Harrison, *The Oresteia* (London: Rex Collings, 1981), p. 9. This lay-out reflects Harrison's published text, as does that in the next quotation.

excuses out of hand – he is in effect executed without trial – but his dilemma is sympathetically depicted by the Chorus. Like Phèdre, he has an almost embarrassing range of potential excuses to choose from: genetic predisposition to violence, consolidated by his upbringing and role models, obedience to a widely-respected higher authority and to a sense of duty, diminished responsibility arising from distress inflicted by his dilemma. Some of these will be discussed more fully in later chapters, but his expression of helpless and baffled rage encapsulates a feeling shared by many tragic heroes.

He does have defenders, at least in Aeschylus' *Agamemnon*. The watchman longs for his return; the members of the Chorus, although they were opposed to the Trojan expedition, are prepared to praise him for its successful conclusion, to welcome him back with due honour, and later to grieve for his death; in comparison with Aegisthus, he is highly dignified. On stage, therefore, the actor must negotiate many tightropes. Is his opening speech pious or complacent? Is his account of the destruction of Troy sympathetic or gloating? Is his treatment of Clytemnestra modestly controlled or offhand? In all of these respects, he is precisely being invited by Aeschylus to strike an ambiguous balance between sympathy and blame, between guilty responsibility and helplessness. This is the view put forward by Hugh Lloyd-Jones,[22] who after reviewing critical interpretations which have insisted either on Agamemnon's boorishness, recklessness and impiety or on his redeeming characteristics of sincerity, moderation and a regal (or at least gentlemanly) bearing, sums up the case: 'Both are right; we have here a character of light and shade'. He compares the impression with that given by Homer's Agamemnon, disagreeable but magnificent and heroic. Later, he draws the conclusion more precisely still: 'Guilty as he is, he is not, like Aegisthus, mean and contemptible; destined as he is to ruin, at once guilty and innocent, he is a truly tragic figure.' At Aulis, because of the machinations of both Zeus and Artemis, he was put in a position where he had no choice but to commit one crime; on his homecoming, he is tricked and flattered by his wife into accepting 'honours due to gods alone' (line 921) by entering the palace on a crimson tapestry.[23] In both these actions, Lloyd-Jones argues, Agamemnon is at once innocent and guilty, responsible and exonerated, partly because there are detailed extenuating circumstances at a human level for his actions – he is victim of a genuine dilemma at Aulis, and of deception and trickery at Argos – and partly because in both instances his responsibility is deliberately and explicitly reduced by the intervention of Zeus to take away his wits and impair his judgment.

---

22   H. Lloyd-Jones, 'The Guilt of Agamemnon', in *Classical Quarterly*, n.s. 12, 1962, pp. 187–199.

23   This rather odd sequence will be discussed further in the final chapter, pp. 205–8.

3   The Seventeenth Century

Nevertheless, Agamemnon's dependence on 'the yoke of Necessity' as an over-riding defence for his shame is liable to produce a position that seems feeble and easy to mock.

> Necessity will make us all forsworn
> Three thousand times within this three years' space;
> For every man with his affects is born,
> Not by might mastered but by special grace:
> If I break faith, this word shall speak for me,
> I am forsworn on mere necessity.
>
> *Love's Labour's Lost*, I, 1, 148–53

Oliver Cromwell was even more crustily unsympathetic:

> Feigned necessities, imaginary necessities [...] are the greatest cozenage that men can put upon the Providence of God, and make pretences to break known rules by.[24]

While Milton[25] made it clear that the Devil's appeal to 'necessity, the tyrant's plea' was an excuse to be rejected, not a satisfactory explanation for 'his devilish deeds'.

The development of seventeenth-century French tragedy can broadly, and risking a degree of over-simplification, be seen as a dialogue about the acceptability of fatalism as an excuse, with Racine – Euripidean and Jansenist – presenting helpless characters with some sympathy, whereas Corneille – Senecan, Stoic and Jesuit – had undermined their pleas as an abnegation of responsibility.[26] Both playwrights, for example, depicted the Athenian King Theseus, but

---

24   Speech to Parliament, 12 September 1654, quoted in *The Oxford Dictionary of Quotations*, third edition (Oxford: OUP, 1980), p. 170.

25   *Paradise Lost*, IV, 393.

26   Once taken as axiomatic, this view has been subjected to critical scrutiny. We have already seen the caution with which Pat Short, as early as 1968, approached the idea that Racine shared the fatalism expressed by some of his characters (see above, note 4), and similar arguments have been strongly put forward since then by John Campbell (see above, note 6) and others. Nevertheless, it is impossible totally to disregard the central thesis inherited from Paul Bénichou, Alban Krailsheimer and others, that the confident moral strength of the 1630s, encapsulated in many typical Cornelian heroes, was displaced by the generation of Pascal and La Rochefoucauld as well as Racine. The confrontation of attitudes between a Racinian and a Cornelian presentation of Thésée which is discussed

whereas Racine's Thésée (in *Phèdre*) joins the chorus of Racinian characters
who insist that events are beyond their control:

> Mais le sort irrité nous aveuglait tous deux.
>
> III, 5, 960

> [But fate in anger blinded both of us.]

> Avec quelle rigueur, Destin, tu me poursuis !
> Je ne sais où je vais, je ne sais où je suis.
>
> IV, 1, 1003–04

> [How harshly you pursue me, destiny.
> I know not where I am, whither I go]

> Inexorables dieux, qui m'avez trop servi !
>
> V, 6, 1572

> [Inexorable, all too helpful gods!]

Corneille's Thésée, sounding quite like Tiberge, confronts no less a character
than Jocasta with the scornful charge that such an attitude is a pathetic and
sloppy equivocation, a delusion if not a downright deceit:

> Quoi ? La nécessité des vertus, et des vices
> D'un Astre impérieux doit suivre les caprices,
> Et Delphes malgré nous conduit nos actions
> Au plus bizarre effet de ses prédictions ?
> L'âme est donc toute esclave, une loi souveraine
> Vers le bien, ou le mal incessamment l'entraîne,
> Et nous ne recevons ni crainte, ni désir
> De cette liberté qui n'a rien à choisir,
> Attachés sans relâche à cet ordre sublime,
> Vertueux sans mérite, et vicieux sans crime :
> Qu'on massacre les Rois, qu'on brise les Autels,
> C'est la faute des Dieux, et non pas des Mortels,
> De toute la vertu sur la Terre épandue,

---

in the next couple of pages adds weight to the position summed up in Bénichou's lapidary
phrase 'la démolition du héros'.

Tout le prix à ces Dieux, toute la gloire est due,
Ils agissent en nous quand nous pensons agir,
Alors qu'on délibère, on ne fait qu'obéir,
Et notre volonté n'aime, hait, cherche, évite,
Que suivant que d'en haut leur bras la précipite.
D'un tel aveuglement daignez me dispenser,
Le ciel juste à punir, juste à récompenser,
Pour rendre aux actions leur peine ou leur salaire,
Doit nous offrir son aide, et puis nous laisser faire.

   Œdipe, III, 5, 1149–70[27]

[What then? Virtue and vice, you say, must follow the whim of an imperious star?

The oracle leads us in spite of ourselves to act in accordance with its crazy predictions?

The soul, quite enslaved, is constantly pulled by a sovereign law towards good or evil?

And we, bound without respite to this overwhelming power, have no freedom to feel fear or desire, no choice? Our virtue has then no merit, our vice no guilty shame.

Do we murder kings, desecrate altars? It is the fault not of mortals but of gods. The glory due to any virtue found across the globe belongs then to these gods! It is they who act in us, when we think we take action; when we suppose we are considering options, we are simply obedient to them; and it is only in response to their goading from on high that our willpower feels love or hatred, seeks or avoids encounters!

If that's what you think, permit me not to share such blind views! Heaven is just in punishment, just in reward, so to grant us the true desserts of our actions it must support us with guidance but then leave us free to act.]

The splendid quality of Corneille's sarcasm here should not conceal the fact that if we remove the 'Quoi?' and the additional question mark, almost all of this speech represents an attitude which Racine's characters are going to put forward seriously for the next twenty years (Corneille's *Œdipe* dates from

---

27 This speech and its context are analysed in D. Dalla Valle, 'Inceste et mythe dans le théâtre français du XVIIe siècle', in J. Morel (ed.), *Littératures classiques*, 16, 1992: *La Tragédie*, pp. 181–197.

1659). Œdipe himself, at the end of Corneille's play, blames destiny – as well as human agents – for his disastrous actions:

> Aux crimes malgré moi l'ordre du Ciel m'attache
> [...]
> Hélas ! qu'il est bien vrai qu'en vain on s'imagine
> Dérober notre vie à ce qu'il nous destine.
>
> > v, 5, 1825, 1829–30

> [In spite of myself, heaven bids me cleave to criminal acts! Alas, in truth it is vain to imagine that we can escape our destiny in this life.]

Corneille had anticipated this debate thirty years earlier in his very first tragedy, *Médée*. Here, it is Jason who urges Médée to resign herself to 'what must be', but she refuses such a 'base' position, insisting on her control of her fate:

> JASON   Lassés de tant de maux, cédons à la fortune.
> MÉDÉE   Ce corps n'enferme pas une âme si commune ;
>   Je n'ai jamais souffert qu'elle me fît la loi,
>   Et toujours ma fortune a dépendu de moi.
>
> > III, 3, 881–84

> [Under the weary burden of so much misfortune, we must yield to fate.
>   This body of mine contains no such base spirit. I have never allowed fate to command me, and my destiny has always been dependent on my own will.]

Characteristically it is from Seneca, not from any Greek source, that Corneille has derived this Stoic assertion of autonomy.[28]

Shakespeare is equally loath to allow his characters too easily to slip into the excuse of helplessness. His characters can be just as scathing as Corneille's Thésée about those who would hide behind various forms of compulsion, divine, astrological or genetic:

> This is the excellent foppery of the world, that, when we are sick in fortune, – often the surfeit of our own behaviour, – we make guilty of our own disasters the sun, the moon, and the stars; as if we were villains by

---

28   Seneca, *Medea*, 520: *Fortuna semper omnis infra me stetit*. See P. Corneille, *Théâtre complet*, ed. G. Couton (Paris: Garnier, 1971), p. 1128.

necessity, fools by heavenly compulsion, knaves, thieves and treachers by spherical predominance, drunkards, liars, and adulterers by an enforced obedience of planetary influence; and all that we are evil in, by a divine thrusting on: an admirable evasion of whoremaster man, to lay his goatish disposition to the charge of a star! My father compounded with my mother under the dragon's tail, and my nativity was under *Ursa major*, so that it follows I am rough and lecherous. 'Sfoot! I should have been that I am had the maidenliest star in the firmament twinkled on my bastardizing.

> *King Lear*, I, 2

There is still an element of evasion in this outburst. Edgar scornfully rejects the responsibility of astronomical influence for his evil nature, but he is still surreptitiously fatalistic, in the same way as is Inès in Sartre's *Huis clos*: both disclaim responsibility for individual evil acts by taking for granted an overall image of themselves as innately – so helplessly – evil.

Shakespeare's *Richard II* has been seen[29] in this regard as marking a critical shift in Renaissance thought about autonomy and self-control. When challenged to study himself in a mirror (IV, 1), he becomes explicitly aware that the forces which seek to destroy him lie not in an external Fate, or the traditionally mean-spirited gods, chance or circumstance, but in himself:

> The shadow of my sorrow! Ha, let's see.
> 'Tis very true, my grief lies all within,
> And these external manners of laments
> Are merely shadows to the unseen grief
> That swells with silence in the tortur'd soul.
> There lies the substance; and I thank thee, King,
> For thy great bounty, that not only giv'st
> Me cause to wail, but teachest me the way
> How to lament the cause.

Shakespeare in such moments is closer to Cornelian Stoicism than to Racine, who often invites us, at least implicitly, to accept a degree of helplessness in those of his characters who are beset with uncontrollable emotions or desires. In his *Préface* to *Phèdre* he states as a given fact that Phèdre's hopeless longing for her stepson is inflicted on her 'par la destinée et par la colère des dieux' ('by

---

29   See Richard Hillman, *Self-speaking in Medieval and Early Modern English Drama* (Basingstoke: Macmillan, 1997), pp. 108–111.

her destiny and by the anger of the gods'), while Hippolyte 'ressent malgré lui' ('feels in spite of himself') his equally doomed love for Aricie.[30] By these words Racine authorizes his actors to present these extenuating circumstances genuinely, and his audiences to accept their sense of helplessness with sympathy, rather than inviting us to expose their feelings of helplessness as mere excuses: 'Racine cherche à excuser ses personnages de s'être laissé emporter par leurs sentiments' ('Racine seeks to excuse his characters for having allowed their feelings to run away with them').[31] Thus his Iphigénie, a willing victim facing sacrificial death, subsumes beneath a wide fatalism several interlocking claims of helplessness, as she addresses her mother Clytemnestre:

> Sous quel astre cruel avez-vous mis au jour
> Le malheureux objet d'une si tendre amour ?
> Mais que pouvez-vous faire en l'état où nous sommes ?
> Vous avez à combattre et les dieux et les hommes.
> Contre un peuple en fureur vous exposerez-vous ?
>
> RACINE, *Iphigénie*, V, 3, 1635–9

> [Under what baleful star did you give birth
> To this poor maid you love so tenderly?
> But in our present plight what can you do?
> You are contending with both gods and men.
> Will you expose yourself to frantic mobs?]

What can a wife and daughter do in the face of the gods, their earthly representatives (oracles and the zealous priest Calchas), vituperative husbands and lovers, the implacable Greek army?

4   Divine Authority

Appeal to higher authority – 'I was only obeying orders' – is another recurrent manifestation of helplessness in both real life and tragedy, and can be equally ambivalent. There is in tragedy a tense relationship between positive and

---

30   Racine, edition, p. 578; translation, pp. 145–46.
31   J.-P. Bigel, 'L'expression de la passion: Etude stylistique et dramaturgique de *Phèdre*', in
       P.L. Assoun (ed) *Analyses et Réflexions sur Phèdre de Racine: La passion* (Paris: Marketing,
       Ellipses, 1983), pp. 34–43 (p. 34).

negative reactions to authority and hence to self-worth. Of course a calling, a vocation, a positive sense of obedience, obligation or service is in a way defining of the human experience, raising us above mere automata. But if blind obedience becomes an excuse for inhuman action, then the world of human interdependency and relationships can rapidly be turned upside down, with disastrous consequences. How can an individual know whether he is Abraham or Agamemnon? Abraham is called to sacrifice his son, and – at least in Renaissance dramatizations of the story such as that by Théodore de Bèze – he has to grapple with the possibility that this urge is not a command of God but a temptation by the Devil. Either way he is in the realm of excuse-seeking: 'Yes, I was ready to kill my son, but I was commanded to do so by God' / 'No, I did not obey the command of God to kill my son, but the command was contradictory and unclear and went against principles of humanity which also appear to be ordained by God'.[32] More confidently, Racine's Joad expresses a sense of compulsion in his question, 'Mais d'où vient que mon cœur frémit d'un saint effroi? / Est-ce l'esprit divin qui s'empare de moi?' ('But why this sacred fear that grips my heart? / Is it the Spirit that comes over me?'),[33] but his use of the violent word 's'emparer' raises questions about autonomy and that irresistible subjugation of the human will to which Racinian characters do seem prone – or perhaps we should say which they are particularly prone to use as an excuse for behaviour about which they feel shame.[34]

For the Greeks, helplessness was largely seen as the result of fate, whereas more modern observers have seen the power of inherited characteristics if not to turn individuals into puppets or automata, at least to inhibit genuine freedom of will and action. The phrase 'genetic determinism' would have meant nothing to Racine, but he unwittingly illustrated it as a force to be reckoned with and scarcely to be resisted, and it is this form of compulsion that was stressed by Racine's Clytemnestre in her vitriolic assault on her husband, Agamemnon:

> Vous ne démentez pas une race funeste.
> Oui, vous êtes le sang d'Atrée et de Thyeste.
> RACINE, *Iphigénie*, IV, 4, 1245–46

---

32   Théodore de Bèze, *Abraham sacrifiant*, edited by Keith Cameron, Kathleen M. Hall and Francis Higman (Genève: Droz, 1967). We will return to this example in more detail in our final chapter, on Scapegoats, pp. 210–11.

33   Racine, *Athalie*, III, 7, 1129–30.

34   See E. Forman, 'Spirit, will and autonomy in Racine's later tragedies', in *Biblio 17* (supplements to *Papers on French Seventeenth-century Literature*), 101, 1997, pp. 273–281 (p. 280).

[Yes, you do not belie your baleful race,
You are of Atreus', of Thyestes' blood.]

It is almost impossible to avoid circular arguments in analysing this situation:
we are what we are because we behave as we do, and we behave as we do because we are what we are. The Greek view was that if a wrong had been committed the pollution caused would have to be cleansed or exorcized, and this
sometimes involved the infliction of suffering on the offspring of the original
sinner. The view represented by Racine's characters is more that the later generations are bound to suffer, not as a punishment for the sins of their forebears,
but rather because they are bound to have inherited a predisposition to sin, to
cause suffering and hence to suffer, in the same way as their forebears. Thus
Agamemnon's contemplation of the sacrifice of Iphigénie is no different in
Clytemnestre's eyes from Atrée's crime of slaughtering his brother's children
and feeding them to him in a pie, just as Phèdre's feelings towards Hippolyte
are precisely equivalent in her own eyes to her mother's monstrous infatuation with a bull. Either way, the characters consider themselves cursed, and
therefore helpless, and spectators can sympathize with the feeling of helplessness even if they dismiss the idea of a curse as superstitious. This does to
some extent neutralize the tortured arguments as to whether Agamemnon is
really guilty. Whatever the rights and wrongs of individual decisions made by
Agamemnon, his fate is sealed: 'From his birth, Agamemnon's fate, like that
of Oedipus or Eteocles, has been determined; he is the son of the accursed
Atreus. Zeus uses him as the instrument of his vengeance upon Troy; but he
uses him in such a fashion that his own destruction must inevitably follow [...].
Such guilt as the king contracts from the sacrifice of his daughter and from the
annihilation of Troy with its people and temples is only a consequence of the
original guilt inherited from Atreus.'[35]

5   Genetic Determinism

It is not always easy to separate out the different strands of tragic helplessness:
genetic determinism, Original Sin (another way of looking at the experience
of apparently uncontrollable human instincts) and the hunt for scapegoats (if
someone else can be found to share the blame, the agent's responsibility is reduced). The project to identify all the genes making up human DNA has given

---

35 See H. Lloyd-Jones, 'The Guilt of Agamemnon', in *Classical Quarterly*, n.s.12, 1962, pp. 187–
199 (p. 199).

new prominence, and some scientific rigour, to the field of genetic determinism since the late twentieth century. Until then, sociology generally supported
the view that human identity was predominantly constructed by social forces:
nurture and environment had a stronger influence than innate nature. This
was particularly espoused by feminist thought, with its assertion that women
behaved in the way they did (and men behaved towards women as they did)
because of centuries of social conditioning and reinforcement: 'on ne naît pas
femme'.[36] The full context of that much-quoted assertion is helpfully explicit:

> On ne naît pas femme: on le devient. Aucun destin biologique, psychique,
> économique ne définit la figure que revêt au sein de la société la femelle
> humaine; c'est l'ensemble de la civilisation qui élabore ce produit inter-
> médiaire entre le mâle et le castrat qu'on qualifie de féminin.

> [No-one is born a woman: it's a process of becoming. There is no biologi-
> cal, psychological or economic destiny that defines the form assumed by
> the human female in society: it is civilization as a whole that continues to
> devise the product, half-way between the male and the castrato, to which
> the term 'feminine' is given]

However, the human genome project reasserted the claim that at least some
aspects of human nature, instinct and behaviour might be biologically determined, that there were indeed 'genes for this' and 'genes for that', until, in
a third phase, that was also called back into question.[37] For the present purpose, the scientific reality matters less than the fact that it has been disputed:
the general theatre-going public is aware that human responsibility, genetic
make-up and cultural formation are problematically related, so the study of
plays in which that relationship is explored opens up a potentially fruitful
debate.

A striking image in Aeschylus' *Agamemnon* supports the inevitability of
what we would now call genetic influence. The Chorus tells a fable (716–735):

> There was a shepherd once who reared at home
> A lion's cub. It shared with sucking lambs
> Their milk – gentle, while bone and blood were young.

---

36   Simone de Beauvoir, *Le Deuxième Sexe* (Paris: Gallimard, 1949), p. 285.
37   See for example Paul H. Silverman, 'Rethinking genetic determinism: with only 30,000
      genes, what is it that makes humans human?', *The Scientist*, 24 May 2004, pp. 32ff. *Gale
      Academic Onefile*, accessed 24 Jan 2020.

> [...]   But in time
> It showed the nature of its kind. Repaying
> Its debt for food and shelter, it prepared
> A feast unbidden. Soon the nauseous reek
> Of torn flesh filled the house [...]
> The whelp once reared with lambs, now grown a beast,
> Fulfils his nature as Destruction's priest!

The phrase here translated as 'the nature of its kind' means more literally 'the temper it had from its parents', and the story suggests an inevitability in the handing on of types and behaviours from generation to generation, not to be overridden by gentleness in upbringing or by good example.

The body of tragic literature is so rich and wide-ranging that it would almost certainly be possible to find examples both to support and to undermine any given position in this debate. Phèdre feels she cannot help behaving like her mother; but what then can explain the difference between Cordelia and her sisters, between Edgar and Edmund?

> It is the stars,
> The stars above us, govern our conditions;
> Else one self mate and mate could not beget
> Such different issues.
> *King Lear*, IV, 3

Kent here replaces one form of determinism with another, but his observation casts doubt on the reliability of either nature or nurture as a basis for predicting character. Perdita, in *A Winter's Tale*, is brought up as a shepherd's daughter and thinks she is a shepherd's daughter, yet she naturally behaves like a princess, which is what she is. A.C. Bradley explicitly noted that Shakespeare 'does not appear to have taken much interest in heredity', and suggested that if the word 'fate' appeals more to Shakespeare's readers than to the author himself, this is precisely because we intuitively interpret Shakespeare's work in the light of Greek tragedy.[38]

In a religious context, the sense of compulsion may be related not only to subservience to an accepted higher authority, but also to the grip of Original Sin. Humans act in ways which others find it difficult to accept, either deliberately

---

38   A.C. Bradley, *Shakespearean Tragedy: Lectures on Hamlet, Othello, King Lear, Macbeth* (London: Macmillan, 1905/London: Penguin, 1991/3rd edition Basingstoke: Macmillan, 1992), p. 22.

because they feel it is the will of God, or helplessly because they are unable to resist the urge to do so. It was Saint Augustine[39] who most influentially transposed the message of the Gospel into the burdensome terms associated with the concept of Original Sin, and furthermore tied that up with physical materiality and with sex. The notion that sinfulness can be inherited leads to an expectation of punishment which feeds a sense of worthlessness as well as of victimization, a sense that is destructive of creativity and freedom. Although Gnosticism (which saw physical matter as the source of evil) was repudiated as heretical, a lot of its associations remained imprinted on the Christian consciousness in both catholic and puritanical cultures. Of course, if it is true that no human individual is free from Original Sin, capable of behaving well by natural instinct, then all must be excused. We are flawed before birth, a fallen species, and this provides a universal excuse for moral failure.

Many of the tragic characters who are based on Old Testament stories are thus portrayed as permanently caught in a cleft stick: emotionally dependent on their sense of belonging to a 'chosen' race, they are destined by that very race to partake in an inherited group shame. The only way to escape from the taint and consequences of Original Sin would be to repudiate one's ancestors and cut oneself off from a promised share in redemption through the inherited line – a predicament comparable to that of Agamemnon, condemned to choose between evils in a tragic dilemma. In Racine's play *Athalie*, the Jewish High Priest Joad sees it as his life's mission to safeguard the young prince Joas, miraculously preserved from the slaughter of his family by Athalie, and concealed in the Temple. Joad foresees in a vision that Joas will later kill Joad's own son Zacharie, yet he feels obliged to save the prince's life to ensure the continuity of the line of David through which alone the Messiah can come. It is unfortunate that the situation is so complex, and the characters' awareness of it so confused, but the tragic impact of this play is dependent at least on the audience's sense that Joad is indeed – uncharacteristically and temporarily, since overall he comes across as an insufferably self-righteous bigot – reduced to genuine uncertainty and suffering by the dilemma he finds himself in.[40] Like

---

39   See for example his *Confessions*, 1, 7 (Harmondsworth: Penguin, 1961), pp. 27–28 – children are inherently evil, driven to anger, jealousy, aggression, tantrums, because they were born into a world inherited from Adam and Eve. This stain must be exorcized by baptism. The argument is built on a quotation from Psalm 51:5: 'From my birth I have been evil, sinful from the time my mother conceived me'.

40   This interpretation has been challenged by those who think that Joad, as well as the chorus, remains oblivious to the significance of his vision. Arguments in favour of that interpretation were brought together in the edition of the play by Peter France (Oxford: Oxford University Press, 1966) and go back particularly to an essay by Annie Barnes, 'La

Abraham (with whom he is explicitly compared at several points in the play) and Agamemnon, he could exclaim with justification, 'Either way, ruin': 'No, I did not act to save the life of the only remnant of David's line, but the cost was too high, and God through the holy spirit made me all too aware of that cost' / 'Yes I condemned my son to eventual death, but I paid the emotional penalty, and I was only obeying orders'. In the same play, both Athalie herself and Joas are also portrayed as victims of genetic determinism: Athalie, as the daughter of Jezebel, is sucked into a cycle of destruction as violent as that to which the Atrides are condemned, and Joas is not only the cherished descendant of David, he is also the son of the murderous king Ochosias, so that the prediction of his ultimate decline into impious treachery and violence is all too credible.

6   The Sense of the Inevitable

People can thus feel helpless if they believe that whatever choice they make they will regret it; if they feel unable to resist a force inside or outside them to act in a shameful way; or if their calculation of the outcome of their decision is wrong and they feel overtaken by events which they could not really be blamed for failing to predict. Helplessness can be an excuse in itself ('I couldn't help it; whatever I had done it would have gone wrong'), or it can be a pendant to other excuses – diminished responsibility or ignorance ('I couldn't help it because I couldn't stop myself, because I didn't know *that* would happen'), buck-passing or scapegoating ('I couldn't help it: my parents made me what I am, X made me do it'). The most fruitful tragic plots to have survived from classical times and to have been re-interpreted as tragedy in different social and cultural contexts are generally open in this way to several interpretations. Phaedra ascribes her disastrous feelings predominantly to a vindictive divinity, Racine ascribes them to human nature, modern audiences to genetics, but the feeling of helplessness is essentially the same. So we can comfortably reject the Classical Greek vision of divine forces manipulating all human activity but still feel sympathy for characters who express belief in it. Hercules' orphaned son Hyllos closes Sophocles' *The Women of Trachis* with the cryptic words:

Prophétie de Joad', in W.G. Moore (ed.), *The French Mind* (Oxford: Oxford University Press, 1952), pp. 90–108. Arguments against this interpretation, supporting the view that Joad is a tragic figure only if he is fully aware of the import of his prophetic vision, were brought together in Edward Forman, 'Lyrisme et tragique dans l'*Athalie* de Racine', in Martine de Rougement et al (eds.), *Dramaturgies/Langages dramatiques* (Paris: Nizet, 1986), pp. 307–313 (pp. 310–11).

> Nothing is here, nothing,
> None of all of it, that is not Zeus[41] –

lines more prosaically but clearly rendered by E.F. Watling as 'And all that you have seen is God'.[42] These words seem to echo the more explicitly fatalistic expressions of Aeschylus in the *Oresteia*:

> Woe, woe, through the act of Zeus,
> Cause of all, doer of all;
> For what is accomplished for mortals without Zeus?
> Which of these things is not god-ordained?
>
> *Agamemnon*, 1484–7

Even Euripides, who is more inclined to ascribe human motives to human actions, reflects a similar sense that humans are not always in control of the outcome of their decisions:

> Zeus assented to all this long ago.
>
> *Bacchae*, 1349

It is Dionysus who speaks these words, himself a god, although one whose make-up in the play consists of conflicting divine and human elements: as god he insists on his superiority to humankind, but as human he craves family intimacy and kinship. There is perhaps some comfort for human audiences if the gods of tragedy – whatever reality they represent – are themselves helpless, subservient to higher forces. In its context, Dionysus' remark can itself seem almost like a lame excuse. Cadmus has admitted human wrong-doing, but claims that the punishment is disproportionate. Dionysus responds with petulance: 'You offended me, me a god', to which Cadmus retorts: 'A god should not show passion like a man'. J.M. Walton comments: 'This response sets even Dionysus back on his heels and gives emphasis to the sheer humanity of Euripides' approach to the story'.[43]

Such a playing down of the contribution of the gods may also be detected in Aristotle's interpretation of the plays he analysed, because he felt that the dramatists of an earlier age had retained a superstitious belief in divine

---

41   Sophocles, *Women of Trachis*, trans. C.K. Williams and Gregory W. Dickerson (New York: Oxford University Press, 1978), p. 70.

42   Sophocles, *Electra and other plays* (Harmondsworth: Penguin Classics, 1953), p. 161.

43   Euripides, *Plays: One*, ed. J. Michael Walton (London: Methuen, 1988), pp. xxxiii.

intervention which his own age rejected.[44] In plays where gods play a significant role (*Agamemnon, Trachiniae, Hippolytus, Herakles, Bacchae*) his focus on
hamartia to the exclusion of *ate* may distort his analysis, but it does so in a way
to which modern readers would mostly relate. Whether the divine intervention takes the form of direct harm done to the human victim, or the blinding
of the human victim (by concealment of facts, or by infliction of a passion) so
that he harms himself, the outcome is usually explicable in human as well as
supernatural terms, and the human victim's sense of helplessness is equally
worthy of pity. The next chapter will look in more detail at the relationship
between external intervention and inherent human choice-making through
the tantalizing but always fruitful concept of hamartia.

---

44   T.C.W. Stinton, 'Hamartia in Aristotle and Greek Tragedy', *Classical Quarterly*, 25, 1975,
        pp. 221–254 (pp. 244 ff).

CHAPTER 2

Flaws, Errors and Excuses: Theories of Hamartia

The ideal tragic hero, according to Aristotle's *Poetics*, should not be 'eminently good and just', nor should he fall into misfortune 'by vice or depravity, but by some error or frailty (hamartia).'[1] When Aristotle wrote that, he was probably unaware of what a complicated and long-running chapter he was opening in the study of excuses. Whether hamartia refers to moral flaws ('frailty'), as was widely believed from the Renaissance to the end of the nineteenth century, or to intellectual miscalculations ('error'), as is more generally argued today, or to both of these in some combination, Aristotle's observations of successful tragic characterization led to a focus on moral ambiguity and extenuation that has inevitably involved students and scholars, the literary equivalents of litigious ambulance-chasers, in a relentless quest for excuses or mitigating factors which will ensure that their chosen hero qualifies as an example of Aristotle's 'character between the two extremes'. 'You can't be a tragic hero,' goes the theory, 'if you are too innocent, so we will have to concede that you carry some share of responsibility for what happened; but you can't be a tragic hero if you are too guilty, so let us present that responsibility in such a way that the audience' – which rapidly assumes the role of jury – 'retains human sympathy and even admiration for you.' Sometimes this has led to a determination to find even the most obviously blameless individual guilty of *something*; in other cases, it has led to a systematic quest for excuses, often going far beyond what the characters themselves would feel comfortable about claiming in extenuation of their own behaviour or decisions. Where the short-hand term 'Aristotelian tragedy' is used, it is almost certainly intending to imply this – 'Man himself causing his fate'[2] – even though Aristotle is by no means consistent or coherent on the point, as we shall find, and other aspects of Greek tragedies are also treated at length in the *Poetics* – including the ways in which they explore 'with their audience the human condition, which may be of "guiltless guilt" rather than hamartia', the latter being defined in this context as 'the transgression of the New Testament'.

Racine, who found it expedient to be considered a loyal disciple of Aristotle, paraphrased the hamartia doctrine helpfully in two important passages: it

---

1 S.H. Butcher, *Aristotle's Theory of Poetry and Fine Art with a Critical Text of the Poetics* (London: Macmillan, 1895, fourth edition 1907 which was reissued eg in 1951), p. 43.

2 John Sayer, *Jean Racine: Life and Legend* (Oxford: Peter Lang, 2006), p. 97.

© KONINKLIJKE BRILL NV, LEIDEN, 2021 | DOI:10.1163/9789004442788_004

is good, he said, if tragic heroes 'aient [...] une vertu capable de faiblesse, et qu'ils tombent dans le malheur par quelque faute qui les fasse plaindre sans les faire détester',[3] and he was later pleased to find in Eriphile a woman 'qui mérite en quelque façon d'être punie, sans être pourtant tout à fait indigne de compassion'.[4] We will return in due course to these quotations, but it is significant that Racine thus pays Aristotle the compliment of basing on his theory the characterization of two significant tragic figures, who are obliged to die by the construction of his plot, and for whom he wishes his audiences to act as critical friends, retaining a degree of sympathy, but sharing the characters' sense of shame. Both Pyrrhus and Eriphile, in short, should come across as guilty, but with extenuating circumstances, and it is no surprise and no coincidence that both, although they fall short of pleading their case directly or blatantly, are experts at implying that excuses exist for their more shameful actions.

The ethical basis of this doctrine was lucidly summed up by Terry Eagleton in his *Sweet Violence: The Idea of the Tragic*:[5]

> If tragedy springs not from chance but from the protagonist's own conduct, then this may risk alienating our sympathies, but it might also serve to temper the injustice of the tragic suffering itself. [...] The problem is not easily settled. Either tragedy results from accident, which is undignified; or from destiny, which is unjust; or from the hero's own actions, which makes him unpalatable.

Eagleton's book exposed to refreshingly iconoclastic reappraisal many of the concepts traditionally associated with the theory and practice of tragedy. Instead of bewailing the demise of tragedy with such as George Steiner, or rejoicing with Mikhail Bakhtin that it had been displaced by a more mature and sophisticated spirit of carnival, Eagleton – in what was described by one reviewer as a 'slash-and-burn rampage' – sought rather to describe 'a new tragic sense, based on a fresh understanding of our contemporary predicament'.[6] To

---

3   *Andromaque, Première Préface*: 'Their virtues should be capable of weakness, and they should fall into misfortune through some error which makes them pitied without making them detested.' References are to Racine, *Théâtre complet*, ed. J. Morel and A. Viala (Paris: Garnier, 1980) (here, p. 131), and for the translations to Jean Racine, *Andromache/Britannicus/Berenice*, trans. J. Cairncross (Harmondsworth: Penguin, 1967) (here p. 41) and *Iphigenia/Phaedra/Athaliah*, trans. J. Cairncross (Harmondsworth: Penguin, 1963).

4   *Iphigénie, Préface* (p. 510): '[...] who in a way deserves to be punished, without being, however, altogether unworthy of compassion' (p. 50).

5   Oxford: Blackwell, 2003, p. 124.

6   Howard Brenton, 'Freedom in Chaos', *The Guardian Review*, 21 September 2002, p. 15, available online at http://www.guardian.co.uk/books/2002/sep/21/highereducation.news, accessed on 19 June 2012.

use the notion of hamartia as a means of helping audiences of tragic drama to come to terms with human guilt is one aspect of tragedy that may be thought particularly relevant to our 'contemporary predicament'; and Eagleton has mild fun at the expense both of those who 'think of hamartia, somewhat implausibly, as a moral transgression' (p. 124) and of those who maintain that a degree of responsibility on the part of the suffering hero is essential to the spectator's empathy – 'not many women are likely to let loose a delighted cry of recognition at the first entry of Medea' (p. 80). He does not, however, devote a lot of space to the matter,[7] and his summary of the theoretical position, while concise and clear, is relatively conventional.

'Tragedy', as Adrian Poole puts it, 'presents situations in which there is a desperate urgency to assign blame'[8] – which again might give it particular relevance in our litigious, compensation-hungry culture – and this is allied to the observation that a balance of guilt must be determined between the protagonist and 'the gods or God, or some force or agency that can be credited with irresistible power' (p. 45). J. Hutton[9] relates this to Aristotle's moral philosophy: in the *Ethics*, it was argued that since *hamartemai* are due not to vice or depravity, but to ignorance of some relevant fact or circumstance, and since the harm that results from them is not intended, we do pardon and pity the perpetrator.[10] Yet since they are done intentionally, they cannot be dismissed as accidents, but involve some degree of responsibility, as is shown by the fact that the doer regrets them and blames himself.[11] As A.H. Gilbert puts it, 'the acts of the tragic hero, resulting from ignorance and error, *seem* like those of a wicked man, but are unlike them because not *deliberately* bad'.[12] Poole, however, contends that 'Aristotle's conception of hamartia [...] doesn't begin to address the intensity and complexity of guilt' (p. 48), so reflection on the ways in which tragic dramatists have addressed issues of responsibility and exoneration must illuminate our own situation in which many factors muddy the waters in respect of the definition of guilt: controversies over genetic and environmental determinism, for example, or feminist and psychoanalytical angles

---

7   Hamartia itself generates only five references in the index.
8   *Tragedy: A Very Short Introduction* (Oxford: OUP, 2005), p. 45.
9   *Aristotle's Poetics*, trans. J. Hutton (New York/London: W.W. Norton, 1982), p. 95.
10 Aristotle, *Nicomachean Ethics*, 5.8, 1136a7, ed. Sarah Broadie and Christopher Rowe (Oxford: Oxford University Press, 2002), p. 171: 'where a person goes wrong in ignorance or because of ignorance, his actions call for sympathy'.
11 *Nicomachean Ethics*, 3.1, 1110b17, p. 124: 'causes the agent pain and involves regret'.
12 A.H. Gilbert, *Literary Criticism, Plato to Dryden* (Detroit: Wayne State University Press, 1962), p. 86, my emphasis. The specific excuse of ignorance will be explored in more detail in the next chapter.

on provocation and diminished responsibility, and legal complexities around such concepts as post-traumatic stress disorder or peer pressure.

1   Aristotle

Aristotle's aim in writing the *Poetics* seems to have been to make the label 'tragedy' more useful by limiting its range of applications. There is a curiously modern flavour to the irritation he conveys towards loose, what we might now call 'journalistic', uses of a word which he implies should be retained for only a limited number of really special literary experiences. He then seeks to define these through the two metaphors of hamartia and catharsis, which have haunted the criticism and theory of tragedy in a troublesome manner ever since. Metaphors are almost bound to achieve their effects impressionistically, so it may be counter-productive to try to be too precise in defining them, but Aristotle suggests that witnessing a tragedy is something like undergoing a ritual or medical cleansing to restore to an individual or community that balance on which health depends (catharsis); and that the most effective tragic hero should be someone a bit like an archer who hits the target but not the bull's-eye (hamartia).

The critical passage of the *Poetics*, chapter 13, reads in full:[13]

> A perfect tragedy should imitate actions which excite pity and fear. It follows plainly that the change of fortune presented must not be the spectacle of a perfectly good man brought from prosperity to adversity: for this moves neither pity nor fear, it simply shocks us.[14] Nor, again, that of a bad man passing from adversity to prosperity: for nothing can be more alien to the spirit of tragedy; it neither satisfies the moral sense, nor calls forth pity or fear. Nor, again, should the downfall of the utter villain be exhibited. A plot of this kind would, doubtless, satisfy the moral sense, but it would inspire neither pity nor fear. [...] There remains, then, the character between these two extremes – that of a man who is not eminently good and just, yet whose misfortune is brought about not by vice or depravity, but by some error or frailty.

---

13   Butcher edn., pp. 41–43.
14   The word used to convey this shock or revulsion, *miaron*, translated as 'stained with blood, defiled with blood' (Liddel and Scott), carries the connotation of 'unclean', in a religious sense. Cf. its etymological link with 'miasma'.

A paragraph later, there is a further reference to a 'change of fortune from good to bad', brought about 'as the result not of vice, but of some great error or frailty.' It is of course impossible to interpret the argument unless we know what the words mean, but equally impossible to translate the words independently of an overall interpretation of the thrust of the passage! In particular, there has been persistent tension between those who wish to translate and interpret hamartia as what in English has come to be known as 'the tragic flaw' – a single moral shortcoming which sullies an otherwise virtuous character – and those who see in its etymology and application to Oedipus and other characters from Greek mythology something more akin to a miscalculation or error of judgment, particularly one brought about in circumstances where the character was obliged to make a crucial decision while ignorant of some essential facts about the situation – like an archer shooting while blindfolded.

Butcher's translation hedges its bets by accepting both 'error' and 'frailty' as alternative translations of Aristotle's single word, but the tension referred to is reflected in the manifold ways in which the word hamartia in the above passage is translated: 'misjudgment', 'error of judgment', 'defect in judgment', 'error', 'mistake', 'shortcoming', 'frailty' and 'flaw' all occur in published translations of the text, while Butcher is not the only editor to play safe by using a double translation, 'some error or frailty' or 'a serious defect in judgment, or shortcoming in conduct'.[15] The terms with which it is contrasted can also affect the weight of the argument: in particular the rejection of the first type of plot, the downfall of an innocent character, may be seen as repugnant either from a moral perspective (*miaron* being translated as 'morally repugnant', or 'abominable') or from an aesthetic one (*miaron* being translated as 'repulsive', or 'revolting'). Some translators retain the ambiguity by using ambivalent terms such as 'shocking' or 'odious'. We shall return to the assertion that innocent suffering is incompatible with tragedy, since it is contradicted elsewhere by Aristotle himself and by many practical experiences of effective theatre, but for now our focus is on the concept of hamartia and how its various interpretations interact with the use of excuses.

The very fact that Aristotle explicitly distinguishes 'vice and depravity' from hamartia suggests that he did not want the latter to mean a moral flaw, and he had plenty of other words available to him for sin or misdemeanour. *Mochtheria*, moral depravity, was applied to someone who simply does not know how to behave, *akrasia* suggests moral instability or deliberate wrong-doing. His choice of hamartia, consciously opposed to *mochtheria*, implies therefore an interest

15   Lane Cooper, *The Poetics of Aristotle: its Meaning and Influence* (first published 1923; Westport, Conn.: Greenwood Press, 1972), p. 48.

in the morally ambiguous area. The logic of chapter 13 makes it clear that something more complicated than straightforward moral wrongdoing must be involved. Tragedy may portray either a person without a true moral flaw, but who makes a mistake of fact or judgment, or one who is not above moral reproach but to whom an objective observer (as opposed to the person himself, his enemies or even his friends) would not wish to apply the more pejorative terms (*mochtheros*, etc). And of course a failure to foresee the consequences of one's actions is itself morally ambiguous. It is often impossible to tell the difference between a person who genuinely does not anticipate the outcome of a decision, and one who calculates that this outcome is sufficiently uncertain to provide him with a reasonable chance of defence. In modern law, the prosecution has to prove that a decision made by the accused *predictably and demonstrably* led to the outcome, without any break in the chain of causation.

Many modern western creators of literary tragedy, their spectators and students of their work, now find it hard to believe that Aristotle himself could be interested in a work of literature which showed too simplistic and unrealistic a regard for poetic justice: the purpose of art is not to reassure us by presenting an escapist picture of a just universe. It is however equally clear, and less surprising than some outraged modern critics have made out, that a significant proportion of commentators on literature through the ages have felt uncomfortable with this view, have sought by almost any means to argue that art, to be worthy of the name, must indeed support their own moral outlook, insisting on and illustrating essential principles of justice, and seeing as its prime purpose the improvement of man's behaviour by vivid demonstrations of what happens if you misbehave – and many of these have sought to turn Aristotle into their ally in this argument. It is perhaps slightly frightening to note the ease with which such moralistic critics could, by focussing on one word, distort Aristotle's line of argument, and the extent to which this distortion was accepted and turned into an authoritative tradition.

Those who believe, or want to believe, or feel they ought to believe, in a personal and benevolent providence governing a well-ordered universe, dare not allow blatant injustice to prevail. So, their argument goes, a character who comes to a catastrophic end must in some sense deserve it, even if the identification of her or his blame involves a degree of legalistic quibbling. Such an attitude, consciously or unconsciously, underlines the apparent world view of both Shakespearean and Racinian characters, and most of their commentators until well into the nineteenth century, and despite the glee with which Classical Greek tragedy itself seems to portray the gods as petty, vindictive and spiteful, a similar basic attitude towards universal justice seems to inform the thought of Aristotle himself. Those, on the other hand, whose motivation is primarily humanist, whether as creators or as critics, are more likely to feel that the status of man is enhanced if he is depicted as rising above a clearly unfair universe, as transcending a hostile fate. Examples can be found of both these interpretations of the tragic, and a distinction has been drawn between the 'tragic victim', 'one whose sufferings have a universal aspect because caused by the flaw in the universe, [who therefore] does not contribute to his downfall' and the 'tragic agent' who does contribute to his downfall 'by a fault of his own'.[16] This leaves open the nature of that fault, and also the root cause of the flaw in the universe – a design fault, or subsequent corruption at the hands of an evil force or of fallen humanity, or an element of randomness in the whole construction from the beginning. It is curious to note that in Euripides' *Hippolytos*, Phaedra is the tragic victim, but that in Racine's *Phèdre* she has become more obviously a tragic agent while Hippolyte (whatever the dramatist himself may say to the contrary) is the victim.

The basic division in the interpretation of hamartia is thus between moral shortcoming and intellectual error. For many, particularly English writers, the standard translation, 'tragic flaw', has reflected and consolidated a predominantly moral interpretation: hamartia is a single moral vice which sullies an otherwise admirable character. Macbeth is a good man except for his excessive ambition, which brings about his downfall. Oedipus is a good man except for his rash hastiness, which leads him to overreact in an early example of road rage; or – perhaps more subtly – he is a good man except for the overweening pride which leads him to assume that he can outwit the divine oracle; or again, he is a good man except for his stubbornness in exposing a truth which would better have remained hidden. A spectator's response is balanced: we are able to admire good qualities, and to respond with sympathetic human understanding to the character's motives while preserving a healthy disapproval of the flaw: Oedipus cannot be blamed for trying to escape from Polybus and Merope, Macbeth's entire upbringing and environment prepared him for a world in which political power was disproportionately prized. In other words, they are in the wrong but not to an inexcusable degree. Modern scholarship, the servant perhaps of a modern outlook, distrusts such an explicitly moral and at times glib interpretation of art, and has turned to philology to argue that the Greek word hamartia need not have moral overtones: it might mean a miscalculation, an error of judgment, a shot in the dark which just misses its target. Macbeth is misled by the ambiguous remarks of the weird sisters into assuming that his quest for power has supernatural backing, and that he has

---

16   R.C. Knight, 'A Minimal Definition of 17th-century Tragedy', *French Studies*, 10, 1956, pp. 297–308 (p. 308, n. 17).

some sort of miraculous protection. Alternatively, he simply miscalculates in his analysis of the benefits and costs of obtaining a certain power.[17] Oedipus is forced to make decisions about his life when he has been misled about his true identity. In other words, they make mistakes, but it easy to articulate specific excuses for their decisions, excuses which may be accepted slightly less grudgingly than those which we accorded them under the first interpretation, since here our sense increases that they are essentially innocent victims trapped by hostile circumstances.

At any rate there is a clear relationship between both these interpretations of hamartia and the theme of excuse, exoneration or extenuation in a tragic context. On the one hand, most obviously, if the tragic hero is misled or misinformed, he can clearly be excused from full responsibility, although we will admire him all the more if he feels and admits some sense of shame for the outcome of his unwitting decisions. On the other hand, we might argue, a morally flawed tragic hero is 'only human', liable to get things out of proportion when under the strain of temper or temptation, but at any rate not a monster. It is on the latter aspect that Aristotle takes most pains to insist, either because he believes it most strongly or because the argument is more subtle and complex. The spectacle of innocent suffering aroused moral outrage, indignation against the universe and the gods, rather than the balanced combination of pity and fear on which catharsis depended. His disciples through the ages – prominent among them, of course, being Racine – have set such store by this argument that it has all but overtaken catharsis itself as the key concept in the definition of tragedy. If hamartia is identified, it is a tragedy: if you want to call it tragedy, you must find an example of hamartia. The enhanced status which tragedy has enjoyed in most literary cultures has thus tended increasingly to widen the application of the term hamartia. But of course a critical term that is applied too widely loses value – the label is only useful if it differentiates its bearer from other things or concepts.

2   Flaw versus Error

Classical scholars have very frequently returned – and felt the need to return – to the battleground to reject the moralistic interpretation of hamartia. One of the most distinguished and influential exponents of the English tradition was

---

17   I. Hyde, 'The Tragic Flaw: is it a Tragic Error?', *The Modern Language Review*, 58, 1963, pp. 321–5 (p. 324).

A.C. Bradley, who referred to the 'tragic trait' in ways and contexts which invite a moral judgment:[18]

> The hero [...] always contributes in some measure to the disaster in which he perishes (p. 7) [...]. The hero's tragic trait, which is also his greatness, is fatal to him. [...] He errs, by action or omission (p. 15) [...]. The critical action is, in greater or less degree, wrong or bad. The catastrophe is, in the main, the return of this action on the head of the agent (p. 23) [...]. The comparatively innocent hero still shows some marked imperfection or defect. (p. 26)

From the Classical tradition, S.H. Butcher, although allowing for the word's ambiguity, explicitly included the moral interpretation:[19]

> [...] limited in its reference to a single act is the moral hamartia proper, a fault or error where the act is conscious and intentional, but not deliberate. Such are acts committed in anger or passion.
>
>   Lastly, the word may denote a defect of character, distinct on the one hand from an isolated error or fault, and, on the other, from the vice which has its seat in a depraved will. This use, though rarer, is still Aristotelian. Under this head would be included any human frailty or moral weakness, a flaw of character that is not tainted by a vicious purpose.

It was from a combination of Butcher and Bradley that this idea was consolidated in the English critical mainstream, so that in 1909, Ingram Bywater felt obliged to correct it:[20]

> It is strange that the *hamartia* or *hamartia megale* of which Aristotle is speaking should have been taken by Tumlirz[21] and others to mean not an error of judgment, but some ethical fault or infirmity of character, like those indicated in *The Poetics*, chapter 15. The Sophoclean Oedipus is a man of hasty temper, but his hamartia was not in that, but in the

---

18   A.C. Bradley, *Shakespearean Tragedy: Lectures on Hamlet, Othello, King Lear, Macbeth* (London: Macmillan, 1905/London: Penguin, 1991/3rd edition Basingstoke: Macmillan, 1992).

19   Butcher, 1895, pp. 296–97.

20   I. Bywater, *Aristotle on the Art of Poetry* (Oxford: Clarendon Press, 1909), p. 215.

21   The reference is to Karl Tumlirz, *Die tragischen Affecte Mitleid und Furcht nach Aristoteles*, first published in 1885 but recently reissued in facsimile, Charleston, SC: Nabu Press, 2009, p. 25.

'great mistake' he made, when he became unwittingly the slayer of his own father.

Bywater went on to give a lucid account of 'error', based on the *Ethics*. Gilbert Murray in a Preface to Bywater's translation[22] made an attempt to inhibit this discussion with his claim that because the Greek language in Aristotle's day was 'unconscious of grammar', not like ours 'dominated by dictionaries', it followed that individual words have insufficient precision for quibbles over the relationship between 'intellectual error' and 'moral flaw' to have any validity. This has not prevented three or four further generations of literary and linguistic scholars from devoting many pages of discussion to the topic. But whether we aim to resolve such quibbles or accept that they must be left unresolved, they do make a difference to our response, both moral and aesthetic, to a tragic character. The surprise expressed by Bywater over the moralistic interpretation did not prevent it from maintaining a firm hold, requiring a succession of scholars ever more tartly to insist that this is not what Aristotle meant: thus Humphrey House, in 1952–53,[23] then Hyde in 1963,[24] Bremer in 1969,[25] Hutton in 1982,[26] all rejected the moralizing interpretation in favour of strong emphasis on mistake of fact, or at least miscalculation. Isabel Hyde's essay begins with a vigorous denunciation of the interpretation of hamartia as 'flaw', although by the end it has raised the real possibility that the concept of tragedy might encapsulate both meanings of the word. In the cases of *Macbeth* and *Dr Faustus*, for example, she concedes that 'the "error" is both intellectual and moral', without making it very clear how a 'moral error' differs from a 'flaw', or at least why that distinction is so fundamental as to justify her earlier dogmatic rejection of the notion of 'flaw' as even a partial interpretation of Aristotelian hamartia. She quotes House's list (p. 94) of 'tragic flaws' as ascribed to various tragic characters – Oedipus is 'hasty in judgment', Samson 'sensually uxorious', Macbeth ambitious and Othello proud and jealous – together with House's assertion that 'these things do not constitute the hamartiai of those characters in Aristotle's sense'.

Bremer's refutation is the most detailed (p. 195):

22　Aristotle, *On the Art of Poetry*, tr. Ingram Bywater, with a Preface by Gilbert Murray (Oxford: Oxford University Press, 1920), pp. 10–11.

23　H. House, *Aristotle's Poetics: A Course of Eight Lectures, Revised with Preface by C. Hardie* (London: Rupert Hart-Davis, 1956).

24　See above, note 17.

25　J.M. Bremer, *Hamartia: Tragic Error in the Poetics of Aristotle and in Greek Tragedy* (Amsterdam: Hakkert, 1969).

26　Aristotle, *The Poetics*, trans. J. Hutton (New York/London: W.W. Norton, 1982).

hamartia here must be understood to mean 'mistake', 'blunder', i.e. a well-intentioned action (or at least one not maliciously undertaken) which proves harmful and therefore wrong because too little was known about its nature or effect.

He observes the discontinuity, if it is not a downright contradiction, in Aristotle's thought on the matter, pointing out (p. 9) that in many Euripidean plays innocent people do suffer; that Aristotle generally if not quite consistently prefers the portrayal of innocent suffering to the portrayal of a simplistic prize-giving, and (p. 12) that the disaster should not be a right punishment for vicious deeds but rather the unexpected effect of a momentous hamartia/hamartema. (The word hamartia does not occur in Aristotle's chapters 14 and 16, but ignorance is an essential element in the situations dealt with in examples in those chapters.)

Throughout the period covered by those studies, some alternative views had continued to be expressed. MacNeile Dixon expressed some perplexity:[27]

> Whether it means a moral or intellectual error, of the heart or head, no one has yet discovered.

T.R. Henn hedged his bets between a moral and an intellectual interpretation:[28]

> I suggest that it may be in different tragedies, either; or both combined.

In 1975, T.C.W. Stinton reopened the debate by putting forward a strong case for a 'both/and' conclusion: the word must be interpreted broadly enough to cover both moral and intellectual shortcomings.[29] Twenty years later, Stephen Halliwell reached the same conclusion, that 'hamartia could cover a range of possible factors in tragic agency'.[30]

Even as this technical argument begins to feel as though it has reached an impasse, if not produced a cop-out, it should help us not only to see the area in which tragedy is problematic, but also to understand its aesthetic and emotional appeal. Tragic playwrights focus their attention precisely on situations in which ethical ambiguity occurs, and tragedy has the ability to persuade

---

27   W. MacNeile Dixon, *Tragedy* (London: Edward Arnold, 1924).

28   T.R. Henn, *The Harvest of Tragedy* (London: Methuen, 1956).

29   T.C.W. Stinton, 'Hamartia in Aristotle and Greek Tragedy', *Classical Quarterly*, 25, 1975, pp. 221–54 (p. 221).

30   Aristotle, *Poetics*, trans. Stephen Halliwell (Cambridge MA/London: Harvard University Press, Loeb Classical Library, 1995), p. 70.

audiences from a wide variety of moral and ethical backgrounds to continue
exploring that ambiguity. It may in fact helpfully be defined by that ability. As
was discussed in the previous chapter, humans may often feel overwhelmed by
the universe, unable to control the result of their actions, aware that matters
over which they have no control impinge much more vigorously on their experience and fate than those which they do control. When that happens, the
spectacle of a tragic hero, drawn with apparent inexorability towards a disastrous course of action which he knows will cause him to lose self-esteem, to
feel shame and inadequacy, but for which he will often seek to find excuses,
extenuating circumstances or at least partial scapegoats, fulfils the function of
true art to enable the ordinary individual to set his and her own experience –
guilty helplessness in the face of an overwhelming and often apparently ab-
surd universe – in a more rational perspective. Healthy encouragement to face
up to and escape from unhealthy and destructive feelings.

It is not too difficult to find examples of plays in which both moral flaws
and intellectual miscalculations occur. Racine's *Phèdre* comes to mind at once:
the eponymous heroine is both lustful *and* misled by her husband's reported
death; Thésée is both rash *and* deceived by Œnone's testimony; Œnone is ready
to divert all blame from her beloved mistress, but cannot be blamed for under-
estimating Thésée's extreme response. In Corneille's *Médée*, most attention is
obviously paid to the crimes of Jason and Médée herself, but miscalculation is
also a factor: a necessary link in the dramatic structure is provided by Créon
who – despite all the previous evidence, as well as warnings from Pollux within
the play – underestimates the power of Médée, and allows her the twenty-four
hours which is all she needs to achieve his undoing:

> Par son bannissement j'ai fait ma sûreté ;
> Elle n'a que fureur et que vengeance en l'âme,
> Mais, en si peu de temps, que peut faire une femme ?
> Je n'ai prescrit qu'un jour de terme à son départ.
>
> IV, 2, 1104–7

> [I've ensured my safety by exiling Médée;
> Her spirit is dominated by frenzy and vengeance,
> But what can a woman do in so little time?
> I've set her departure for tomorrow.]

Créon does take Pollux's warning seriously enough to test out the possibility
that the robe offered by Médée to Créuse might be poisoned: he insists that
a female criminal, Nise, try on the dress first. However, we already know from

Médée's instructions to her confidante Nérine (IV, 1, 1049–54) that the poison will be ineffectual against all except Créuse and Créon.

3   Renaissance and Pre-Classical

Renaissance and early modern Europe was less comfortable than either the ancients or the post-Enlightenment world with the notion that the universe might simply be unfair. If the world is controlled by divine providence, the argument would go, innocent suffering is impossible to explain, and so if something goes wrong, humanity must in some sense be to blame. This, coupled with an exaggerated hero-worship for the ideas of Aristotle, makes it easier to see why theorists of drama in that period should have resuscitated the concept of hamartia and attached considerable importance to it. It was clearly articulated in French as early as 1572, with the publication of Jean de la Taille's treatise *De l'Art de la tragédie*, amounting to little more than a paraphrase of Aristotle:[31]

> Que le sujet aussi ne soit de Seigneurs extrêmement méchants, et que pour leurs crimes horribles ils méritassent punition ; ni aussi par même raison de ceux qui sont du tout bons, gens de bien et de sainte vie.

> [Tragedy should not deal with extremely vicious lords, who deserve to be punished for their terrible crimes; nor yet, similarly, with altogether good men of virtuous and saintly life.]

A more significant treatise on tragedy from the first part of the seventeenth century in France, Hippolyte-Jules Pinet de la Mesnardière's *Poétique* of 1639 presents a predominantly moralistic view of tragedy, and although his debt to Aristotle is clear, La Mesnardière has great difficulty in accepting any interpretation of hamartia that risks being perceived as unjust:[32]

---

31   Jean de la Taille, *Dramatic Works*, edited Kathleen M. Hall and C.N. Smith (London: Athlone, 1972), p. 20.

32   Hippolyte-Jules Pilet de La Mesnardière, *Poétique* (Paris: Sommaville, 1639), pp. 107–108. For a more detailed analysis of La Mesnardière's treatment of hamartia, see Tomoki Tomotani, 'La faute tragique dans le théâtre classique français: La Mesnardière, Corneille, Racine', available online (17 October 2017) at http://www.waseda.jp/bun-france/pdfs/Vol18/Tomotani.pdf.

Le poème tragique, étant toujours obligé de récompenser les vertus et de châtier les vices, ne doit jamais introduire des personnes très vertueuses et absolument innocentes qui tombent en de grands malheurs, ni des hommes fort vicieux qui soient heureux parfaitement.

[The tragic poem is always obliged to reward virtue and punish vice, so it should never deal with altogether virtuous and innocent individuals who fall into misfortune, nor highly vicious men who achieve total happiness.]

La Mesnardière seems aware of the tensions in his argument: the 'faute' that brings about a disastrous dénouement for a more-or-less virtuous hero must deserve punishment but should also be at one level excusable. The best – and most socially useful – tragedy should be characterized by the justice of its dénouement (p. 141):

Ce fruit [l'utilité merveilleuse de la tragédie] est attaché à deux rameaux opposés, à la punition des méchants, et plus encore aux bonnes mœurs des héros qui ne sont coupables que par quelque fragilité qui mérite d'être excusée.

[The reason that tragedy is so marvellously beneficial to society springs from two opposing sources of moral nourishment: from the punishment of evil-doers, but even more from the virtuous behaviour of its heroes whose guilt stems from a single weakness for which they deserve to be excused.]

Corneille did not devote a lot of time to arguments about tragic guilt. Reflecting in 1660 on his dramatic output so far, he translated Aristotle's crucial passage quite literally, and discussed it in terms that seem to us of an independence verging on the dismissive:[33]

Il reste donc à trouver un milieu entre ces deux extrémités, par le choix d'un homme qui ne soit ni tout à fait bon, ni tout à fait méchant,[34] et qui par une faute, ou faiblesse humaine, tombe dans un malheur qu'il ne

---

33   'Discours de la tragédie'. Corneille, *Théâtre complet*, ed. G. Couton (Paris: Garnier, 1971, 3 vols.), I, p. 35.

34   This formulation, which interprets rather than translates Aristotle's text, is a striking foreshadowing of those used by Racine in his *Préfaces* to *Andromaque* and *Phèdre*. Nevertheless taken overall, Corneille's response to Aristotle's doctrine is much less passive and more argumentative than Racine's.

mérite pas. Aristote en donne pour exemples Œdipe et Thyeste, en quoi véritablement je ne comprends pas sa pensée. Le premier me semble ne faire aucune faute, bien qu'il tue son père, parce qu'il ne le connaît pas, et qu'il ne fait que disputer le chemin en homme de cœur contre un inconnu qui l'attaque avec avantage. Néanmoins, comme la signification du mot grec *hamartia* peut s'étendre à une simple erreur de méconnaissance, telle qu'était la sienne, admettons-le avec ce philosophe, bien que je ne puisse voir quelle passion il nous donne à purger, ni de quoi nous pouvons nous corriger sur son exemple.

[It remains then for us to find a mean between these two extremes, by choosing a man who is neither totally good nor totally wicked, and who falls through some fault or human weakness into a misfortune that he does not deserve. Aristotle gives Oedipus and Thyestes as examples of this type, and in this regard I must say I cannot understand what he is getting at. The former does not seem to me to be guilty of any sin, even though he kills his father, because he does not know who he is, and does no more than defend his right of way spiritedly against a stranger who has attacked him with superior numbers. However, since the Greek word *hamartia* can be taken as meaning a straightforward mistake of recognition, like the one Oedipus makes, let us agree with Aristotle that this is a case of *hamartia*, even though I cannot see what passion it purges us of, or how we can use it as a moral example.]

Corneille's dismissal of Thyestes as a figure characterized by hamartia is even more peremptory: in the back story to the play which bears his name[35] Thyestes is an incestuous and abusive adulterer, so would forfeit all sympathy; whereas within the play itself he is the victim of calculating deceit on the part of the wronged brother with whom he believes himself to have been reconciled. Corneille was indeed suspicious not only of Aristotle's examples, but also of the principle of hamartia itself, since he argued (p. 39 of the same text) that it was not hard to find examples of innocent suffering, or of the punishment of wickedness, which he claimed were entirely appropriate for the tragic stage: perhaps, he argued rather disingenuously, these were 'not available in the theatres of Aristotle's day'. Corneille sought, for example, innocent victims who are persecuted by an opponent who is nevertheless not so unpalatable

---

35   Aristotle had been writing about a lost play by Euripides, but it was not unreasonable for Corneille to extrapolate his characterization of Thyestes from the play by Seneca which he himself knew.

as to alienate the audience completely – 'qui montre plus de faiblesse que de crime dans la persécution qu'il lui fait' ('who demonstrates more weakness than villainy in the persecution he imposes on [his victim]'). Thus in his own martyr play, *Polyeucte*, Corneille argued that our detestation of the actions of Félix were tempered by an appreciation of his position – he is weak but can be excused because of the power and hold that Sévère has over him. Corneille's position here, however, is not so distant from Aristotle's as he was trying to make out: by giving excuses to his villains he is precisely aligning them with Aristotle's theory, presenting them as characters who deserve their fate but are not entirely unworthy of our pity. At any rate, in comparison with the rather slavish obeisance of his contemporaries La Mesnardière, d'Aubignac and even (in theoretical terms) Racine, it is refreshing to find Corneille arguing the toss with Aristotle when it comes to the analysis of individual cases.

4   Racine

Against such a background, Racine's Jansenist religious upbringing imbued him with a particularly strong sense of human worthlessness, and he frequently defended tragedy in general on the basis that it demonstrates how severely humanity needs to be punished for even mild transgressions. Indeed, several of Racine's discussions of the principle of hamartia include an explicit reference to *punishment* that is not found in Aristotle himself.[36] *Phèdre*, he argues, is the most 'virtuous' of his works because 'les moindres fautes y sont sévèrement punies',[37] and relevant passages from the *Préfaces* to *Andromaque* and *Iphigénie* also use the word 'punition' ('punishment') to refer to the suffering of Pyrrhus and Eriphile. For Racine's spectators, familiar with the sacrament of confession, the notion of 'faute' (particularly, perhaps, that of 'ma faute') was almost inextricably linked with concepts of sin. 'Derrière le cas intermédiaire défini par Aristote entre le bon et le méchant se profile le cas du pécheur d'occasion qui se sait et se sent coupable, différent à la fois de l'homme juste et du pécheur endurci qui persévère dans un mal dont il n'a plus conscience.'[38] The French word 'faute' does retain its moral ambiguity, covering many types of error, lack

---

36   See Roger Duchêne, 'Punition et compassion: tragédie et morale chez Racine', in Madeleine Bertaud (ed.), *Travaux et Littérature: offerts en hommage à Noémi Hepp* (Paris: Adirel, 1990), pp. 85–93.

37   Racine, p. 578. '[In this tragedy], the slightest transgressions are severely punished' (p. 146).

38   Duchêne, p. 88. 'In the background to the intermediate case between good and evil as defined by Aristotle can be detected the figure of the opportunistic sinner, who

or moral flaw, although Duchêne is right to point out that Aristotle concentrates on actions, whereas Racine is concerned with states, with essences that define a character once and for all.

In several key moments in his defensive and polemical *Préfaces*, Racine refers explicitly to Aristotle's doctrine of hamartia to answer criticisms made about individual characters in his tragedies by his rivals or enemies. He seldom identifies these critics, hiding behind such indignant expressions as 'Encore s'est-il trouvé des gens …,'[39] and at times it appears as though he has invented criticism in order to give himself a platform for a statement of orthodoxy to which his works do not adhere as faithfully as the *Préfaces* themselves imply. Thus it was in response to unnamed critics whom modern scholarship has been unable to identify that Racine, in the first *Préface* to *Andromaque*, made his first appeal to the principle of hamartia. Their reproach, that Pyrrhus had been too brutal in his treatment of the heroine, drew from Racine a clear summary of the Aristotelian position:[40]

> Aristote, bien éloigné de nous demander des héros parfaits, veut au contraire que les personnages tragiques […] ne soient ni tout à fait bons, ni tout à fait méchants. Il ne veut pas qu'ils soient extrêmement bons, parce que la punition d'un homme de bien exciterait plus l'indignation que la pitié du spectateur; ni qu'ils soient méchants avec excès, parce qu'on n'a point pitié d'un scélérat. Il faut donc qu'ils aient une bonté médiocre, c'est-à-dire une vertu capable de faiblesse, et qu'ils tombent dans le malheur par quelque faute qui les fasse plaindre sans les faire détester.

> [Aristotle, far from asking us to provide perfect heroes, asks on the contrary that tragic characters (…) should not be entirely good or entirely evil. He does not want them to be completely good, since the punishment of an upright man would arouse the indignation rather than the pity of the spectator; nor that he be a scoundrel, or excessively wicked, since nobody would feel pity for a scoundrel. They should therefore be not too good and not too bad, that is, their virtues should be capable of weakness, and they should fall into misfortune through some error which makes them pitied without making them detested.]

---

acknowledges his sin and feels guilty, but who is distinguished both from the just man and from the hardened sinner who perseveres in evil of which he is no longer conscious.'
39   *Andromaque, Première Préface*, p. 130. 'And yet there have been people who […]' (p. 40).
40   P. 131; trans. pp. 40–41.

On the face of it, this is not very promising terrain for Racine to fight his first major critical battle. He does not make it easy for the actor playing the part of Pyrrhus, characterized as he is by the cold-blooded murder of Priam at the climax of the Trojan War, to evoke any sympathy. Remaining true to his reputation for callous brutality, Pyrrhus breaks his promises to Hermione, forswears his loyalty to the Greeks and tortures Andromaque with extreme moral blackmail. Such attempts as he himself makes to inspire pity strike modern audiences as unspeakably misogynistic, as when he bluntly informs Andromaque that he 'souffre tous les maux que j'ai faits devant Troie' (I, 4, 318: 'suffered all the ills I did to Troy') and is 'brûlé de plus de feux que je n'en allumai' (I, 4, 320: 'Burned with more blazing fires than e'er I lit') – in other words he sees a precise equivalence between his bloody destruction of Andromaque's home and family and her current withholding of sexual favours.

There is thus an apparent discrepancy between the actual characterization and Racine's claim in the *Préface*. When Craig Raine adapted the play to a post-war Europe in which Hitler and Mussolini had won, in his *1953*,[41] he found it so unbelievable that his Andromache (Annette) would trust the triumphant Vittorio (his Pyrrhus, the son of Mussolini) to stand by a gentleman's agreement to defend her son, if she died between the ceremony of their marriage and its consummation, that she had to contrive that the suicide appeared to be an accident. Pyrrhus could of course benefit from several of the excuses that are customarily available to exonerate the protagonists of tragedy: his upbringing, role models and inheritance had all prepared him for a tendency to violence, the effect of Trojan War had no doubt been traumatizing, and his passion for Andromaque and guilt over Hermione might be thought to diminish his responsibility. Like Agamemnon, too, he is in a genuine dilemma, obliged either to betray those he now loves or to fall short of his public duty. 'Either way, ruin' – although he does not precisely articulate it in those terms. In this case, the discussion presupposes a moral interpretation of hamartia. Pyrrhus's downfall is brought about by a moral flaw in his nature[42] which deserves a degree of punishment (so his fate is not unjust) but does not arouse fundamental antipathy (so he is not too unpalatable). Racine's choice of words, *faute* and *faiblesse*, linked to the explicit mention of punishment, invites a straightforwardly moral interpretation: hamartia as a fatal flaw. At any rate, the case

---

41   London: Faber & Faber, 1990. See Guy Snaith, 'Andromache, Annette and Andromaque: A Look at two recent Translations', *Seventeenth-century French Studies*, 13, 1991, pp. 139–152 (pp. 144–150), and '*1953*: An *Andromaque* for our Times', *French Studies Bulletin*, 59, 1996, pp. 15–16.

42   He had in the *Préface* been described as 'violent de son naturel' ('violent in his very nature').

remains problematic both practically and theoretically: Pyrrhus *is* too unpalatable to be an entirely satisfactory tragic character, and Racine's suggestion that he can be considered to possess 'une vertu capable de faiblesse' does not correspond to our experience.

In the prefatory matter to his next tragedy, *Britannicus*, Racine made only one passing reference to Aristotle, but some of the discussion does focus on similar issues. His (still unnamed) detractors had complained that Britannicus himself was a man 'too young to be a tragic hero', to which Racine responded rather inconsequentially by reminding us that the tragic hero must have 'some imperfection'.[43] Opposed to Britannicus was the young Emperor Nero, whose reputation as a brutal tyrant was, if anything, even more firmly established than Pyrrhus's, while his mother Agrippina was described by Tacitus (in a reference quoted by Racine himself) as 'burning with all the delirium of maleficent power'.[44] Racine implicitly appealed again to the theory of hamartia in arguing that his depiction of them is in conformity with sound Aristotelian principles. In the first *Préface* he wryly points out that since his critics attacked him from both directions – Néron is 'too cruel' for some, 'too good' for others[45] – he must in practice have struck the balance perfectly, and he used the idea of a 'monstre naissant' (a 'fledgling' monster, or a monster 'in the process of becoming such') to bind the character into the argument that he is not (yet) so unpalatable as to become a pantomime villain rather than a tragic agent. Britannicus and Junie are, by any normal definition, innocent victims of evil. Britannicus's credulity is no more worthy to count as a tragic flaw than Hamlet's indecisiveness. It would be more persuasive to bring in the concept of hamartia as miscalculation to define the tragedy here: all the characters, Agrippine as well as Junie, Burrhus as well as Britannicus, simply underestimate the depth of Néron's emerging evil. However, Racine does not argue this, and the fact remains that this is the most polarized of his tragedies; the conflict between the sage Burrhus and the manipulative Narcisse over the soul of Néron is reminiscent of a morality play.[46]

Racine returned to hamartia, in terms closely reminiscent to those used in the *Préface* to *Andromaque*, when he considered his 1674 play *Iphigénie*. The character Eriphile was virtually invented by Racine but plays a significant role in the tragedy: since we learn in the last act that her real name is Iphigénie,

---

43   Racine, p. 255, trans. p. 130.
44   *Seconde Préface*, p. 258, trans. p. 136.
45   P. 254, trans. p. 129.
46   We will return to these issues in more detail in our final chapter, on Scapegoats, particularly pp. 195–97.

and she is the only one who dies during the play, she could have some claim
to be the central if not the title character. Racine wrote of her that 'tombant
dans le malheur où cette amante jalouse voulait précipiter sa rivale, [elle]
mérite en quelque façon d'être punie, sans être pourtant tout à fait indigne de
compassion'.[47] The usual delicate balance between sympathy and blame is
evoked, and it seems that Racine has worked quite hard, both in his characterization and in his argument, to achieve the aim of reflecting the Aristotelian
theory in his fated figures. Indeed, he went so far as to state that that he would
have felt unable to write his play had it not been for his 'discovery', in the
ancient writers Stesichorus and Pausanias, of an Iphigenia who was not the
daughter of Agamemnon, but whose sacrifice satisfied the conditions set by
the gods for the Trojan expedition to take place.

Eriphile is herself quite an expert in excuses, sometimes delivered pre-
emptively. Even before she has done or contemplated anything to feel ashamed
or guilty about, she speaks and behaves defensively. In her first scene, II, 1,
her confidante Doris expresses surprise at her continuing unhappiness, when
things seem to be going so well. The terms in which Eriphile explains her mel-
ancholy mood sound like excuses for inadequacy:

> Et moi, toujours en butte à de nouveaux dangers,
> Remise dès l'enfance en des bras étrangers,
> Je reçus et je vois le jour que je respire,
> Sans que père ni mère ait daigné me sourire.
>> II, 1, 423–6

> [And I, always exposed to dangers new,
> Placed among strangers from my earliest days,
> Neither at birth nor later have I seen
> Mother or father ever smile on me.]

– not just from a broken home, she is a helpless orphan deprived of parental
affection.

> J'ignore qui je suis
>> II, 1, 427

> [I know not who I am.]

---

47   See above, p. 50, note 4. Racine, p. 510: 'As she meets the fate which, in her jealousy, she
      wished to bring upon her rival, [she] in a way deserves to be punished, without being,
      however, altogether unworthy of compassion' (trans. p. 50).

– an overwhelming excuse for any irresponsibility: if the self does not grasp
its own identity, on what basis can it make decisions or actions? Freewill depends on a sense of self knowledge.

> [...]   et pour comble d'horreur
> Un oracle effrayant m'attache à mon erreur,
> Et quand je veux chercher le sang qui m'a fait naître,
> Me dit que sans périr je ne me puis connaître.
>   II, 1, 427–30

> [... and crowning woe,
> An oracle binds me to ignorance,
> And when I seek to learn my origin,
> Says I must die to find out who I am.]

'Horreur' (weakened in the translation as 'woe') surely comes as something of
a shock there. The previous lines may have elicited pity, but they have scarcely
prepared us for a sense of the horrific. Eriphile's final excuse brings in a supernatural element with its mysterious premonition that self-knowledge will
for her spell death. In terms of its connection with Racine's Aristotelian sense
of the tragic, the passage anticipates a climax involving both catharsis and
anagnorisis, deriving from a situation based on hamartia. Racine's use of the
word 'erreur' – rather contrived as here applied to mere ignorance – suggests
that he feels a need to express Eriphile's sense of inadequacy in those terms.
Furthermore the overall expression of line 428 confirms the impression that
the weakness in Eriphile's make-up, or in her grasp of the situation, is forced on
her against her conscious will. In all of this she explicitly contrasts her position
with that of Iphigénie:

> Je vois Iphigénie entre les bras d'un père ;
> Elle fait tout l'orgueil d'une superbe mère
>   II, 1, 421–2

> [Iphigenia in her father's arms,
> The idol of her haughty mother's love.]

Eriphile projects her feeling of being hard done by in a way that suggests she
will seek to escape responsibility for the pernicious effects of her jealousy.
Racine may here be giving an intelligent actress a chance to win some sympathy by hinting at the excuses Eriphile has for a sense of inadequacy, without
descending to whinging or unattractive self-pity.

The same tone continues in her next speech, confirming her sense of help-lessness with a striking image of imprisonment and frustration:

> Ton père, enseveli dans la foule des morts,
> Me laisse dans les fers à moi-même inconnue,
> [...]
> Vile esclave des Grecs [...]
>> II, 1, 449/51

> [Your father, buried in a heap of dead,
> Left me in fetters, to myself unknown –
> (...) a poor Greek slave.]

In the second half of the scene, the romantic side of her weakness is explored: her helpless, irrational passion for her conqueror Achille. She describes her-self as 'possédée' by a 'fatal amour' (482: 'by this mad love possessed'), and she makes it clear that she blames her woes on a supernatural force, vaguely defined but clearly perceived as conscious and acting deliberately:

> Le ciel s'est fait sans doute une joie inhumaine
> A rassembler sur moi tous les traits de sa haine.
>> II, 1, 485–6

> [Heaven, it is certain, with inhuman joy
> Mustered against me all its thunderbolts!][48]

As elsewhere, the sense of helplessness is depicted by means of an image of the divided personality: referring to her love as a 'faiblesse' (478: 'a weakness'), Eriphile says she hoped to conceal it behind total silence,

> Mais mon cœur trop pressé m'arrache ce discours.
>> II, 1, 479

> [But my full heart forces these words from me.]

---

48   More literally 'all the tokens of its hatred': whatever 'heaven' refers to in Eriphile's mind, it is a form of consciousness capable of hatred, spite and glee over the suffering it can cause.

This reflects the feeling that she associates with her first glimpse of Achille:

> Je sentis contre moi mon cœur se déclarer.
>> II, 1, 499

[I felt my heart declare against me.]

Finally, like Oreste in Racine's *Andromaque*, she appears to reveal a certain doubt or confusion in the source of her feelings, trapped as she is between external fate and her own internal impulses. Where Oreste said,

> Je me livre en aveugle au destin qui m'entraîne.
>> *Andromaque*, I, 1, 98

[I follow blindly my impelling fate.]

Eriphile distances herself slightly but not totally from the decision to let fate take its course:

> Au sort qui me traînait il fallut consentir –
>> *Iphigénie*, II, 1, 515

[I yielded to the fate that drove me on.]49

And she ascribes her departure to 'une secrète voix' which 'm'ordonna de par-tir' (561: 'a voice within me ordered me to go') with vague promises that her misfortune might prove infectious to Iphigénie and Achille.

After she has silently witnessed Agamemnon's cold and painful greeting of his daughter, Eriphile's second scene (II, 3) recapitulates her initial excuse, the absence of warm parenting and of reciprocated love, in contrast to Iphigénie:

> Hélas! à quels soupirs suis-je donc condamnée,
> Moi qui de mes parents toujours abandonnée,
> Etrangère partout, n'ai pas même en naissant
> Peut-être reçu d'eux un regard caressant !
> Du moins, si vos respects sont rejetés d'un père,
> Vous en pouvez gémir dans le sein d'une mère,

---

49   See above, 'Helplessness', p. 27.

Et de quelque disgrâce enfin que vous pleuriez,
Quels pleurs par un amant ne sont point essuyés ?

    II, 3, 585–92

[Alas! to what deep sighs am *I* condemned!
Always abandoned by my parents, and
A stranger everywhere; even at birth
Perhaps I was not given the least caress.
You at least, if the King rejects your love,
You can seek comfort on a mother's breast!
And whatsoe'er the mishap you bemoan,
Tears are dried swiftly by a lover's hand.]

She is then once more a silent witness to Iphigénie's perplexing relationship with her parents, this time Clytemnestre who brings the news that
Agamemnon's invitation had been superseded by the instruction not to come.
All the women believe or assume that this decision reflects a change of heart
in Achille, which leads to Eriphile's scornful taunting of Iphigénie (II, 5), but
which is soon corrected by Achille's own insistence to Eriphile of his continuing love for Iphigénie.

    Eriphile's final position in this act is defined by shame:

Dieux, qui voyez ma honte, où me dois-je cacher ?

    II, 8, 756

[Ye gods who see my shame, where can I hide?]

This seems to be generated both by the feeling that Achille still rejects or ig-
nores her own love, and by the realization that she has behaved badly towards
Iphigénie in what she had considered, briefly, to be her own moment of triumph.
This is a different form of hamartia: shameful behaviour triggered by a mistaken
appreciation of the situation. Eriphile was both overpowered by an impulse to
hurt another person (tragic flaw) and she was misled by Clytemnestre (tragic
error). She therefore has an excuse for her haughty treatment of Iphigénie, but
still feels ashamed of it, and fears a tit-for-tat response on the part of Iphigénie
(whose character she misreads) who will triumph over her:

Orgueilleuse rivale, on t'aime, et tu murmures ?
Souffrirai-je à la fois ta gloire et tes injures ?

    II, 8, 757–8

[He loves you, haughty one, yet you complain.
Can I abide your glory and abuse?][50]

Eriphile's exemplification of Aristotelian hamartia is also revealed in the way
Racine handles her decision to publicize the terms of the oracle, and to expose Agamemnon's and his family's plots to save Iphigénie if possible. This
decision, whether a tragic flaw or a tragic miscalculation or both, needs to be
presented as devastating but excusable if a tragic impact is to be generated.
The first stage of her action is dominated by claims of diminished responsibility. She almost wills herself to get carried away, to be given an excuse to claim
helplessness – 'Consultons des fureurs qu'autorisent les dieux' (IV, 1, 1140:
'Exploit wild passions that the gods approve') and is finally driven by jealousy
to expose to the Greek army Clytemnestre's plan to escape with Iphigénie,
supported by Achille and sometimes by Agamemnon. She can thus in human
terms be condemned for spitefulness, and for disloyalty towards one who
has befriended her when she was herself a helpless victim. The contrast with
the virtuous Iphigénie makes her an unsympathetic character whose death the
audience will not regret as deeply as they would that of Iphigénie. But at the
moment of announcing the sentence of death, Calchas pays no attention to
her own shortcomings, explaining the need for her death in liturgical rather
than judicial terms. To enable the expedition against Troy to succeed, the gods,
through the mysterious oracle, have demanded a sacrificial payment, which
should relate to the crime on which the expedition is based. 'Une fille du sang
d'Hélène' (I, 1, 59: 'a maiden pure of Helen's race') must perish if the army is to
succeed in reclaiming the guilty wife of Menelaus and punishing her abductor.
In so far as Eriphile's death is a punishment meted out by divine forces, therefore, it is a punishment on her mother rather than on herself. Since she is the
fruit of a previous illicit union between Helen and a different Greek prince
(Theseus), the punishment may seem fitting, but only by turning Eriphile into
a helpless pawn, a victim with the same low status as is accorded to Iphigénie
throughout the play. In that way, for all Eriphile's moral shortcomings and un-
pleasant character, Racine can indeed claim that he has presented her as not
'tout à fait indigne de compassion' (Préface: '[not] altogether unworthy of compassion'). It seems at least plausible, as is the case with Phèdre, to interpret
this role in proto-feminist terms. Racine portrays a world in which women are
the possessions of their fathers until handed over to their husbands, in which

---

50   Cairncross's translation here slightly misleads by substituting a present-tense verb for the
      future. The haughty abuse from Iphigénie exists only in Eriphile's imagination, and the
      force is more 'Will I have to put up with it?' than 'Can I stand it?'

women are destroyed by men for the sake of masculine ideals and objectives which they do not share, and (whatever Racine himself may consciously have thought) his plays demand that we reconsider the values of that world.

The character of Eriphile has not generally won the degree of sympathy from critical readers that this interpretation invites, but this is more because Racine does not quite rise to the challenge of his conception than because of a fundamental flaw in the conception itself. Iphigénie appears to be the tragic victim but does not die; Eriphile dies but is too unpalatable to invite pity. However, it is certainly an over-simplification of the ending to interpret it as 'happy' for Iphigénie herself: she ends the play isolated and weeping,[51] disillusioned with her parents and her lover, completely alienated from the cheerful rejoicing with which she is surrounded, the epitome of that 'tristesse majestueuse' ('majestic sadness')[52] in which Racine sees the essence of the tragic. If a production is to grasp the play's tragic resonance, *both* Iphigénies must convey this *tristesse* to the audience, and the key to that in Eriphile's case is to follow Racine's lead in using the theory of hamartia to inspire a balanced response to her fate and her actions from spectators – we must be encouraged and allowed to '[la] plaindre sans [la] détester'. Her role in this respect anticipates some aspects of that of Phèdre. In both characters, ignorance and helplessness are combined to generate pity, and love for which the woman takes no responsibility becomes overwhelming under the influence of jealousy. It may be that the construction of Eriphile was too deliberate, too much a question of analysing the Aristotelian principles and applying them, so that the fluency with which all the elements in Phèdre's character combine is missing in her case. But an interpretation in performance of the role that brought out what it had in common with Phèdre would have a good chance of imbuing the role, and the play itself, with a genuine tragic spirit.

Œnone is another case where Racine delicately balances blame and extenuation, and the two interpretations of hamartia as both moral flaw and error. Her action in accusing Hippolyte of a crime he did not commit (the rape or attempted rape of Phèdre, with violence) is clearly morally reprehensible, as she herself comes close to admitting: 'pour sauver votre honneur combattu, / Il

---

51   John Cairncross, whose translation is being referenced here, is one of several critics whose interpretation of the play defines the ending as 'happy': see for example his edition, pp. 40–41. But the tone generated by the conclusion suggests otherwise: 'La seule Iphigénie / Dans ce commun bonheur pleure son ennemie' (V, 6, 1785–6: 'Alone amidst the rejoicing, Iphigénie weeps over her enemy'). In Racine's text, the audience does not see Iphigénie at this point; perhaps it would be helpful if the ending were staged with her in sight.

52   *Bérénice, Préface*, p. 324; translation p. 223.

faut immoler tout, et meme la vertu' (III, 3, 907–8: 'To safeguard your honour, everything, / Yes even virtue, must be sacrificed'). But even for her, attenuating circumstances can be put forward.[53] She acts out of devotion to the beloved princess whom she suckled and has protected throughout her life, and puts forward her despicable plan only when Phèdre has violently rejected the much more sensible response initially offered by Œnone: 'Il faut d'un vain amour étouffer la pensée, / Madame. Rappelez votre vertu passée' (III, 3, 825–6: 'Your love is vain and you must stifle it, / O Queen, and summon up your former strength'). Phèdre's dismissal of this sound advice amounts to an abnegation of the responsibility that should be hers rather than her servant's, and she couples it with a renewed and very credible threat of suicide, which triggers Œnone's despair.

Œnone's action is also a miscalculation. She works out the consequences of her advice with precise logic:

> [...] Thésée, aigri par mes avis,
> Bornera sa vengeance à l'exil de son fils.
> Un père, en punissant, Madame, est toujours père,
> Un supplice léger suffit à sa colère.
>   III, 3, 899–902

> [Despite his wrath, the King
> Will do naught to his son but banish him.
> A father when he punishes is still
> A father, and his judgment will be mild.]

Œnone, in short, is suggesting no more than what Phèdre herself had inflicted on Hippolyte when she first met him (see I, 3, 291–6, and we have just been expressly reminded of this precedent in 892). She is, at this stage in her argument, balancing not Hippolyte's life against Phèdre's honour, as might at first appear, but Phèdre's certain death against relative discomfort for her stepson. This is a miscalculation in two respects: she underestimates the depth of Thésée's fury, and she overlooks the possibility that his tutelary god Neptune might remove from his shoulders the burdensome responsibility for carrying out the execution which as a father he can reasonably be expected to baulk at.

---

53   The case for her defence was most cogently argued by L.-L. Naneix, *Phèdre l'incomprise* (Paris: La Pensée universelle, 1977), pp. 165–175.

Hippolyte himself is considered by Racine to exemplify Aristotle's theory of hamartia explicitly:[54]

> On reprochait à Euripide de l'avoir représenté comme un philosophe exempt de toute imperfection, ce qui faisait que la mort de ce jeune prince causait beaucoup plus d'indignation que de pitié. J'ai cru lui devoir donner quelque faiblesse qui le rendrait un peu coupable envers son père [...]. J'appelle faiblesse la passion qu'il ressent malgré lui pour Aricie, qui est la fille et la sœur des ennemis mortels de son père.

> [The Ancients reproached Euripides with having portrayed him as a sage free from any imperfection. As a result, the young prince's death caused much more indignation than pity. I felt obliged to give him one weakness which would make him slightly guilty towards his father [...]. I regard as a weakness the passion he feels in spite of himself for Aricia, who is the daughter and sister of his father's mortal enemies.]

This, however, may turn out to be the most problematic of all Racine's applications to his own characters of the theory of hamartia, calling into question what Aristotle said and meant, how Racine himself interpreted it, and how it affects our reaction to tragic suffering. This is because, although few would question that Hippolyte's love for Aricie makes him a more *sympathetic* character than Euripides' misogynistic prig, even fewer are at all comfortable with considering that love as a 'weakness', let alone a moral failing which would make him remotely 'guilty' towards his father or anyone else.[55] Hippolyte's love does not turn him from a man into a villain, but from a superman into a man, 'asservie sous la commune loi, [...] au rang du reste des mortels' (II, 2, line 535 and I, 1, line 63: 'in bondage to the common law ... with the throng of ordinary mortals'). In Euripides, Hippolytos' superhuman self-control alienated audience sympathy, making him too good to be true, or at least too good to be likeable. Racine brings him down to the level of the audience – sinful man, perhaps, in a conventional sense, but with no necessity to be obsessed with inadequacy – and thus allows the normal operation of human sympathy on which tragedy depends. In short, Racine may be justified in arguing that it is

---

54   *Phèdre*, Préface, p. 577, translation p. 146.

55   See Edward Forman, '"Je commence à rougir": Shame, Self-Esteem and Guilt in the Presentation of Racine's Hippolyte', in Keith Cameron and Elizabeth Woodrough (eds.), *Ethics and Politics in Seventeenth-century France* (Exeter: University of Exeter Press, 1996), pp. 233–43, particularly for what follows here, p. 239. Some sections of that essay are repeated in the next few pages.

the invention of Aricie that turns Hippolyte into a satisfactory tragic hero, but he seems most unfair in calling his love for her a 'faiblesse' (weakness) and in going on to use the adjective 'coupable' (guilty) to describe this weakness and its victim. Such a characterization is undermined within the play itself, where Hippolyte, Phèdre and Œnone all use the word 'innocence' of the prince (996, 893, 903, 1238, 1617). However disorientated and uneasy Hippolyte feels about the unfamiliar feelings that seem to be detaching him from his self-image, he never refers to himself as guilty.

Insofar as he does nevertheless feel shifty about his feelings for Aricie, he has a number of excuses available. His father has had a reputation as a philandering he-man, so can be blamed for encouraging his son by example to adopt similar attitudes. And when, comparing himself to his father, Hippolyte explicitly draws a connection between heroic exploits and sexual gratification:

> [...] Qu'un long amas d'honneurs rend Thésée excusable,
> Qu'aucuns monstres par moi domptés jusqu'aujourd'hui
> Ne m'ont acquis le droit de faillir comme lui !
>
> I, 1, 98–100

> [Since countless exploits plead on his behalf,
> Whereas no monsters overcome by me
> Have given me the right to err like him.]

his tutor Théramène takes no advantage of the opportunity to explain to his pupil the difference between appropriate and inappropriate sexual desires or between reciprocal love and exploitation. Besides all of which, his father must shoulder some blame for bestowing on Aricie the enticing quality of forbidden fruit.[56]

If, then, hamartia as moral flaw does not shed much light on the interpretation of Hippolyte as a satisfactory tragic character, is hamartia as miscalculation any more helpful? We can certainly feel sympathy for the extent to which he is misled, by fate and others, about the context of all the decisions he has to make. He as much as Phèdre suffers from ignorance as to the real situation of Thésée as the play starts; he is oblivious of Phèdre's initial feelings for him and visits her in Act II under a misapprehension; he misreads Phèdre's ambiguous speech after the arrival of Thésée in Act III (fearing not that he is going to be falsely accused, but that Phèdre is going to blurt out the truth); and he is *never* told what it is that Thésée is berating him for in Act IV. So almost all

---

56   These issues will be discussed further in our chapter on Scapegoats, pp. 197–9.

his decisions and actions are the result of miscalculations about the motives and likely reactions of the other characters, including his closest friends, allies and divine protectors. Buoyed up but confused by human love, he fails to see the rash temper of his father, the lack of moral control in his step-mother, the potential of Œnone to intervene and the blind inhumanity of the supernatural forces in which he misguidedly puts his faith. Most intriguingly, he seems to overlook a fundamental miscalculation that lies at the heart of his own situation. Thésée's decree that Aricie should not marry, lest her offspring revive the claim of the descendants of Pallas to the throne of Athens, is neither illogical nor criminal, but if the descendants of Pallas and the descendants of Thésée were the same, then that blood feud would be neutralized. Hippolyte is thus in fact the one person that Aricie *could* be allowed to marry, and it is one of the many tragic ironies underlying this complex situation that neither he nor anyone else grasps this potential way out. The most relevant instance of hamartia here is neither the illicit passion of Phèdre herself nor that of Hippolyte, but this error of judgment, arising because the characters are kept in total or partial ignorance of the whole picture, an error for which no single person is obviously to blame but for which everyone carries a share of responsibility.

The case of Hippolyte opens up an even more fundamental debate about the very basis of Aristotle's theory of hamartia. Is it really true that an innocent victim of fate or circumstance is an inappropriate figure for the operation of catharsis and the sense of the tragic? Hippolyte insists not only that he is innocent, but that the gods will respect and protect him because of it:

> Mais l'innocence enfin n'a rien à redouter.
>> III, 6, 996

> [But innocence has surely naught to fear.]

> Sur l'équité des dieux osons nous confier.
>> V, 1, 1351

> [Let's trust the justice of the gods above.]

At a pinch one could define this as another miscalculation: Hippolyte's blind faith in the justice of the universe is misguided. But that was not the basis on which Racine sought to apply to Hippolyte the term 'coupable'; nor is it easy to trace a logical argument that that sort of fundamental misreading of the nature of the universe is what Aristotle could have had in mind in defining the special characteristic of tragedy. The spectacle of a totally innocent character

driven to distraction or particularly to death, his argument goes, provokes
in an audience a moral repulsion which undermines the effects of pity and
fear on which catharsis depends. It is that argument that has often led, as we
have seen, to a scurry to find hamartia at all costs, a quest with which not
everyone agrees:[57]

> Seul le destin immérité est tragique. Nous faisons fausse route en voulant
> trouver chez Antigone une faute qui justifierait sa fin, en rendant Œdipe
> ou Deianeira coupables.

> [*Only* undeserved fate is tragic. It is misguided of us to seek in Antigone
> some fault that would justify her fate, or to try to make Oedipus or
> Deianeira guilty of anything.]

5   Hamartia Re-Assessed

Martha Nussbaum considered that 'despite the thousands of pages that have
been written on [hamartia], we still need an account that is fully responsive to
the ways in which, for Aristotle, practical error can come about through some
causes other than viciousness of character and still matter to the value of a
life'.[58] As we saw (above, pp. 56–61, particularly around notes 18 and 21), many
of those thousands of pages were devoted to a perceived tension between interpretations of hamartia as 'tragic flaw' and as 'tragic error', and Nussbaum's
fresh insight is that this tension may be resolved if we see that a character imperfection might be relevant to the audience's response to the tragic hero without necessarily having to be implicated as a cause of his downfall: 'The tragic
hero should not fall through wickedness; but his being less than perfectly good
is important to our pity and fear' (p. 387). Terry Eagleton expressed it similarly:
'You can interpret the tragic flaw less as a defect which causes the tragedy than
as a blemish which makes the hero's sufferings more palatable'.[59] For most
tragic victims, even if we are able to prove that their disgrace and suffering are
the result of some specific (or indeed general) stupidity or sinfulness on their
part, this scarcely allays our uncomfortable sense that they get a raw deal. But

---

57   Ion Omesco, *La Métamorphose de la tragédie* (Paris: Presses Universitaires de France,
      1978), p. 85.
58   *The Fragility of Goodness: Luck and Ethics in Greek Tragedy and Philosophy* (Cambridge:
      Cambridge University Press, first published 1986, revised edition 2001), p. 382.
59   *Sweet Violence*, p. 124.

the fact that they are liable to stupidities and weaknesses is what enables us to avoid thinking of them as supermen or superwomen whose fate is of no concern to us, and to try to grapple alongside them with the perplexities generated by their misfortunes. A.D. Nuttall, in exploring the question, 'Why does tragedy give pleasure?' argued that it is problematic only because we are not in fact all sadists, even (*pace* Freud) subconsciously.[60] He bluntly rejected any notion of fairness in the outcomes of tragedy: 'Poetic justice is one of the first casualties of tragedy' (p. 34). I believe that the re-evaluation through modern eyes of ancient human stories, superimposing our conceptions of justice and injustice on those of earlier periods, provides a basis for appreciation of the sorts of pleasure that Nuttall defined as characteristic of tragedy – relief, a sense of rebalancing, a renewed faith in the value of human endeavour – and that the theory of hamartia, related as it can be to the notion of extenuated guilt, provides a useful framework for analysing this appreciation. It is one of the more enticing paradoxes of literary study that one can perfectly well use the theory of hamartia to explain why one believes that *Phèdre* is one of the pinnacles of tragic drama, even whilst proclaiming that Racine himself misunderstood Aristotle on the subject, and that Aristotle was inconsistent and incoherent in expounding the theory.

---

60   *Why Does Tragedy Give Pleasure?* (Oxford: Clarendon Press, 1996), p. 1, p. 54 and p. 74.

CHAPTER 3

Ignorance

The law acquits me, innocent, as ignorant of what I did[1]

∴

The maxim that 'ignorance is no excuse for breaking the law' is firmly embedded in almost every legal system, if only for the pragmatic reason that ignorance would otherwise be a universal excuse – it would be impossible for a prosecutor to prove that a suspect who claimed ignorance was simply lying.[2] Nevertheless, it is difficult to avoid a sense of injustice in contemplating this rule: one might genuinely have failed to see a speed-limit sign, or be genuinely unaware of local regulations about smoking, or spitting, in a public space. From around the time of the Enlightenment in 18th-century Europe, as a rapidly increasing corpus of national legislation was applied to a citizenry that was still largely illiterate, it became increasingly clear that the presumption of knowledge worked in favour of lawyers rather than citizens. As the lifestyle of the average citizen has become increasingly complex, the excuse of a degree of ignorance has become correspondingly more plausible, and although society must be based on the broad presumption that citizens have a responsibility to be well informed and to act according to established local practice, lawyers in practice continue to make a great deal of money by exploiting the ignorance of many in the face of the complex contemporary world, its rules and regulations. It also chimes in with human experience – if only at the level of Murphy's Law – that we cannot predict precisely what consequences our actions and decisions are going to have. To that extent, a tragic dramatist who can contrive some ambiguity in this regard is likely to achieve a striking moral effect. The person whose misfortune comes about because of some unforeseen detail, some hidden secret about his own or his protagonists' identity or

---

1 Sophocles, *Oedipus at Colonus*, lines 546-48, in *The Theban Plays*, trans. E.F. Watling (Harmondsworth: Penguin, 1947), p. 88.
2 One clear, recent exposition of the history and basis of the maxim, and some difficulties presented by it, is Arnold Nciko, 'Ignorance of the Law is no Defence', *Strathmore Law Review*, 3, 2018, pp. 25–47.

© KONINKLIJKE BRILL NV, LEIDEN, 2021 | DOI:10.1163/9789004442788_005

motivation, some link in the chain of causation which he cannot be blamed for failing to anticipate, will seem less blameworthy, and so more pitiable. Other nuances may add complexity: was the victim deliberately deceived, did he overlook what should have been obvious, or can the miscalculation be considered simply 'one of those things' – and how does this affect the moral responsibility of the parties involved? Does the central character himself manipulate the position, *calculating* that the outcome of his action is sufficiently uncertain to provide him with a reasonable chance of successful defence – and is this calculation deliberate or at most semi-conscious? Even if the claim of ignorance is accepted, a replacement charge of negligence, wilful blindness or sheer stupidity might restore the balance in favour of a guilty verdict, or at least ensure, within the context of classical tragic theory, that the balance between blame and exoneration is maintained at a level that produces hamartia and generates catharsis.

Ignorance is less pervasive in classical tragic drama than other forms of extenuation, such as diminished responsibility, provocation or determinism, but it was emphasized by Aristotle, and is central to *Oedipus tyrannos*, which he held up as the best model. A theorist of tragedy who prioritizes the notion of anagnorisis may sense that the discovery of something hidden – an identity or relationship, or some less tangible factor underlying a decision or action – can be as central to the generation of tragic intensity as is the evocation of pity or fear. It is not difficult to find examples of tragedies, from all periods, in which actions or statements are blamed and/or regretted, but excused on the basis that the character involved was not at the time in full possession of relevant facts. Agave does not recognize Pentheus as she dismembers him. Deianeira is deceived into believing that a deadly poison is a love-charm. Hercules in his madness believes that he is making an assault on the heavens, whereas in fact he is slaughtering his own wife and child. Macbeth is misled as to the nature of his enemy and the guarantees he is offered of prosperity. Othello is simply lied to. Phèdre (in Racine's play) genuinely thinks Thésée is dead. Athalie is ignorant of the identity of Joas. Stella Kowalski (in *A Streetcar Named Desire*) cannot straightforwardly be blamed for her inability to accept what her husband has done to her sister. 'I wouldn't have done it if I'd known ...' is indeed a widespread tragic 'if only'.

1   Theories

There is some classical support for exculpation on the basis of ignorance. In his *Nicomachean Ethics*, Aristotle deals rather legalistically and precisely with degrees of guilt and extenuation, drawing distinctions between innocent and culpable ignorance. 'Ignorance constitutes grounds for penal correction, if the agent seems to be responsible' or 'ignorant through carelessness'.[3] The agent, although not vicious, may seem reckless, careless or impulsive, and to that extent blameworthy. Oedipus knew that he was killing an old man (and he knew that he had been warned that he would kill his father) but he had grounds for not believing this man to be his father, so in a sense he killed the man voluntarily, but he killed his father involuntarily. When at Thebes he first discovered the reality of his action, he was pained and ashamed. This retrospective pain may make no difference to his legal responsibility but it does provide the onlooker with 'valuable ethical information about the agent'.[4]

Ovid maintained that 'ignorance will provide a pardon for earlier sins',[5] although doubt has been cast on the general validity of this defence under Roman law: 'Ignorance, or an error concerning the existence or meaning of a legal norm [...] does not afford an excuse, and the person who acts from lack of knowledge of the law has to bear the consequences of his ignorance. Some persons, however, such as women, minors, soldiers, inexperienced rustic persons, may be excused.'[6] On the other hand, *error facti*, 'ignorance or false knowledge of a fact, may be alleged as an excuse, and may in certain instances produce the nullity of the act', although this rule 'was not generally applied' (p. 456). A similar degree of relativism can be found in Mosaic law: *Numbers*, 15:22–31, for example, distinguishes between those who 'sin through ignorance' – for whom atonement is still necessary but who will receive forgiveness – and those who 'sin presumptuously', whose 'soul shall be cut off from among his people'. Psalm 19:12–13 asks 'Who is aware of his unwitting sins?' but the psalmist acknowledges that cleansing is needed for 'secret' as well as for wilful transgressions. That legal framework was inherited by the Judaeo-Christian tradition; Christ is reported in *Luke* 12:47–48 as differentiating between those who sin in ignorance of their master's wishes, and those who knew them 'yet made no attempt to carry them out' – the former will still be flogged, but 'less severely' than the latter. To this may be added a third strand, summed up in the words attributed – although only by Saint Luke[7] – to Christ on the cross:

3   3.5, 1113b30ff. Edited and translated by Sarah Broadie and Christopher Rowe (Oxford: Oxford University Press, 2002), p. 130.

4   *Nicomachean Ethics*, edn. cit., pp. 39–40.

5   Ovid, *Heroïdes XX*, 187.

6   A. Berger, *Encyclopedic Dictionary of Roman Law* (Philadelphia: The American Philosophical Society, 1953), p. 491.

7   *Luke*, 23:34. These words are not found in all early manuscripts of Luke's gospel, and where they occur they seem to break the narrative flow in an obtrusive way, as though the speech

Father, forgive them: for they know not what they do.

Although forgiveness is not the same as exculpation, this suggests that ignorance can be accepted as a valid excuse for an act of extreme injustice, indeed
that it was willingly offered as such by the victim of the crime. The parties for
whom Christ pleads forgiveness had calculatedly bribed one of his intimate
followers, had manipulated the legalistic framework of the time and had deliberately stirred up a volatile crowd to violence. What, therefore, did Christ
mean? Who was ignorant, and what were they ignorant of? Are they to be forgiven for the action only because they do not know the identity of the victim? If
so, the implication is that the behaviour of the torturers was acceptable in the
normal way of things, but made criminal or sinful by being inflicted on God's
son – just as Oedipus' road rage would be excusable against an anonymous
stranger, but becomes monstrous when the victim is revealed to be his father,
even though the latter shared some responsibility for concealing their relationship. An equivalent in modern British law would be the offence of assaulting a
police officer, which is more serious than assaulting someone else, and which
will carry a guilty verdict even if it is clear that the accused was unaware, at
the time of the assault, of the officer's identity and status.[8] Does this apply
even if the police officer is disguised specifically as an *agent provocateur* or for
purposes of entrapment? At the time of the crucifixion of Christ, there was no
shortage of evidence available to the Jewish leaders to indicate who it was that
they were dealing with: so if that is the key, were they not culpably negligent in
ignoring it? Or are there greater truths about the nature of reality or human relationships, which the people needed to know in order to subdue their violent
instincts? Was Christ saying (or Luke suggesting) that humankind, in general,
is not in full possession of information necessary to rational decision making?
That may correspond to the experience of many people most of the time, and
is comforting to the extent that it releases us from a sense of full responsibility
for the results of our decisions, but it raises awkward questions about freedom
and autonomy, and seems out of tune with a great deal of the moral teaching
of Christ and his church from the earliest times.

---

was an interpolation. Some modern Biblical scholars therefore believe that the words were
not spoken by Christ, others that they were not even recorded by Luke. See for example,
C.F. Evans, *Saint Luke* (London: SCM Press, 2008), pp. 867–68, which includes (p. 868) the
statement, 'Ignorance as a ground of forgiveness is fairly widely attested in Hellenistic
literature'.

8   This legal precedent dates back to 1865, Reg. v Forbes and Webb: 'it is not necessary that the
defendant should know that he was a constable'. See E.W. Cox, *Reports of Cases in Criminal
Law*, vol. X (London: Law Times Office, 1868), p. 362.

Saint Paul considered himself 'the first of sinners'[9] even though he 'acted in the ignorance of unbelief'.[10] On that basis, he does not seem to claim exoneration for his actions, but is grateful to be 'dealt with mercifully'.[11] Elsewhere, he suggests an understanding attitude towards ignorant humans who cannot be expected to grasp in full the 'hidden wisdom' of God: 'None of the powers that rule the world have known that wisdom; if they had, they would not have crucified the Lord of glory'.[12] Saint Augustine, whose views may have had an influence on the thought of Racine through his Jansenist upbringing, emphasized that it was possible to be guilty of sin even if you were unaware of the true nature of justice.[13] The Jansenist and the Jesuit who debate this point in Pascal's *Lettres Provinciales* produce sharply polarized arguments: the Jesuit doctrine that an action 'ne peut être imputée à péché, si Dieu ne nous donne, avant que de la commettre, la connaissance du mal qui y est, et une inspiration qui nous excite à l'éviter' ('cannot be deemed sinful if God, before we commit the act, has not given us insight into its evil quality, and provided us with inspiration to avoid it', p. 55) is dismissed by the Jansenist as typical moral laxness: 'jamais les Pères, les Papes, les Conciles, ni l'Écriture, ni aucun livre de piété, même dans ces derniers temps, n'ont parlé de cette sorte' ('the Holy Fathers, Popes, Councils of the Church, the scriptures and other pious works, even in recent times, have never made this claim', p. 56). This was a genuinely thorny issue for Renaissance thought, faced with pagan virtue – if members of classical or of recently colonized societies were to be excused from sin on the basis of ignorance, it would be too easy for the negligent or the calculating to let themselves off the hook, a position mercilessly caricatured by Pascal: 'tous les péchés de surprise, et ceux qu'on fait dans un entier oubli de Dieu, ne pourraient être imputés' ('sinful actions that creep up on us unawares, or are undertaken in total forgetfulness of God, could not be taken into account', p. 55), and 'peut-être n'avez-vous guère vu de gens qui aient moins de péchés, car ils ne pensent jamais à Dieu' ('you could scarcely envisage less sinful people than those who never spare God a single thought', p. 59). Pascal does provide his Jesuit with some popular contemporary sources for his more casuistic approach, but the Jansenist insists that biblical precedent and the authority of the Church Fathers are overwhelmingly on his side: ignorance is no excuse.

---

9   *I Timothy*, 1:15.

10   *I Timothy*, 1:13.

11   *Ibid.*

12   *I Corinthians*, 2:8.

13   See B. Pascal, *Les Provinciales*, ed. by L. Cognet and G. Ferreyrolles (Paris: Bordas, 1992), 4th Letter, pp. 53–71.

2   Oedipus at Thebes and at Colonus

Given the ethical background current in ancient Greece, and the general tendency in law to downplay the validity of ignorance as an exoneration, Oedipus' claim at Colonus is quite startlingly explicit:

> A wretch, but innocent
> In the law's eye, I stand without a stain.[14]

He does not here claim ignorance as a partial mitigation, or as the basis for a plea of forgiveness, but as a total exculpation. This is not a claim he had made at Thebes:

> Now I've exposed my guilt, horrendous guilt,
> Could I train a level glance on you, my countrymen?[15]

By the time he reached Colonus, he saw things differently – or Sophocles' perspective had changed when he wrote his later play. Antigone is first to mention Oedipus' lack of deliberate ill intent, but she does not expect him to be granted special favours or acquittal:

> Though you refuse to hear my poor blind father,
> Because of the things he is known to have done –
> Although they were none of his own devising –
> Yet have some pity on *me*, I beseech you![16]

Oedipus himself appears increasingly bitter in his denial of responsibility:

> Was I the sinner?
> Repaying wrong for wrong – that was no sin,
> Even were it wittingly done, as it was not.
> I did not know the way I went. *They* knew;
> They who devised this trap for me.
>
>   270–74, p. 74

---

14   Sophocles, *Oedipus at Colonus*, 548, in Sophocles, *Oedipus the King, Oedipus at Colonus and Antigone*, trans F. Storr (Cambridge, MA: Harvard University Press, 1912), p. 201.

15   Sophocles, *Oedipus tyrannos*, 1384–85, in *The Three Theban Plays*, trans. Robert Fagles (Harmondsworth: Penguin, 1984), p. 243.

16   Sophocles, *Oedipus at Colonus*, 237–40, trans. E.F. Watling, p. 78.

If he had committed guilty actions, he had done so unwittingly, in a form of self-defence, and he does not admit that his identity is shameful. Later his expression of outraged innocence on the basis of ignorance, as well as provocation, self-defence and diminished responsibility, becomes explicit:

> I tell you, then, I have endured
> Foulest injustice; I have endured
> Wrong undeserved; God knows
> Nothing was of my choosing.
>> 521–2, p. 87

> He whom I killed
> Had sought to kill me first. The law
> Acquits me, innocent, as ignorant
> Of what I did.
>> 546–48, p. 88

Even before the truth has been revealed, the attitude of those around him towards Oedipus is hard to pin down. At one point, Jocasta explains why she has come to the temple to pray:

> The King is over-wrought
> With fancies, and can no longer sanely judge
> The present by the past, listening to every word
> That feeds his apprehension. I can do nothing
> To comfort him.[17]

The predominant tone of these lines in that translation, surely, is 'Poor Oedipus: the impossible position he has been put into has rendered him paranoid' – if he makes injudicious decisions, or prefers good advice to bad, he is excused by perplexity. However, that interpretation has not been unanimous. Robert Fagles's translation of the very same lines introduces a stronger note of condemnation:

> Oedipus is beside himself. Racked with anguish,
> no longer a man of sense, he won't admit
> the latest prophecies are hollow as the old –
> he's at the mercy of every passing voice

---

[17]   Sophocles, *Oedipus tyrannos*, 913–7, trans. E.F. Watling, p. 50.

if the voice tells of terror.
I urge him gently, nothing seems to help.[18]

'He won't admit' suggests a refusal to look rather than a cruelly inflicted blindness. And Frederick Ahl pushes this negative interpretation of the speech, and of Oedipus's character, to an extreme:

> Oedipus lets his emotions run too high
> whenever stressed or pained. Unlike the thinking man,
> he doesn't assess the new from past experience.
> He's always owned by anyone who spells things out
> for him – provided that man spells out things he fears.[19]

The unobtrusive but powerful introduction of the words 'whenever' and 'always' turns this into a generalized statement about the king's character rather than an expression of temporary sympathy, and the formulation of the last line suggests more powerfully than other translations that Oedipus is stubbornly refusing to listen to any voice that does not feed his paranoia.

Although the speech is about Oedipus it also reveals truths about Jocasta. She, too, is blinded, clinging obstinately to her logic: *her* oracles about the death of Laius did not come to pass, so why should they believe Tiresias's condemnation of Oedipus? Whether she is expressing sympathy for her husband or blaming him, it is unfair of her to suggest that her response is more rational than his: even before the messenger from Corinth arrives, he is right to be disconcerted by the strange news they are uncovering, and it is rather ironic that when she cannot reassure him, her response is to come to a different temple to pray, as though a different oracle might provide a less troubling message:

> For Oedipus is exciting his mind in excess with every kind of grief, and he is not interpreting new happenings by means of earlier ones like a rational man, but he is at the mercy of the speaker, if he speaks of terrors. So since I do no good by trying to counsel him, I come as a suppliant to you, Lycian Apollo ...[20]

---

18   Fagles translation, p. 211.
19   Frederick M. Ahl, *Two Faces of Oedipus: Sophocles' Oedipus Tyrannus and Seneca's Oedipus* (Ithaca NY: Cornell University Press, 2008), pp. 169–70.
20   Sophocles, *Ajax, Electra, Oedipus tyrannus*, edited and translated by Hugh Lloyd-Jones (Cambridge, MA: Harvard UP, 1994), p. 417.

They both struggle to make sense of strange new[21] discoveries in the light of their memories – and interpretations – of past events; neither has a monopoly either of reason or of unreason.

It has been argued that there is a relevant difference from this point of view between Sophocles' Oedipus and that of Seneca.[22] Because Sophocles' king is 'a commanding presence, forthright and bold', the spectator is more likely to view his self-confidence as hubris, and therefore to criticize his apparent or claimed ignorance: 'his ignorance of the fact that he is implicated might appear naivety or obtuseness or an ostrich-like attempt not to know'. Seneca's hero, in contrast, is 'conscience-wracked, filled with foreboding', and 'comes to seem less culpable because of his apprehensions'. We have already noted[23] this aspect of the dramatist's skill: the manipulation of the audience by playing with a tendency, potentially rather perverse, of observers to show sympathy in inverse proportion to a character's self-pity: Seneca's ruler, argues McEachern, 'earns our fellowship by confiding his unease [...]. We feel allied with him against the forces that best us.'

3   Deianeira

Another Classical figure who killed in a state of ignorance was Deianeira, the virtuous wife of Heracles, who unwittingly caused his death. This event was turned into a tragedy by Sophocles in his *Trachiniae*, by Seneca in his *Hercules Oetaeus* (*Hercules on Mount Oeta*), and by the seventeenth-century French baroque dramatist Jean Rotrou in his *Hercule mourant*. Although there are striking differences between the three treatments, all of them make some dramatic and ironic play with the ambiguity surrounding the degree of guilt that may be attached to Deianeira for her action. During an earlier adventure, she and Heracles had been deceived by the monstrous centaur Nessus who agreed to carry the woman across a swollen river, but then proceeded to assault her. Although Heracles could not reach them, he killed the monster with a poisoned arrow – at which Nessus tricked Deianeira into believing that his own blood would be an effective love-philtre should she ever need to regain her husband's affection. These perfidious instructions condemn her beloved

---

21   In the speech under consideration, the Greek word *kaina*, translated as 'present, new, latest', actually means both 'recent' and 'strange'. See Sophocles, *Oedipus Rex*, edited by R.D. Dawe (Cambridge: CUP, Cambridge Greek and Latin Classics, 1982), p. 188.
22   Claire Elizabeth McEachern, 'Two Loves I have: Of Comfort and Despair in Shakespearean Genre', *British Journal of Aesthetics*, 54, 2014, pp. 191–211 (pp. 201–203).
23   'Introduction', pp. 14–15.

husband to intense agony and death, since what had been represented to her by Nessus as a love potion was in fact a deadly poison.

In Sophocles' version of the story, Deianeira genuinely does not foresee, let alone intend, the outcome of her action; although jealous of Heracles' new amour Iole, she is neither vindictive nor destructive, but simply wants her husband back. As she herself rationalizes:

> Love has his own way with the gods themselves.
> [...]   It would be madness
> To blame my husband for catching this infection. [...]
> I shall not blame them [...] I cannot be angry with him.[24]

Other jilted wives might have been glad to have poison to administer, and might, like Medea, have claimed diminished responsibility or provocation as their excuse for killing either party. Both Seneca and Rotrou, as we shall see, present her as more embittered and confrontational than Sophocles, but Sophocles' Deianeira is simply duped.[25]

Ignorance in the abstract, combined with a general sense of helplessness, is a recurrent theme of Sophocles' play, sometimes in rather conventional terms:

> If we are not blind, we cannot but fear
> Today's success may be tomorrow's fall.
> 296–97, p. 129

Generalizations of this sort are characteristic of anagnorisis-based tragedies, and Deianeira herself is not above platitude:

> Call no man happy, unhappy; you cannot tell
> Till the day of his death. [...]
> 2–3, p. 119

---

24 Sophocles, *Electra and Other Plays*, trans. E.F. Watling (Harmondsworth: Penguin Classics, 1953), lines 441–49 and 543–44, pp. 134 and 137. Some critics consider this speech to be insincere, a means of extracting the truth from Lichas, but the portrayal of Deianeira in the rest of the play does not support that degree of calculation.

25 See Jennifer R. March, *The Creative Poet: Studies on the Treatment of Myths in Greek Poetry* (London: Institute of Classical Studies, Bulletin Supplement 49, 1987), pp. 47–77; she demonstrates, pp. 49–60, the prevalence in Hesiod and other pre-Sophoclean sources of a bloodthirsty and vengeful Deianeira.

> O let this be a warning to everyone
> Not to rush blindly into an act whose consequence
> Cannot be foreseen!
>> 669–70, p. 141

However, Sophocles seems to have gone out of his way to present her as haunted by ignorance in a way that generates sympathy. It is a Leitmotif of her opening speech:

> What kind of battle it was, I cannot tell you;
> I never knew. [...]
>> 21–2, p. 120

> But where my husband is, who knows?
>> 41–2, p. 121

As a child she had not known her future; as a bride she never knew where her husband was or what he was up to; within the play, she is woefully unable to interpret messages or situations accurately. The herald Lichas presents her with an all but invented story of Heracles' enmity towards Eurytus, the basis of his most recent triumph, and brazenly denies all knowledge of the name and identity of Iole, who herself remains disconcertingly silent under questioning.

The situation is further complicated by a number of misleading or ambiguous messages and oracles. Heracles knows the date on which 'his labours will come to an end', and believes that he can never be killed by a living creature; Deianeira has been told that the charm 'will bind the heart of Heracles'. Both might therefore be charged with a degree of credulity or complacency, but Sophocles is at pains to ensure that they do not lose the audience's sympathy altogether. Even when Deianeira herself admits that it was imprudent of her to believe that 'the monster at his death / Would wish to do me good' (707–08, p. 142), she is likely to appear naïvely innocent rather than stupid, and the Chorus reinforces this impression: 'Yet anger mellows / In the presence of innocent fault, as it will for you' (727–28, p. 143).

The fact remains that as soon as she learns the dreadful truth, Deianeira is filled with horror and remorse, and kills herself. Ignorance is in her own eyes an inadequate excuse, especially coupled with credulous faith in an untrustworthy source. Her son Hyllus and Heracles both assume initially that her action was deliberate and calculated, and condemn her outright:

> This is what you have done, mother, to my father;
> Done it deliberately; and your guilt is known.
>   807–08, p. 145

The Chorus is more charitable, distinguishing between the willed action and the unintended outcome:

> What she did
> She did deliberately; the consequence
> Was not her doing.
>   844–46, p. 147

These lines are difficult to reconstruct and to interpret, and translators have expressed in slightly different ways the distinction being made: 'The remedy was destructive, but only through her blindness',[26] and 'Part of the deed she herself supplied, but part came from another's will'.[27] At any rate it is clear that the position adopted by the Chorus reflects Aristotle's differentiation between 'acting because of ignorance' and 'acting in ignorance'[28] – Deianeira is not befuddled in her decision-making by drunkenness or even passion, which would transfer her culpability to a lack of self-control, but genuinely unaware of what will happen. When in due course Hyllus learns the truth, 'that what she had done was all a mistake', he weeps with regret that he himself has caused *her* death through his anger. Part of the pathos of this tragedy is generated by the fact that Heracles himself never receives that illumination, but dies in the belief that his wife has deliberately killed him in revenge for his infidelity.

Although Seneca and Rotrou both retain the story of Nessus, and both present Deianeira as intending the robe she sends to Hercules to act as a love potion, they depict her as violently jealous of Iole and motivated to destroy her husband as an act of vengeance. This makes her subsequent remorse over the unintended outcome of her action more bitter, and the excuse of ignorance – more often expressed by others on her behalf than by the queen herself – less convincing. Both authors are true to their times in suggesting a strong desire that the outcomes of tragedy should not be manifestly unjust, yet they retain an awareness of the basic principle of Aristotelian hamartia, that her fate would not be appropriately tragic or cathartic if she were either too innocent

---

26   Trans. J. M. Walton, in *Six Greek Tragedies* (London: Methuen Drama, 2002), p. 105.
27   Trans. Hugh Lloyd-Jones, in Sophocles, *Antigone, Women of Trachis, Philoctetes, Oedipus at Colonus* (Cambridge, MA: Harvard University Press, 1994).
28   *Nicomachean Ethics*, 3.1, 1110b16–26, edn. cit., p. 124.

or too guilty. She must not appear as totally a puppet of the gods or of an evil influence, nor as totally calculating and vengeful.

Seneca's Deianeira opens the play in a distraught frame of mind, aware that her impulses are violent but claiming, in effect, diminished responsibility:

> I myself admit that it is an enormous crime, but my pain insists on it.[29]

It is only through an apparently chance remark by her nurse that she is reminded of the substance given to her by Nessus and its alleged powers: although she contemplates the possibility that Hercules will return to her, she is still talking about killing him, if not with the sword, then with guile (436–38, p. 371). Her subsequent reaction to the news that her robe is torturing Hercules to death is to feel and acknowledge guilt: 'Use your thunderbolts, father-in-law, to destroy your criminal daughter-in-law. [...] Strike me like some unexampled scourge, like an evil worse than the angry stepmother' (847–52, p. 407). Only in passing does she distinguish between her intention and the outcome: 'my spirit is innocent, but my hand bears the crime. Oh, for my credulous mind!' (964–65, p. 417) and it is Hyllus and the nurse who expound the excuse of ignorance on her behalf: 'What iniquity exists here is entirely due to error. A person is not guilty unless guilty by intent' (886–87, p. 409). 'Many whose guilt lay in their mistake, not their act, have been allowed to live. Who passes sentence on his own fate?' (900–01, p. 413) and 'At least vindicate your action, ill-fated woman: let him know the deed arose from treachery, not his wife' (932–33, p. 415). Hercules himself has little doubt that Deianeira was the willing and deliberate agent of his death: indeed for him (and for Juno, in his view) the ultimate shame is that it is a mortal woman who defeats him (1174–1207, pp. 433–35). Although this play ends with the apotheosis of Hercules and a degree of reconciliation, the residual moral is not that ignorance constitutes an acceptable excuse: 'Only death establishes the innocence of those that were duped' (890, p. 411) – in other words those who have been ensnared into sin may be guilt-free but must still atone for their action.

When Jean Rotrou adapted Seneca's play for the French stage as *Hercule mourant* around 1631,[30] he increased the love interest. Hercule has a rival for the love of Iole, Arcas, and Rotrou made space for this by excluding Hercule's son Hyllus from the action. He sharpened the hostility between Déianire and

---

29   Seneca, *Hercules on Oeta*, 330–31, in Seneca, *Tragedies*, trans. J.G. Fitch (Cambridge, MA: Harvard University Press, 2004), vol. 2, p. 361.

30   Ed. D.A. Watts (Exeter: University of Exeter, 1971). The French text is also available online at http://gallica.bnf.fr/ark:/12148/bpt6k72394w.

her husband in the opening scenes, which depict a confrontation between them and a bitter monologue from Déianire. Her spite is soon translated into direct threats:

> Mais son espoir est vain, et le cours de cet âge
> Qui m'ôte des attraits, me laisse du courage ;
> Si ma force n'est vaine en cette occasion,
> Je paraîtrai ta femme à ta confusion.
>
> I, 2, 137–40

> [But his hope is in vain, and as my increasing age
> Detracts from my beauty, it increases my courage;
> If now my force is not in vain,
> I will appear as your wife, to your ruin.]

These become still more explicit in act II:

> O Junon ! Perds ce traître, envoie un monstre ici
> Qui te satisfaisant, me satisfasse aussi ;
> S'il est quelque serpent, horrible, épouvantable,
> Capable d'étouffer ce vainqueur redoutable,
> Et qu'à cette action tu puisses provoquer,
> Qu'il vienne, qu'il paraisse, et qu'il l'aille attaquer.
> Ou s'il n'est point de monstre assez fort pour ta haine,
> Fais-moi capable d'être et son monstre, et sa peine.
>
> II, 2, 327–34

> [Oh, Juno! Destroy this traitor, send down a monster
> who will satisfy both you and me.
> If there is a snake, monstrous and terrifying
> Who can overcome this redoubtable champion,
> And whom you can inspire to act against him,
> Let it come, let it appear, let it attack him!
> Or if no monster has the strength to reflect your hatred,
> Grant me that capacity, so that I may be Hercule's monster and his
>   punishment.]

Rotrou's Hercule is a good deal more antipathetic, at least to a modern reader, than his classical counterparts in his heroic misogyny:

Parce que j'aimais trop, je fus un peu cruel,
Et ta seule beauté causa notre duel.
[...]
Quoi ? Possédant Hercule, Iole est malheureuse ?
[...]
Quoi ? Toute chose cède à ma force indomptée [...]
Et je reconnaîtrais un si faible vainqueur ?
Je nourrirais sans fruit le brasier qui me brûle,
Et l'on dirait, Iole a triomphé d'Hercule ?

> I, 3, 175–76, 182, 205, 208–10

[Because I loved too much, I was a little cruel,
And it was your beauty which caused our dispute.
What? Commanding Hercule, Iole is unhappy?
What? Everything bows before my unvanquished force,
And I am to acknowledge defeat at such weak hands?
I am to submit to the burning flames with no reward?
It is to be alleged that Iole triumphed over Hercule?]

In this version, almost all the attention, particularly in the second half of the play, is focussed on Hercule himself, whose physical agony we witness on stage, and whose repetitive self-pity is hardly calculated to engage our sympathy. His peremptory execution of the herald Lichas prepares us for the rage with which he seeks to punish Déianire for what he sees as a clear and deliberate crime. Any sense that she might have made a simple mistake or miscalculation is reduced to passing references, for example her servant Luscinde's attempts to reassure her that 'Celui ne pèche pas qui pèche sans dessein' ('It is no sin to sin without intent', 880), which she dismisses as a 'frivole raison' ('frivolous argument'):

En un malheur semblable,
La plus pure innocence est encor trop coupable.
> III, 4, 881–82

[when the consequence is so dire,
The purest innocence is still filled with guilt.]

Although her dying words will appear to exonerate her –

> Agis, m'a-t-elle dit, un seul point me console :
> J'ai sans intention tramé cet accident,
> Et mon dessein fut moins criminel qu'imprudent.
>> IV, 3, 1130–32

> ['Go ahead,' she said, 'I am consoled by the sole thought
> That unwittingly I unleashed this disaster,
> And my intention was not criminal but rash.']

– she more generally accepts responsibility for the results of her decision:

> Cette main, cette main a donné le poison,
> Le fils de Jupiter meurt par ma trahison.
> [...]
> O traître sang de Nesse ! ô femme trop crédule
> De ne soupçonner pas un ennemi d'Hercule !
>> III, 4, 831–32, 873–74

> [This hand, my own hand, handed over the poison,
> Through my betrayal, Jupiter's son has met his death.
> Oh treacherous blood of Nessus! How credulous I was
> Not to suspect one of Hercules' enemies.]

These observations do bear out to a certain extent a thread that has emerged in previous chapters, that the ancient classical tragedians, Greek and Latin, were seeking a fine balance between responsibility and exoneration that can be allied to the notion of hamartia, whereas the baroque (pre-Racinian) period in France was more inclined to dismiss facile exoneration as mere abnegation of responsibility. Excuses may be sought for a tragic decision or outcome, but they will not be too readily accepted either by the perpetrator or by witnesses within the play or in the audience.

4   Hercules, Agave and Others

All of these versions of the Deianeira story make some ironic reference to the fact that Heracles, here the victim of an unintended act of killing, had himself been the unwitting agent of murder: in an earlier phase of his life, struck blind by Hera/Juno, he had massacred his previous wife Megara and their children. This episode is recounted in Euripides' *Heracles* and in Seneca's *Hercules furens*, and again the defence of ignorance is adduced, allied to a more general sense of human helplessness in the face of divine spite. Here, too, although there is no doubt that Heracles is in a state of total confusion, he feels deep guilt and distress on learning the truth of his actions, and can only with difficulty be dissuaded from an expiatory suicide. Euripides' Heracles accepts Theseus's offer to go to Athens for purification, rationalizing in his own mind that suicide would in fact be the more cowardly option. He entrusts the bodies of his wife and children to Amphitryon: 'Give them a burial, and the proper clothes, honour them with your tears (for by law I may not do so) and put them in their mother's embrace against her breast in a fellowship of misfortune, the mother I killed, unhappy man that I am, unwittingly.'[31] Despite this use of the word 'unwittingly', most commentators agree that Euripides' Heracles makes little claim to 'innocence of intention'.[32]

In Seneca's play, the debate is more open. It is Amphitryon who seeks to reassure, if not exonerate Hercules: 'The grief is yours, the guilt your stepmother's. Bad luck is not your fault'[33] and again 'Juno used your hands to fire this shot' (1297, p. 176) – but such words have no effect on Hercules who rages in his shame and guilt and demands death as punishment. In a further exchange he makes it explicit that 'ignorance is no excuse': to Amphitryon's 'Who has ever called an accident a crime?' (1237, p. 174) Hercules retorts 'Major accidents are often crimes' (1238, p. 174). Shifting his position slightly, Amphitryon suggests that Hercules may be guilty but forgivable: 'No: remember all your world-renowned good deeds; forgive yourself for just this one bad act' (1265–66, p. 175), but Hercules is still insistent in assuming responsibility for his action: 'I did good under orders. Only this is mine' (1268, p. 175).

Blindness thus deliberately inflicted on a mortal by a god is a recurrent theme of ancient myth.[34] 'Athene interfered with Ajax's sight [in Sophocles' *Ajax*] so that he mistook animals for men, slaughtering and tormenting them instead of the Greek leaders' (p. 106). 'Poseidon casts a mist over Achilles' eyes

31   Euripides, *Heracles*, 1360-64, in Euripides, *Suppliant Women, Electra, Heracles*, trans. D. Kovacs (Cambridge, MA: Harvard University Press, 1998), p. 447. It is not clear whether the object of 'killed' is the mother or the broader sense of family or fellowship evoked, but all translations depict Heracles as accepting his responsibility for the destruction of something valuable, unknowingly or involuntarily.

32   See Seneca, *Hercules furens: A Critical Text with Introduction and Commentary* by J.G. Fitch (Ithaca, NY: Cornell University Press, 1987), pp. 426 and 434.

33   Seneca, *Hercules furens*, 1200–01, in Seneca, *Six Tragedies*, trans. E. Wilson (Oxford: Oxford World's Classics, 2010), p. 173.

34   See R.G.A. Buxton, 'Blindness and Limits: Sophocles and the Logic of Myth', in Harold Bloom (ed.), *Sophocles: Modern Critical Views* (New York: Chelsea House Publishers, 1990), pp. 105–126.

[in *The Iliad*, 20] and removes it when the danger to his favourite Aeneas is over' (p. 112). A final example from the ancient world of a figure who destroys what is dearest to her in ignorance of what she is doing is Agave in Euripides' most bitter tragedy, the *Bacchae*. Blinded by Dionysus as a consequence of a spiteful feud, Agave rips apart her son Pentheus in the belief that he is a lion cub. At a legalistic level, her excuse is watertight, since her will has been totally destroyed: she has no choice, no genuine moral feeling or awareness left at the time of her action. Her responsibility is not at issue: she is merely the instrument of Dionysus' revenge on his foe. Her ignorance is demonstrated in scenes of powerful dramatic irony, particularly when she asks for Pentheus to come and hang up the 'trophy' which is in fact his own mutilated head. For this very reason, the *Bacchae*, although an overwhelming dramatic experience, appears less effective as a tragedy than the presentations of the other myths. There is a greater mismatch between the opponents (a pitiless and vengeful god versus an innocent mortal) and a greater disproportion between the crime and the punishment (the rejection of Semele and her reputation by her sisters, and the subsequent failure of Theban society to worship Dionysus, set against the vindictive destruction of social order, the murder of Pentheus and the shameful destruction of the personalities of Cadmus and Agave). There is no very strong sense of a moral conflict, simply an opposition between two sorts of selfishness. Since Agave has already left Thebes under the influence of Dionysus when the play opens, we have no chance to form a relationship with her or appreciate her normal state of mind.

Dionysus makes it quite plain that the actions of the women throughout the play, and those of Pentheus when he allows himself to be dressed as a woman to spy voyeuristically on the maenads on Mount Cithaeron, are only explicable because the humans have been sent mad, blinded or possessed:

> I have driven them mad [...] out of their senses, witless and homeless.[35]
>   We will pay him out, but first befuddle his wits, make him mad. Never in his right mind would he put on a dress. Possessed, he will.
>
> 850–53, p. 134

In other words it is within the power of Dionysus – as god of wine, as god of animal instinct, and as god of theatre – to derange, to incite and to inspire ecstasy. The shameful action may thus be excused by a combination of ignorance and

---

35   Euripides, *Bacchae*, 33-36, trans. J.M. Walton in Euripides, *Plays: One* (London: Methuen, 1988), p. 115.

diminished responsibility, but this sort of example provides one basis under which a kind of ignorance is indeed a valid excuse for helplessness.

5   Credulity – Macbeth and Others

In the case of Macbeth, sympathy for the extent to which he is misled by cryptic prophecies must be tempered by his failure to calculate more carefully the outcome of his actions. His early soliloquies do not indicate mature consideration of costs and benefits so much as an agonized attempt to intuit what the different suggestions made to him by the Weird sisters and by his wife really mean: tiresome hesitation is thinly disguised as moral debate.

> This supernatural soliciting
> Cannot be ill, cannot be good. If ill,
> Why hath it given me earnest of success,
> Commencing in a truth? I am Thane of Cawdor.
> If good, why do I yield to that suggestion
> Whose horrid image doth unfix my hair ...?[36]

Macbeth's vision of a dagger also generates an image of perplexity in his mind: 'Mine eyes are made the fools o'th'other senses' (II, 1, 45, p. 124). Although this is the language of confusion rather than ignorance – 'Nothing is, but what is not' (I, 3, 142–3, p. 107) – it reminds us that Macbeth, like other victims of ignorance, is forced to take action without being allowed access to the full facts. Whatever the Weird sisters are, and whatever the power they represent, every one of their cryptic predictions does come true. Could he therefore with any justification argue that their words leave him with the impression that his actions are supported by supernatural authority and as such seem to be justified? In practice, he does not claim for himself the degree of helplessness associated with Greek or Racinian tragic figures: on the contrary, he knows in the first act that he has a decision to make, and almost makes the right and moral one. Nevertheless, there is a sense in which the sisters represent Fate or the Fates – that is what the word weyward or Weïrd meant in Anglo-Saxon mythology – and so we cannot altogether dismiss the possibility that they inflict on Macbeth an inescapable urge to act. They take away his wits as fearfully

---

36   Shakespeare, *Macbeth*, I, 3, 131-6, ed. Nicholas Brooke (Oxford: Oxford University Press, 1990), p. 107.

as Ate takes away the wits of Agamemnon, and they mislead him as sharply as the oracles mislead Oedipus.[37]

Macbeth and Deianeira are by no means the only tragic victims whose unwitting actions are influenced by obviously untrustworthy sources. Thésée refuses to believe the evidence of his eyes, but believes the evidence of Œnone:[38]

> Ah! le voici. Grands dieux ! à ce noble maintien
> Quel œil ne serait pas trompé comme le mien ?
> Faut-il que sur le front d'un profane adultère
> Brille de la vertu le sacré caractère ?
>
> [Ah, it is he. Great gods! what eye would not
> Be duped like mine by such nobility?
> Must needs the brow of an adulterer
> Be bright with virtue's sacred character?]

Othello refuses to believe the evidence of his eyes, but believes the evidence of Iago:

> Look where she comes:
> If she be false, O then Heav'n mocks itself!
> I'll not believe't.
> [...]
> Now do I see 'tis true. Look here, Iago,
> All my fond love thus do I blow to heaven:
> 'Tis gone![39]

This is a remarkable change of perspective in so short a time, on the evidence of a missing handkerchief, and with no cross-examination or defence. So are Thésée and Othello to be blamed as credulous fools, or excused and pitied as victims of deception? To what extent can it be considered a valid excuse for inappropriate behaviour if the perpetrator is misled about the real situation, whether by gods, villainous humans or coincidences? This category shares with other sorts of ignorance the complication that one may be genuinely ignorant,

---

37 We will return in the final chapter to consideration of the extent to which the weird sisters represent genuine demonic sources of evil inspiration, or whether they are rather scapegoats, mere excuses for decisions made consciously by Macbeth.
38 Racine, *Phèdre*, IV, 2, 1035–38.
39 *Othello*, III, 3, 282–3, 447–9.

but still blameworthy, either for not checking one's sources carefully enough, for believing untrustworthy sources recklessly, or for negligently failing to take account of the possible repercussions of actions.

6   *Phèdre*

All the characters in Racine's *Phèdre* are as prone to plead ignorance, misinformation or miscalculation as they are to depend on other forms of excuse for the outcomes of their decisions. 'I (Phèdre) wouldn't have done it if I'd known Thésée was still alive.' 'We (Œnone and Phèdre) wouldn't have done it if we'd known that Neptune might intervene.' 'I (Thésée) wouldn't have done it if I'd known how unreliable Œnone was as a witness.' 'I (Hippolyte) would have spoken and reacted differently if I'd ever been told what Œnone and Phèdre had said about me.' The characters' lack of control over their emotional responses is exacerbated at every turn by their failure to perceive the real truth of any situation, which blights all their attempts at rational decision-making. Some of the most bitterly ironic moments of the play are those where individuals express incredulity at the 'truths' they have been persuaded of. The sort of misinformation that traps a tragic agent in ignorance is often seductive, and we may conclude that the so-called victims of misleading information are often precisely culpable for their eagerness to believe the rumours that suit them, and ignore evidence that would point in an opposite direction.[40]

The report of Thésée's death is an interesting case, revealing how characters latch on to rumours that suit them. Hippolyte seems to vary in his response according to the company he is in: with Aricie he is quite dogmatic – 'Mon père ne vit plus' ('My father is no more', 465) because it suits his relationship with the princess to believe it, whereas with Théramène throughout the opening scene and with Phèdre (621–22), he insists on keeping open the possibility of his father's survival. This inconsistency makes it slightly more difficult for Phèdre herself to depend on the false report of her husband's death as an excuse for her inappropriate declaration to Hippolyte of her passion. Daniela Dalla Valle, however, supports the view that the erroneous news of Thésée's death brings about a fundamental change in the division of responsibilities, and that it does give Œnone and Phèdre a degree of extenuation.[41]

40   Vincent Grégoire, 'Bruits et rumeurs dans les tragédies de Racine', *Papers in French Seventeenth-century Literature*, 24, 1997, pp. 383–94.

41   D. Dalla Valle, 'Inceste et mythe dans le théâtre français du XVIIe siècle', in Morel J. (ed.) *La Tragédie, Littératures Classiques*, 16 (1992), pp. 181–97 (pp. 194–95).

7   **Oedipus Revisited**

Many early modern and modern authors have re-opened the question of
Oedipus' culpability. In the French classical period, Corneille and Voltaire both
wrote tragedies on the story, and although both felt the necessity to complicate
it with extraneous love plots, their consideration of ignorance as an excuse for
guilty actions is explicit. Corneille[42] deliberately made it easier for his Œdipe
to plead ignorance, by reducing the number of oracles referring to his fate,
and although in general the Stoic Corneille was scathing about an attitude of
fatalism,[43] he allows his Œdipe to utter the lines:

> Aux crimes malgré moi l'ordre du ciel m'attache ;
> Pour m'y faire tomber à moi-même il me cache ;
> Il offre, en m'aveuglant sur ce qu'il a prédit,
> Mon père à mon épée, et ma mère à mon lit.
>
> > v, 5, 1825–28, p. 71

> [It is against my will that heaven's command binds me to crime;
> It hides me from my very self to attract me to criminality,
> And blinding me to the truth of its predictions, it offers up
> My father to my weapon and my mother to my bed.]

Voltaire was critical about the extent to which Oedipus and Jocasta, as presented
by Sophocles and Corneille, overlooked the obvious: for him, the hero might be
ignorant, but only through culpable negligence. His own Œdipe appears rather
squeamish about the degree of ignorance he is obliged to admit to:[44]

> Et je ne conçois pas par quel enchantement
> J'oubliais jusqu'ici ce grand événement ;
> La main des dieux sur moi si longtemps suspendue
> Semble ôter le bandeau qu'ils mettaient sur ma vue.

> [I cannot conceive what enchantment it was
> That made me forget such a significant event;
> God's hand has been hanging over me all this time

---

42   *Œdipe*, 1659, in his *Théâtre complet*, ed. M. Rat (Paris: Garnier, 1971), vol. III, pp. 1–77.

43   See above, 'Helplessness', pp. 36–8.

44   *Œdipe*, 1718, in his *Œuvres complètes* (Paris: Garnier, 1877), vol. 2. IV, 1, p. 96.

And only now removes the blindfold it seems to have placed over my
eyes.]

Voltaire himself comments on this device as infelicitous: 'Il est triste d'être
obligé de supposer que la vengeance des dieux ôte dans un temps la mémoire
à Œdipe, et la lui rend dans un autre' ('It is distressing to have to assume that
the vengeful gods obscure Oedipus' memory on one occasion and then restore
it on another', p. 39). This Œdipe also explains that he wished to save Jocaste's
feelings by not asking awkward questions about the death of Laius, and Voltaire
is similarly self-critical in that regard: 'Ce compliment ne me paraît point une
excuse valable de l'ignorance d'Œdipe. La crainte de déplaire à sa femme en
lui parlant de son premier mari ne doit point l'empêcher de s'informer des cir-
constances de la mort de son prédécesseur; c'est avoir trop de discrétion et
trop peu de curiosité' ('This compliment does not seem to me a valid excuse
for Œdipe's ignorance. The fear of distressing his wife by speaking to her of her
former husband should not prevent him from investigating the circumstances
surrounding his predecessor's death; he shows too much discretion and too
little curiosity', p. 36). In the end, for all his attempts to rationalize his presentation, Voltaire sums up his characters' sense of responsibility in a rather
conventional way: Jocaste says of her husband:

> Vous êtes malheureux, et non pas criminel ;
> Dans ce fatal combat que Daulis vous vit rendre,
> Vous ignoriez quel sang vos mains allaient répandre.
>   IV, 3, p. 100

> [You are not a criminal but a victim of misfortune;
> In that fatal conflict witnessed at Daulis
> You were unaware whose blood it was you would spill.]

Œdipe does no more than echo a similar fatalism:

> Et je me vois enfin, par un mélange affreux,
> Inceste et parricide, et pourtant vertueux.
> Un dieu plus fort que toi m'entraînait vers le crime ;
> Sous mes pas fugitifs il creusait un abîme ;
> Et j'étais, malgré moi, dans mon aveuglement,
> D'un pouvoir inconnu l'esclave et l'instrument.
>   V, 4, p. 107

[At last I now see myself in a hideously confused state:
Incestuous and parricidal, yet with untainted virtue.
A god stronger than you pushed me towards my crimes,
Digging an abyss beneath my restless feet as they tried to escape,
And it was against my will, in my blindness,
That I became the slave and the instrument of an unknown power.]

Gide[45] transposed the story into a context that is very recognizably catholic. Although Antigone gives voice to the defence of ignorance on his behalf – 'Mon père n'a pas sciemment commis son crime' ('My father did not commit his crime wittingly', III, p. 299) – Gide's Œdipe had actually been given more relevant information than many previous Oedipuses. He was, most notably, told by Polybe before leaving Corinth that he was adopted (II, p. 271), so his decision to travel was not a despairing attempt to outwit the oracle but a deliberate quest for self-fulfilment. The journey to Thebes, the killing of Laius, the defeat of the Sphinx and marriage to Jocaste were all symptoms of that human pride which is identified as the cause of his blindness. He complains not that the gods have kept him in ignorance, but that key facts have been withheld from him by humans – Jocaste, Créon and Tirésias – for essentially human and political reasons. 'Tu ne m'avais pas dit,' he reproaches Jocaste ('You never told me', I, p. 257), turning Greek fatalistic helplessness into a rather peevish marital squabble. So far from claiming ignorance as a legalistic excuse, he confesses that he has joined what amounted to a conspiracy to cultivate it: 'J'ai compris l'art de faire, de cette ignorance même, ma force' ('I understood the art of turning my very ignorance into a source of power', II, p. 287). Tirésias characterizes this attitude as 'ce parti pris d'indifférence' ('a decision to embrace indifference'). Jocaste in this version has been part of the same conspiracy: 'J'ai fait ce que j'ai pu pour t'empêcher de déchirer le voile qui protégeait notre bonheur' ('I did all I could to prevent you from tearing back the veil that protected our happiness', III, p. 297), so she is more likely to be charged with wilful negligence, and indeed condemned for wilful concealment of known truths, than pitied for ignorance.

A similar line was taken, slightly more subtly, by Jean Cocteau in his *La Machine infernale*,[46] whose innovative treatment of the Oedipus story employs a comic tone and an array of witty anachronisms but achieves a real intensity of feeling at the denouement. His consideration of Œdipe's and Jocaste's guilt is not without some tension. On the one hand, he stresses the total and arbitrary

---

45   *Œdipe*, 1930, in his *Théâtre* (Paris: Gallimard, 1942), pp. 249–304.
46   1934. Ed. W.M. Landers (London: Harrap, 1957).

power of the forces – whatever they represent – that control this universe: 'Obéissons,' insists Anubis when the anthropomorphized Sphinx expresses disgust at her role, 'Le mystère a ses mystères. Les dieux possèdent leurs dieux' ('We must obey. Mystery has its mysteries, the gods have their gods', 11, p. 46). Humanity is thus genuinely helpless in the face of one of the 'plus parfaites machines construites par les dieux infernaux pour l'anéantissement mathématique d'un mortel' ('the most perfect mechanisms constructed by the infernal gods to bring about the mathematical annihilation of a mortal') and should therefore be exonerated from responsibility. Œdipe may be an overbearing boor here, but he acts from good intentions and aspires to heroism. On the other hand, in depicting the meeting, courtship and even the wedding night of the couple, rather than making them unpick their decisions years later, Cocteau undermines to an almost comic extent any hope they might have of convincing the audience that their potential plea of ignorance has any validity. Both Œdipe and Jocaste spend act III frustrating the spectators by their apparently wilful refusal to see the obvious. The act is filled with ironies: innuendo-laden references to their ages; Œdipe's wounded ankles; the presence in the bridal chamber of a cot; ominous dreams; a ludicrous confusion in Jocaste's subconscious between a young soldier with whom she had flirted outrageously in act I, her son with whom she had compared him, and Œdipe whom she now says she was 'reminded' of at a time before she had met him. These all contribute to the sense of excruciating frustration on the part of the viewer as these brittle and troubled characters lumber blindly into an act of which we can scarcely believe that they do not grasp the significance.

'As long as a man knows the good,' said Socrates, 'he will do it. All that is necessary is that he has really recognized the nature of the good.'[47] If we accept Socrates' contention that knowledge and virtue are equivalents, it should follow that their opposites, ignorance and evil, are also equivalent. This is almost tantamount to suggesting that an individual who behaves badly *must* have been in some way ignorant of the right path – ignorance becomes a universal let-out clause, and our examples have illustrated that it is indeed one of the tragic ways by which fate, fortune or vindictive divinities render human victims impotent to avert disaster. It has been suggested[48] that Sophocles essentially accepted Socrates' thesis, by allowing Deianeira and Oedipus the excuse

---

47   This summary of Socrates' theory of knowledge and virtue, argued particularly in the
      Meno, is from Bruno Snell, *The Discovery of the Mind in Greek Philosophy and Literature*
      (New York: Dover, 1982), p. 182.

48   For example by T.B.L. Webster, 'The Classical Background to Racine's *Phèdre*', in
      T.E. Lawrenson et al (eds.), *Modern Miscellany presented to Eugène Vinaver* (Manchester:
      Manchester University Press, 1969), p. 298.

of ignorance, but that Euripides challenged this, demonstrating the extent to which characters do choose an evil path even in full knowledge of the facts and situation. His Medea famously embraces 'the nature of the awful act I face', asserting that 'rage masters all, as conscience never can'[49] – opening up, clearly, the defence of diminished responsibility, but not that of ignorance. A fragmentary quotation from a lost Euripides play, identified as *Chrysippus*, was sufficiently quoted in antiquity to become almost proverbial: 'Alas, this truly is a godsent evil for men, when someone knows the good but does not practise it'.[50] This curiously anticipates a confessional statement by Saint Paul: 'The good which I want to do, I fail to do; but what I do is the wrong which is against my will; and if what I do is against my will, clearly it is no longer I who am the agent, but sin that has its dwelling in me.'[51] Both Saint Paul and Euripides, then, accept that individuals can deserve pity for transgressing even if they are fully aware of the wrong they are doing. Euripides' Phaedra, similarly but more problematically, concedes that 'we know what's good and we recognize it' but adds that 'we don't toil to accomplish it'[52] – so she at this stage and in this version of her story explicitly rejects the excuse of ignorance, blaming such failures on idleness and the distraction of enticing pleasures. However she goes on within the same speech to admit to some confusion, amounting to a sort of ignorance: 'if what is appropriate were clear, there would not be two with the same letters' (386–87, p. 85). It is not certain whether Phaedra is here drawing a distinction between good and bad sorts of shame (the more general view) or good and bad sorts of pleasure. In either case, however, she is asserting that even agents who have complete information about the basis of their actions are not adequately equipped to judge them, because of the limitations inherent in human language. Although well aware that her attraction to Hippolytos was wrong, and having done all she could to resist it, she was in the end powerless, and this in part was because she could not tell the difference – no-one could – between 'virtuous modesty, which is good, and an excessive respect

---

49   Euripides, *Medea*, 1079–81, as translated by Jeremy Brooks in *Plays: One* (London: Methuen, 1988), p. 40.

50   Fragment 841, as given in Euripides, *Fragments: Oedipus-Chrysippus and Other Fragments*, edited and translated by C. Collard and M. Cropp (Cambridge, MA: Harvard University Press, 2008), pp. 468–69. The word translated here as 'godsent', θεῖον, is elsewhere given as δεινόν, 'terrible'.

51   *Romans*, 7:19–20, *The Revised English Bible* (Cambridge: Cambridge University Press, 1996).

52   Euripides, *Hippolytos*, 380–81, as translated by Michael Halleran in his edition of the play (Oxford: Aris and Phillips, 1995), p. 85.

for other people's opinions and feelings, which is bad'.[53] This rather metaphysical kind of ignorance is not the same as the factual ignorance of Sophocles' Phaedra and Racine's Phèdre regarding the current whereabouts of Theseus/Thésée: Euripides' character is deprived of that excuse, but she is still denied clear insight. Socrates' equation of knowledge and virtue is not dissimilar to the modern liberal view that *anyone* who commits violent crime, especially murder, must in some sense have lost control of themselves – diminished responsibility as a universal excuse. The different sorts of ignorance we have investigated suggest in a similar manner that all human transgression is to some extent explained if not excused by perplexity amounting to helplessness. Our examples suggest that the western tradition of tragic drama can help us, at least as well as legalistic or philosophical enquiries, to negotiate with greater confidence the borderline between blame and extenuation.

---

53   This is Richard Rutherford's gloss on John Davie's translation of line 387, in Euripides, *Alcestis and Other Plays* (London: Penguin Books, 1996), p. 180, n. 20.

CHAPTER 4

Diminished Responsibility: Medea and the *Crime passionnel*

'Je voulais faire souffrir Philippe' ('I wanted to make Philippe suffer'). With these chilling words, Aurore Baumgartner appears to put beyond doubt the calculated nature of her motivation in killing, in autumn 2013, both of her infant children by a man who had abandoned her and had subsequently entered into a liaison with another woman. At her trial three years later, evidence was brought forward that she had announced in advance by text message to the children's father that he would never see them again, and had weighed up the means by which she could most readily achieve her intention (drowning as opposed to suffocating so that she would be able avert her gaze from the dying children). On that basis, despite attempts by her counsel to suggest mental deficiency or diminished responsibility, she was found guilty of murder and sentenced to twenty-five years imprisonment.[1]

Medea, who went further than Aurore Baumgartner in killing her husband Jason's new fiancée as well as her own infant children, may thus seem the least excusable villainess in world literature, and yet many modern productions of plays about her appear to be aimed at a degree of exoneration, or at least understanding, of her terrible actions. Indeed, there seems to be little point in depicting her for any other purpose. Medea clearly was driven to desperation. Jason, whose life she had saved and whose reputation she had enhanced on several occasions by the use of her magic powers, abandoned her for a younger woman, the princess of Corinth, Glauke (called Creusa by Seneca, and therefore Créuse in French adaptations). When she dared to complain about her husband's desertion, the king, Creon, reacted with vindictive harshness, banishing both her and her children, so she may be excused for responding with frenzy.

The question of diminished responsibility arises not infrequently in modern law. When an individual has started a cycle of violence by bullying behaviour, threats or coercive control, and ends up becoming the victim of his (or occasionally her) own victim, prosecutors or juries may consider diminished responsibility, provocation or self-defence as excuses for an uncontrolled

---

1 See for example http://www.estrepublicain.fr/edition-de-vesoul-haute-saone/2016/04/27/vesoul-25-ans-de-reclusion-pour-le-double-infanticide.

violent reaction on the part of the eventual perpetrator, and reduce the charge or sentence accordingly. 'Affection [...] makes possible things not so held.'[2] The technical details of laws providing such partial defences to murder vary from jurisdiction to jurisdiction. The law in England and Wales was controversial in the 1980s and 1990s, as we shall see in the next chapter, and was reviewed in a Law Commission discussion paper in 2006.[3] Also in the UK, Section 76 of the Serious Crime Act 2015 created a new offence of controlling or coercive behaviour in an intimate or family relationship.[4] The same area of law has also been particularly controversial in Australia since 1987,[5] and similar issues are addressed in almost all modern legal systems.[6] This widespread acceptance of loss of self-control as an extenuating factor for at least some acts of violence – not necessarily unpremeditated, although this will normally help – encourages us to look more closely at parallels between the legal treatment of 'crimes of passion' and the depiction in classical and modern tragedy of similar violent actions. In one twentieth-century French version of the Clytemnestra story, even her apparently cold-blooded murder of her husband Agamemnon is exonerated, as one commentator within the play wryly puts it: 'Vous savez, avec un bon avocat, quand on plaide le passionnel ...' ('Well, of course, if you get a good lawyer and call it a crime of passion ...').[7]

In the French classical period, as we have seen,[8] the critic La Mesnardière in his *Poétique*[9] grappled with the central problem of tragedy: his instinctive

---

2 Shakespeare, *A Winter's Tale*, I, 2, 139. See Paul Hammond, *The Strangeness of Tragedy* (Oxford: Oxford University Press, 2009), pp. 21–22 for further elucidation of this speech.

3 Law Commission, *A New Homicide Act for England and Wales?: A Consultation Paper*. London: Stationery Office, Law Commission Consultation Paper no. 177, 2006.

4 https://www.cps.gov.uk/legal-guidance/controlling-or-coercive-behaviour-intimate-or-family-relationship.

5 See Phil Cleary, *Just Another Little Murder* (St Leonard's, NSW: Allen and Unwin, 2002).

6 See for example: Dominique Rouch, *Amour à mort: enquête sur les crimes passionnels* (Paris: Hachette/Carrère, 1992); Ralph Slovenko, *Psychiatry and Criminal Culpability* (New York: Wiley, 1995); Stanley Yeo, *Unrestrained Killings and the Law: A Comparative Analysis of the Laws of Provocation and Excessive Self-defence in India, England and Australia* (Delhi/Oxford: Oxford University Press, 1998); Edward E. Tennant, *The Future of the Diminished Responsibility Defence to Murder* (Chichester: Barry Rose Law Publishers, 2001); Cynthia Lee, *Murder and the Reasonable Man: Passion and Fear in the Criminal Courtroom* (New York/London: New York University Press, 2003); Véronique Jaquier and Joëlle Vuille, *Les femmes et la question criminelle: Délits commis, expériences de victimisation et professions judiciaires* (Zurich/Genève: Editions Seismo, 2017); Katherine O'Donovan, 'Defences for Battered Women Who Kill', *Journal of Law and Society*, 18 (1991), pp. 219–240.

7 Jean Anouilh, *Tu étais si gentil quand tu étais petit*, in his *Pièces secrètes* (Paris: La Table Ronde, 1977), p. 17.

8 'Hamartia', pp. 61–2.

9 Paris: Sommaville, 1639. Consulted online at http://gallica.bnf.fr/ark:/12148/bpt6k50691s.pdf.

belief that the universe is just made it difficult for him to accept the artistic representation of innocent suffering, so those who suffer catastrophe must share some responsibility for their suffering, even though, as Aristotle insisted, they should not be straightforwardly to blame. With reference to diminished responsibility, La Mesnardière referred to criminals 'qui après avoir balancé entre les bons sentiments et les méchantes actions, ne prennent le mauvais parti que parce qu'ils sont aveuglés de la passion qui les transporte' ('who hesitate between good impulses and evil actions, and only follow the wicked path because they are blinded by the passion that carries them away', p. 225). La Mesnardière was troubled by this, insisting that the dramatist must always ensure that the tragic figure remains aware of the voice of reason and gives way to passion only after a struggle, although he concedes that in the case of 'de simples meurtres et d'autres violences que produisent dans le poème la colère et la jalousie, leur soudaineté les excuse presque entièrement à cause que ces émotions ne donnent pas le loisir à l'âme en qui elles s'élèvent de faire aucune réflexion sur le crime qu'elle va faire' ('where anger and jealousy give rise within a play to straightforward murder or other violence, they can be almost entirely exonerated as on-the-spot impulses, because these emotions do not give the subject space or time to consider the criminal action they propose to take', p. 230). This formulation nicely invites a parallel with the modern legal notion of the reasonable man, and ensures that a jury, like a theatre audience, is always being asked to discern a balance between a degree of residual guilt and an appeal to circumstances beyond the control of a normal moral being.

Medea is often described as 'mad', with or without direct reference to the possibility that her actions can be excused on that basis. It is the thesis of Seneca's play about her that 'no soul, once love had entered it, could safely guarantee that hostility, rage and murder would not follow', and that 'the one who really loves properly, loyally, will be the most derailed by the loss of love',[10] and French versions frequently define her as 'furieuse'. In a rather melodramatic depiction of her by a minor contemporary of Racine, the baron de Longepierre (Hilaire-Bernard de Requeleyne, 1659–1731),[11] the title character describes herself thus at her first entrance (II, 1, 269) and observes the stages by which her frenzy mounts: 'Ma rage s'est accrue, et ce torrent fougueux / Va plus rapidement se déborder contre eux' ('My frenzy has increased, and its overwhelming torrent will engulf them ever faster', III, 4, 843–44). By the end

---

10   Martha Nussbaum, 'Serpents in the Soul: A Reading of Seneca's *Medea*', in James Clauss and Sarah Johnston, eds., *Medea: Essays on Medea in Myth, Literature, Philosophy, and Art* (Princeton, N.J.: Princeton University Press, 1997), p. 224.

11   *Médée*, 1694. Ed. T. Tobari (Paris: Nizet, 1967).

of act IV, she does appear to show greater self-control in deliberating over her decision, and argues that her proposed action is a sort of mercy killing – she expects her children to lose their mother as well as their father, and to be enslaved, so they have nothing more to live for. But this logic seems so twisted as to call her true sanity into question. More modern French interpreters similarly stress her frenzy: for Anouilh, as for Seneca, *all* love is destructive, and the painter Delacroix labels her 'furieuse', calm and beautiful though his portrayal may look – to an innocent eye she could as easily be defending her children against an unseen assailant as preparing to attack them herself.[12]

1   Euripides

In a dramatization of this situation, any attempt to defend her actions on the basis of diminished responsibility is likely to depend on the degree to which an observer is first alienated by Jason's cruel insensitivity, to emphasize Medea's role as the victim of him individually and of patriarchy generally. It seems clear enough that in the early part of his play, Euripides wished to excite at least some sympathy for Medea, so his portrayal of Jason is designed to be provocative. Euripides may never want to *excuse* Medea's action, but perhaps he wants to explain it, and hence invites the audience, at least initially, to see the world from her point of view. Given that perspective, it is plausible that diminished responsibility brought about by extreme provocation would have provided a defence worth considering if Medea's retaliation had limited itself to an assault – even a murderous one – on Jason and his new bride. That would be a conventional crime of passion, and seems to be what Medea initially contemplates:[13]

> Oh, let me see him and his bride destroyed
> And all his house brought down in ruins.

When it comes to the infanticide, however, Euripides went to some lengths to ensure that his Medea was not too easily allowed to claim the excuse of madness. He makes Medea remind the audience (167–68) that she has previously murdered her own brother Apsyrtus for Jason's sake. He distinguished

---

12   Amy Wygant, *Medea, Magic and Modernity in France* (Aldershot: Ashgate, 2007), p. 12.
13   *Medea*, 163–64, trans. Jeremy Brooks, in Euripides, *Plays: One* (London: Methuen, 1988), p. 10.

between her and other infanticides, such as Ino,[14] to stress that since *their* mad blindness was inflicted on them by gods, her own actions appear more calculating. He ensured that she is given ample time and some encouragement to reconsider her plan before carrying it out. The arrival of Aegeus facilitates her action by giving her a bolthole; it also triggers it by drawing her attention to the pain of childlessness, enabling her to increase the suffering inflicted on Jason to avenge her own slight. The calculation involved in refining this torture, however, seems to reduce Medea's chance of exoneration. Edith Hall's statement that 'even to raise the question of diminished responsibility in the case of Euripides' Medea may seem fundamentally misguided' is scarcely less disconcerting for the fact that her article brilliantly surveys ways of doing precisely that.[15]

In Euripides' version of the story Jason, in attempting to justify his action, argues that marriage to Glauke would enhance his status in Corinth, and ensure an appropriate lifestyle and future not only for him but for his sons and Medea herself, although in view of the disputes for status between Hippolytos and the sons of Phaedra, we may feel he is on doubtful ground, if not downright insincere, in making such a claim. In that context, cruelly, he taunts Medea with the assertion that the only thing which makes her furious about his plan is her sense of being sexually slighted – and in this respect he generalizes from her to the whole of womankind:[16]

> [...] You women
> Have such strange ideas; you seem to think
> That if your sexual rights are not infringed
> Then everything is well. But if some little thing
> Ruffles your ownership, then all that once was good,
> All that was valuable, means nothing to you.

That is Jeremy Brooks's translation: the one by James Morwood is even more judgmental and provocative, at least to a modern audience: 'You would agree with me if the matter of sex were not provoking you. But you women have sunk so low that, when your sex life is going well, you think that you have everything, but then, if something goes wrong with regard to your bed, you consider the

14   *Ibid.*, 1284, p. 46: 'Ino, by the gods driven mad'.
15   Edith Hall, 'Medea and the Mind of the Murderer' in Heike Bartel and Anne Simon (eds.), *Unbinding Medea* (London: MHRA, 2010), pp. 16–24 (p. 20).
16   Euripides, *Medea*, c568–572, edn. cit., p. 23.

best and happiest circumstances utterly repugnant.'[17] The explanatory notes (p. 174) refer to this speech as 'breathtaking crass insensitivity', and although it is risky to impose an anachronistic reading on the text through modern perspectives, such an assault on Medea's sensitivity must invite some sympathy, as though she is being punished for the extent of her affectionate attachment to Jason, which might indeed have seemed unusual if not unhealthy to an element of Euripides' audience.

Medea herself, later in Euripides' play, alludes to this category of excuse, although she does so dishonestly. Having reacted with justifiable anger to his insensitive handling of their initial confrontation, she pretends to repent, and suggests excuses for her previous outburst:[18]

> Jason, I beg your forgiveness for the words I spoke.
> We two together once endured much love;
> So now you should endure that burst of passion.
> [...] I saw how foolish,
> How senseless my rage had been.
> [...] I was mad. [...] I am a woman,
> Not evil, perhaps, but frail.

Again, James Morwood translates the last line slightly differently: 'But we are what we are – I won't call us evil – we women'.[19] So the argument is not so much 'Let me off because I got carried away' as 'Let me off because I could not help getting carried away because – as you yourself, Jason, hinted a little while ago – women are like that'. And it is true that before the twentieth century, the story of Medea was always told from a male perspective, and the picture of women as inherently flawed made the heroine a useful scapegoat. Indeed, it has been suggested that in the original version of the story, Medea's children had actually been killed by the Corinthian population in revenge for her murder of Creon and Glauke, and that their descendants bribed Euripides into presenting a version in which she carried out that atrocity as well as those she did commit. In other words, Medea could plead provocation and diminished responsibility in the cases of Creon and Glauke, so the Corinthians needed her to kill the infants too to ensure she was condemned. Christa Wolf was to make this explicit in her novel, *Medea: A Modern Retelling*: the Corinthian

---

17 Euripides, *Medea and Other Plays*, trans. James Morwood (Oxford: Oxford University Press, Oxford World Classics), 1998, p. 16.

18 869–890, Methuen edition, p. 33.

19 Oxford edition, p. 24.

mob killed her children expressly in order to brand her for posterity as a child murderess.[20] So, too, Tony Harrison, in his libretto for an unfinished opera, *Medea: Sex War*, presented Euripides as bribed by male murderers to present the crime as the work of Medea:[21]

> Men's hatred had to undermine
> MEDEA's status as divine
> and to reduce her
> to a half-crazed children-slayer
> making a monster of MEDEA
> like the Medusa.

George Tabori's 1984 dramatization of the story under the title *M* was even more subversive, suggesting that Jason himself, perhaps bribed by the Corinthians, killed his children to make M(edea) look guilty.[22]

At the climax of Euripides' play, Medea is given a speech which seems to encapsulate the paradox of diminished responsibility as a defence:[23]

> I cannot bear this pain.
> Now it is here. Now I embrace
> The nature of the awful act I face.
> But rage, that fuels the foulest deeds of man,
> Rage masters all, as conscience never can.

Expressed in these words, the statement articulates the loss of control, but its very articulation, and the acknowledgement of conscience as an opposing pressure, exposes it as an excuse rather than a true justification for her action. If Medea is to be allowed to excuse her action on the basis of loss of control – 'rage' or 'frenzy' overwhelming her real intention – she cannot also 'embrace' her action in advance. That is in fact a problematic word in a problematic speech, both in its text and in its interpretation, and the way it is translated is liable to pre-empt a full discussion of what it actually means. David Kovacs, in an edition which explicitly aims to prioritize accuracy over elegance, translates

---

20   Trans. John Cullen (London: Virago, 1998), p. 186.
21   Tony Harrison, *Dramatic Verse 1973–1985* (Newcastle upon Tyne: Bloodaxe Books, 1985), p. 432. The capitalization of Medea's name is a feature of that text.
22   *M: nach Euripides* (*M: after Euripides*) (Berlin: Kiepenheuer, 1995).
23   1077–80, trans. Brooks, Methuen edition, p. 40.

that line 'I know well what pain I am about to undergo',[24] which steers the performer and viewer firmly in the direction of Medea's victimhood. Michael Collier and Georgia Machemer, on the other hand, frame the line in a confessional mode: 'The horror of my evil overwhelms me. Horror of what I'll do'.[25] Brooks's 'the awful act I face' manages a certain ambiguity, but most translators do include or stress the sense of acts which Medea will 'commit'. The problem of interpretation and translation arises partly because the speech is dominated in the original Greek by derivatives of the word κακος or κακία, which occur three times in four lines (translated above as 'pain', 'awful act' and 'foulest deeds') and which – rather like the English word 'ill' – can have, but need not have, moral overtones. This ambiguity is retained in the above translation with the word 'awful', but 'foulest' and 'conscience' steer this interpretation of the speech firmly in the direction of a moral judgment: 'I know I am going to do a dreadful thing, but it may be blamed on a loss of control so the real me may be exonerated'. Reflecting on the passage, Donald Mastronarde comments: 'Medea is primarily concerned with the harm she will do to her sons and to herself; this is based primarily on a calculation of pain and suffering'[26] – in other words, her determination is to harm Jason and she undertakes a cost/benefit analysis as to the amount of collateral suffering she and her sons must undergo to bring about that desired end. In a way this begs the very question we are investigating: things which cause harm are not necessarily 'evil' but they are so, precisely, unless a valid excuse can be found for them. But here, since Medea herself has earlier characterized the contemplated killings as 'unholy' (line 796), purely moral considerations cannot be altogether excluded: the action she is contemplating will damage her, *and* it is evil. To complicate matters further, she has also referred to it as a 'sacrifice' (line 1053), although it is not clear that this would gain sympathy from her original audience, who might regard this claim as sacrilegious.[27] Translators and performers cannot but interpret as they proceed, in ways which are bound to influence the audience's reaction to and judgment on the character. Is the tone predominantly 'Poor me, I am defeated by evils, overcome with sorrows, the helpless puppet of my

---

24   Euripides, *Plays: I*, ed. David Kovacs (Cambridge, MA: Harvard University Press, Loeb Classical Library, 1994), p. 383.

25   Euripides, *Medea*, trans. Michael Collier and Georgia Machemer (Oxford: Oxford University Press, 2006), p. 71.

26   Euripides, *Medea*, ed. Donald J. Mastronarde (Cambridge: Cambridge University Press, 2002), p. 344.

27   See Morwood in the Oxford edition, p. 177: 'It is a blasphemous distortion of the real nature of this act of vengeance upon Jason for her to regard the murder of her children as a sacrifice.' This judgment is perhaps too categorical.

barely conscious passions, like all people, destined to perpetrate unreasonable horror', or is it rather 'Unspeakable me, logic tells me that what I am about to do is dreadful, but I am governed by rage rather than reason'? George Theodoridis stresses the element of calculation:[28] 'I know only too well how horrible the crime I am about to commit is. Logic makes it clear for me but anger, the only cause of man's most terrible suffering, anger, conquers my logic.' This invites us to admire Medea's lucidity under great stress, but does not make it easy for us to exonerate her.[29]

It is relevant to make a distinction between diminished responsibility – 'my situation sent me into a frenzy which might excuse a violent reaction' – and righteous indignation – 'what was done to me was so horrible that a violent reaction was just'. Seneca's treatment of the Medea story explores the relationship in her between anger ('ira') and frenzy ('furor'), and hence between retribution and the blind lashing out that characterizes diminished responsibility and provocation as excuses.[30]

2   Early-Modern and Modern Medeas

The link between the Medea story and legal debates has sometimes been made explicit. As well as Aurore Baumgartner, mentioned at the beginning of this chapter, Susan Smith in South Carolina in 1994 and Lamora Williams in Atlanta in 2017 killed their children when estranged from their partners. Margaret Garner, a real slave woman who killed her child to prevent her being returned to slavery, was celebrated in painting by Thomas Satterwhite Noble as 'the modern Medea',[31] and this became a source for Toni Morrison's 1987 novel *Beloved*, and Jonathan Demme's film of the same name. In Jules Dassin's 1978 film *A Dream of Passion*[32] Melina Mercouri appears as an actress portraying Medea who seeks out Brenda Collins, a mother in prison for the recent murder of her children. In a version performed in Bristol in 2017, a translation of Euripides' text by Robin Robertson was framed within the fictional story

---

28   His 2005 translation is available online at http://www.poetryintranslation.com/theo doridisgmedea.htm.

29   I am indebted to the Revd Philip Seddon, formerly of Sarum College, for help in elucidating this speech.

30   See Seneca, *Medea*, ed. A.J. Boyle (Oxford: Oxford University Press, 2014), pp. liv ff.

31   See Isabelle Torrance, 'The Infanticidal Mother in Alejandro Amenábar's film *The Others*', in Bartel and Simon, pp. 126–27.

32   This is the title under which it was distributed in the English-speaking world, although the original Greek title *Kravgi gynaikon* literally means 'the cry of women'.

of a modern army wife, Maddy, whose husband Jack abandons her, leaves her to face eviction and the loss of custody of her children, and is only foiled when Maddy, taking a ruthless Medea as her inspiration, uses her knowledge of his character and army career to have him convicted and imprisoned for reckless bullying of his subordinates. It is no doubt significant that the adaptation of Euripides' text by Rosanna Lowe performed in 1998 was mounted by a company called *Not Without Cause* – a name which may deliberately evoke the legalistic overtones of Alfred Bates's judgment: 'Medea is criminal, but not without cause, and not without strength and dignity'.[33]

In a context defined by such adaptations, the thrust of several productions of Euripides' play and other modern retellings of the story – the Diana Rigg *Medea* at the Almeida (London, 1992), the 1998 *Not Without Cause* adaptation just referred to, Deborah Warner's production of 2000–01 (Dublin and London) with Fiona Shaw, and the adaptation by the *Actors of Dionysus* in early 2001 – was indeed to encourage the audience to understand Medea's perspective and sympathize with her nightmare. Amy Wygant was in no doubt that as early as the seventeenth century Corneille and his audience 'take [Medea's] side',[34] and expanded this to say that 'while it is true that she commits every kind of horrific crime, audiences, from the very first information that we have about them in France, seem to have forgiven her' (p. 12). Corneille himself supported that claim in his *Examen* of the play, written reflectively some twenty-five years after the play's performance and publication: conceding that (under Aristotle's conception of hamartia), Créon and even Créuse are too guilty to arouse our passion, he contends that their unworthy treatment of Médée exonerate her to some extent for her crimes, at least towards the king and his daughter:[35]

> [Créon et Créuse] importunent plus par leurs cris et par leurs gémissements, qu'ils ne font pitié par leur malheur. La raison en est qu'ils semblent l'avoir mérité par l'injustice qu'ils ont faite à Médée, qui attire si bien de son côté toute la faveur de l'auditoire, qu'on excuse sa vengeance après l'indigne traitement qu'elle a reçu de Créon et de son mari, et qu'on

---

33   *The Drama: Its History, Literature and Influence on Civilization.* London: Historical Publishing Company, 1906. Vol. 1, pp. 192–196. http://www.theatrehistory.com/ancient/bates018.html.

34   Wygant, p. 9.

35   Pierre Corneille, *Théâtre complet*, ed. G. Couton (Paris: Garnier, 1971), I, p. 566. The chronology is significant here: the play was written and performed in 1635, published with a dedicatory epistle in 1639 (so after the *querelle du Cid*), and Corneille's *Examen* was written for a revised publication in 1660.

a plus de compassion du désespoir où ils l'ont réduite, que de tout ce
qu'elle leur fait souffrir.

[Créon and Créuse, with their cries and groans, are tiresome rather than
arousing pity for their misfortune. This is because they seem to have deserved their fate through the injustice they inflict on Médée, who attracts
for her part all the audience's sympathy; we excuse her vengeance after
the unjust treatment she has received at the hands of Créon and her husband, and we have more pity for the despair into which she is plunged by
their actions, than for all the suffering she inflicts on them.]

In this respect, Corneille seems to have shifted his view slightly between 1639
and 1660: when the play was first published he made it clear that he was not
trying to justify Médée's behaviour:[36]

Ici vous trouverez le crime dans son char de triomphe, et peu de personnages sur la scène dont les mœurs ne soient plus mauvaises que bonnes.
[...] Il n'est pas besoin d'avertir ici le public que celles de cette tragédie ne
sont pas à imiter.

[Here you will find evil mounted on her triumphal chariot, and characters on stage, with few exceptions, who are more marked by evil than by
good. There is no need in this case to point out to the public that their
behaviour and morals are not to be imitated.]

For Medea to be exonerated, she must be obviously victimized by Creon and
betrayed by Jason. Other modern retellings of the story have explored the extent to which post-colonialism, genetic determinism or feminism can help us
to understand even this degree of anguished frenzy. Some, for example, have
seen Medea almost as a freedom-fighter: alien, unsupported and made to feel
unwelcome by what amounted to a colonial power. Hélène Domon has pointed
out how truly Medea is 'l'autre', the stranger, the outsider, whose isolation from
the normative human institutions of society is underlined by the breaking
of vows, or, as Domon calls them, 'epacts'.[37] The vows of marriage, broken by

---

36   Ibid., p. 563.
37   Hélène Domon, 'Médée ou l'Autre'. *Cahiers du Dix-Septième. An Interdisciplinary
Journal*, 1987, pp. 88–93. Referred to by Joy Sylvester, 'Will the Real Médée Please Step
Forward?' in *Didaskalia: The Journal For Ancient Performance*, 1, 1994, accessed online,
12 September 2017 at http://www.didaskalia.net/issues/supplement1/sylvester.html.

Jason, lead to Medea's expulsion by the state. The political vows, first made by Creon, when he accepted both Jason and Medea into Corinth and gave them sanctuary and safety from their enemies are broken by him when he decides to offer only her up as the sacrifice necessary to save his state. More and more, she stands alone, cut off from all she has known and loved. She has given up everything; country, family and her royal status, for love of Jason. As she now stands in splendid isolation against the powerful forces amassed against her, what remains to her is herself. This theme was touched on in Euripides and was strongly built up by the Austrian dramatist Franz Grillparzer,[38] whose character made particular efforts to learn the culture into which she had been transported (with Creusa initially as a sympathetic tutor), so had a stronger sense of injustice when she was nevertheless rejected. It recurs with renewed force in twentieth-century versions by Hans Henny Jahnn, whose 1925 Medea was a black North-African; by Robinson Jeffers, whose 1946 adaptation positively affirms the disruption caused by Medea as 'indeed culture-founding';[39] and by Jean Anouilh whose Médée (written 1946, performed 1953) exemplifies social alienation by living in a gypsy caravan – one production of this play was set in Haiti. In Brendan Kennelly's 1991 work the implied opposition is between Dublin and England, whereas Liz Lochhead sets the story in a rough Scotland with Medea as an educated-sounding English-speaker.[40] In all, the thrust is of a minority figure persecuted beyond endurance.

3 Corneille

In seventeenth-century France it was Pierre Corneille who adapted Seneca's treatment of the Medea story as a tragic drama.[41] His Médée enters the stage with a powerful soliloquy which makes up I, 4 and contains a clear and almost gleeful acceptance of evil: she remembers, without ducking responsibility, her betrayal of her father and her murder of her brother, and adds:

> Des crimes si légers furent mes coups d'essai :
> Il faut bien autrement montrer ce que je sais ;

---

38 *Medea*, 1821. Ed. Friedrich Schreyvogl (Salzburg: Bergland-Buch, 1984).

39 See Isabela Capeloa Gil, 'Femininity as Trauma in R. Jeffers' *Medea* and G. Tabori's *M*', in Pascual Nieves, *Witness to Pain: Essays on the Translation of Pain into Art* (Bern: Peter Lang, 2005), pp. 186–208 (p. 188).

40 *Medea* (London: Nick Hern Books, 2000).

41 *Médée*, 1635. *Théâtre complet*, ed. G. Couton (Paris: Garnier, 1971), I, pp. 555–618 (p. 576). References to this play will be given by Act, scene and line numbers.

Il faut faire un chef-d'œuvre, et qu'un dernier ouvrage
Surpasse de bien loin ce faible apprentissage.

I, 4, 251–4

[Such trifling crimes were my first ventures;
I must now show my true colours in quite a different way;
I need a masterpiece of crime, a final foray
That will far surpass such a feeble first attempt.]

Elsewhere, too, this Médée comes across as coldly calculating: she lays particular stress on Créon's unfairness and inconsistency as excuses for her own bitterness:

O d'un injuste affront les coups les plus cruels !
Vous faites différence entre deux criminels !
Vous voulez qu'on l'honore, et que des deux complices
L'un ait votre couronne, et l'autre des supplices !

II, 2, 455–8

[How cruel are the blows of this horrid injustice!
You draw a distinction between two criminals:
Jason is to be honoured, and the two co-conspirators
Should receive, one the throne and the other torture!]

She also reminds Créon that his attitude at the start of the play is inconsistent with his earlier knowing acceptance of her as a refugee:

Mais vous les saviez tous quand vous m'avez reçue ;
Votre simplicité n'a point été déçue :
En ignoriez-vous un quand vous m'avez promis
Un rempart assuré contre mes ennemis ?

II, 2, 477–80

[But you knew all of this when you welcomed me here;
We did not lull your naivety with deception.
Were you unaware of any of my crimes
When you promised to defend me against my enemies?]

Later, hearing that her attack on Créon and his daughter has been successful, she wonders whether this punishment is sufficient for Jason:

Est-ce assez, ma vengeance, est-ce assez de deux morts ?
Consulte avec loisir tes plus ardents transports.
[...]   Immolons avec joie
Ceux qu'à me dire adieu Créuse me renvoie.

> V, 2, 1327–34

[Are these two deaths enough to satisfy my vengeance?
Take time to consider yet more extremes of passion:
(...) Take joy in destroying the very people
Whom Creusa is sending to me for a farewell.]

At that point Médée can certainly be portrayed as arguing herself into a position in which the murder of her children appears logical, rather than being
carried away by a helpless and overwhelming passion. Her weighing up of the
pros and cons, the urge to revenge versus her maternal instinct, may seem to a
modern audience unacceptably calculating, reflecting Corneille's tendency to
force the human individual to accept responsibility for the outcome of such
deliberations. Jesuit and Stoical, he was less prone than the Jansenist Racine to
accept pleas of helplessness or fatalism on behalf of his characters.[42]

In any dramatic context, if Medea's thought-process is to be explored, she
must reveal it to the audience, and if she is given an extended speech in which
she agonizes about her decision, or even simply reflects on it, it will be difficult
to distinguish between despair and calculation. Seneca's Medea says: 'my madness shall never cease its quest of vengeance and shall grow on for ever'[43] –
which sounds more like a rational attempt to claim madness as an excuse,
than a mad outburst. The demonstration of a mind being torn apart can sound
disturbingly similar to a rational balancing act – particularly perhaps if the
vehicle is the French classical alexandrine. Early in the play, Corneille's Médée
seems to spell out the logical consequences of her rage:

Déchirer par morceaux l'enfant aux yeux du père
N'est que le moindre effet qui suivra ma colère ;
[...]
Il faut bien autrement montrer ce que je sais ;
Il faut faire un chef-d'œuvre [...]

> I, 4, 249–50, 252–53

---

42   Acknowledging again that this formerly consensual view has been scrutinized and chal-
     lenged, see above, 'Helplessness', p. 28 (note 8).

43   Lines 406–07: 'numquam meus cessabit in poenas furor / crescetque semper.'

[To tear apart the child (her brother Apsyrtus)
     under the very eyes of his father
Is but the slightest effect of my rage;
I must find another way to reveal my understanding,
A masterpiece of revenge ...]

(In practice the ambiguous line 249 might combine the allusion to the old story of Apsyrtus with a reference to the current situation as regards Créon and Jason – in both cases she is minded to murder a child in the presence of its parent.) Much will always depend on directorial decisions and the actress's own personality, but at moments like that, a performance can be tilted towards or away from an interpretation which suggests either that the character is genuinely premeditating future action or is thrashing around in a confused state of mind. Brendan Kennelly's character, for example, is given much less chance to portray genuine despair, so is almost bound to come across as matter-of-fact to the point of resignation: 'There are consequences. Passion strangles all my love. My children will fall into murderous hands. Whichever way the wheel turns, my children must die. And if they must, I will kill them.'[44] It is perhaps a moot point whether fluency and verbosity convey greater agony than this tongue-tied coldness; at any rate, this is a key decision for a hypothetical jury – whose position the theatre audience is in a sense occupying. Will they be more sympathetic to a Medea who conveys helpless anguish ('My children are going to die anyway, better at my hand than at those of the cruel Corinthians'), or one who claims diminished responsibility in the most conventional sense ('I am so wretched that I cannot control my actions'), or one who claims victim status and tries to shift the responsibility for her state of mind and consequent actions onto Jason ('he has treated me so badly that he does not deserve the love of children to console him')?

As Corneille's play reaches its climax, his Médée seems to have to make a superhuman effort to overcome her last vestiges of pity and maternal loyalty: an intellectual victory for will over instinct, rather than a pathetic inability to control her passion:

Cessez dorénavant, pensers irrésolus,
D'épargner des enfants que je ne verrai plus.
Chers fruits de mon amour, si je vous ai fait naître,
Ce n'est pas seulement pour caresser un traître :
Il me prive de vous, et je l'en vais priver.
     V, 2, 1347–51

---

44   *Medea* (Newcastle-upon-Tyne: Bloodaxe Books, 1991), pp. 65–71.

[Irresolute thoughts, from now on no longer
May you spare my children whom I will not see again.
Beloved fruits of my love, I gave you life,
But not so that you may caress and console a traitor:
He is depriving me of you so I will deprive him of you.]

This sounds more like calculating punishment than uncontrolled revenge, despite what Médée claims in the ensuing lines:

Mais ma pitié renaît, et revient me braver ;
Je n'exécute rien, et mon âme éperdue
Entre deux passions demeure suspendue.
N'en délibérons plus, mon bras en résoudra.
Je vous perds, mes enfants; mais Jason vous perdra ;
Il ne vous verra plus ...

    V, 2, 1352–57

[But now my pity returns and starts to defy me again;
I cannot take action – my soul is lost in the balance
Between two conflicting emotions.
No – no more anguished deliberation,
      my hand will cut through the arguments.
Oh, my children, I will see you no more – but nor will Jason,
He too will lose you.]

The logic of revenge necessitates the killing of the children: they would console Jason, and they would transmit his seed. Her suffering may or may not blind her to the fact that they are her children also: what she sees clearly is that they are *his* children, and her liberation from him – and in a modern perspective from patriarchy generally – involves the destruction of his legacy.[45]

As a sort of counterpoint to this position, it is noteworthy that Corneille's Jason also has the idea of killing the children as a means of getting at Médée. This idea is unique to Corneille, and it does not really let Médée off any moral hooks since it is a passing idea, quite independent of her thought processes, and nothing comes of it because it is pre-empted by her own murder of the children. Nevertheless, the very fact that a 'non-barbarian' conceives of the idea may subtly steer the audience towards finding it less absolutely abhorrent,

---

45   See Marianne McDonald, 'Medea as Politician and Diva: Riding the Dragon into the Future', in J.J. Clauss and S.I. Johnston (eds.), *Medea: Essays on Medea in Myth, Literature, Philosophy and Art* (Princeton NJ: Princeton UP, 1997), pp. 297–324 (p. 301).

or at least marginally less incredible,[46] and the notion of Jason as a role model
for Médée's actions is touched on:

> Indignes rejetons de mon amour passée,
> Quel malheureux destin vous avait réservés
> A porter le trépas à qui vous a sauvés ?
> C'est vous, petits ingrats, que, malgré la nature
> Il me faut immoler dessus leur sépulture.
> Que la sorcière en vous commence de souffrir ;
> Que son premier tourment soit de vous voir mourir.
>
> v, 5, 1530–36

> [Ye wretched offshoots of my former love,
> By what sad fate were you destined
> To cause the death of the very persons who saved you?[47]
> Against all nature, thankless children, it is you
> Whom I should sacrifice upon the tombs
>   (of Créon and Créuse).
> Let the witch discover torment through you,
> And let her first taste of torture be to witness your deaths.]

Although we can scarcely on this basis consider Jason and Médée as co-
conspirators to kill the children, it is clear that they had been active accomplices in earlier bloody exploits, notably the murders of Apsyrtus and of Pelias.
Much of the debate during their confrontations in Corinth centres on mutual
recriminations over who carries ultimate responsibility for those earlier acts.
If Jason can blame Medea for all that had gone on before, it gives him a pretext for disowning her now, but leaves him guilty of ingratitude, since she had
clearly acted in his interests if not on his behalf. Corneille's Médée may want
to have this both ways. When taxing Jason with ingratitude (either in soliloquy
or to his face), she does accept responsibility for the earlier misdeeds, because
this gives her a lever to apply moral blackmail to Jason, and confidence in her
ability to punish him in like manner:

---

46   Zoé Schweitzer, '"Si vous ne craignez rien que je vous trouve à plaindre". Violence et pou-
     voirs dans la *Médée* de Corneille' in *Comparatismes en Sorbonne*, 2, 2011, pp. 5–18 (p. 15).
     Accessed online, 17 September 2017 at http://www.crlc.paris-sorbonne.fr/pdf_revue/
     revue2/Spectacle4.pdf.
47   As in other versions, it was the children who had delivered the poisoned robe to Créuse.

Croit-il que m'offenser soit si peu de chose ?
Quoi ! mon père trahi, les éléments forcés,
D'un frère dans la mer les membres dispersés,
Lui font-ils présumer mon audace épuisée ?

     I, 4, 234–7

[Does he treat it so lightly to cause me offense?
The betrayal of my father, the control of the elements,
The limbs of my brother scattered across the sea –
Does he assume from these that I have run out of daring?]

Similarly in her confrontation with Créon (II, 2) she is not abashed to describe herself and Jason as 'complices' (accomplices), demanding equivalent punishment for equivalent crimes. On the other hand, she does want to insist that whatever she did it was for Jason, and that she sought no direct gain for herself:

Je n'en ai que la honte, il en a tout le fruit :
[...] Aucun de tant de maux ne va qu'à son profit.

     II, 2, 472/6

[I carry all the shame, he has all the benefits:
None of the evil I have done was not intended for his profit.]

Similarly in the central confrontation with Jason himself (III, 3) she is anxious to insist that he carry his share of the blame, since the gain was all his:

JASON	Toi, qu'un amour furtif souilla de tant de crimes,
	M'oses-tu reprocher des ardeurs légitimes ?
MÉDÉE	Oui, je te les reproche, et de plus ...
JASON	Quels forfaits ?
MÉDÉE	La trahison, le meurtre, et tous ceux que j'ai faits.
JASON	Il manque encor ce point à mon sort déplorable,
	Que de tes cruautés on me fasse coupable.
MÉDÉE	Tu présumes en vain de t'en mettre à couvert ;
	Celui-là fait le crime à qui le crime sert.

     III, 3, 853–60

[After all of the crimes caused by your furtive love,
You dare to reproach me now when my love is legitimate?
Yes, I reproach you and furthermore ...

What crimes have I committed?
Treachery, murder, all my crimes are yours.
My pitiful fate needs only this to crown it,
That I should be held guilty of your cruel acts.
In vain do you seek to shield yourself from them –
Whoever benefits from a crime is guilty of it.]

Both these scenes are fairly direct translation from Seneca.[48] Although
Euripides had made much of the fact that everything Medea had done had
been undertaken 'for Jason' he did not explicitly argue that Jason therefore
carried any culpability for Medea's earlier crimes. Seneca turned this into a
legal axiom, 'cui prodest scelus is fecit' (500–501), translated by Corneille in his
line 860, which, as editors have noted, has gone on in certain jurisdictions to
become a valuable maxim in the forensic investigation of crime, if not necessarily in a judicial process.[49]

Although Corneille was broadly faithful to Seneca in the construction of
his plot, he incorporated elements from Euripides (notably the significance
of Aegeus) and some independent inventions, many of which have the effect
of diminishing at least to some extent the guilt and responsibility of Médée
herself. As Racine was to do for Phèdre, he furnished her with a few extra
excuses,[50] and, as we have already seen, made this explicit in his *Examen* of the
play.[51] Corneille's Jason uses the language of excuse-making in his own early
admission of a strong sense of shame for his betrayal of her:

Mon cœur, qui se partage en deux affections,
Se laisse déchirer à mille passions.
Je dois tout à Médée, et je ne puis sans honte
Et d'elle et de ma foi tenir si peu de compte :
Je dois tout à Créon, et d'un si puissant roi
Je fais un ennemi si je garde ma foi :
Je regrette Médée, et j'adore Créuse ;
Je vois mon crime en l'une, en l'autre mon excuse ;

---

48   Corneille's II, 2 reflects Seneca's lines 190–300; Corneille's lines 455–58 and 472–76,
      quoted above, are a close imitation of Seneca's lines 275–80; Corneille's III, 3 reflects
      Seneca's lines 447–520; Corneille's lines 854–882 are a close imitation of Seneca's lines
      497–520.

49   See for example, Georges Couton's edition (Paris: Classiques Garnier, 1971, 3 vols.), I,
      p. 1128.

50   Schweitzer, p. 7.

51   See the passage quoted on p. 117 and referenced in note 35.

Et dessus mon regret mes désirs triomphants
Ont encor le secours du soin de mes enfants.
    I, 2, 163–172

[Two sources of tenderness split my heart
Which is indeed torn apart by a thousand conflicting emotions.
I owe all to Medea, and it is shameful
That I set so little store by her and by my faithfulness to her.
I owe all to Creon, and if I remain faithful to Medea,
Such a powerful king becomes our enemy.
I mourn the loss of Medea, and I adore Creusa.
The former is my source of guilt, the latter my excuse.
And over and above the regrets I feel,
The need to protect my children supports my desire
        (to be with Creusa) which will emerge triumphant.]

A director who wished to maximize sympathy for Médée here would have no difficulty in portraying this speech as a self-justificatory rationalization of a decision all but made: Jason's sense of shame is expressed in rather forced and unconvincing language and is easily overcome by his desire, as he evokes his own diminished responsibility in the face of the lust which grips him, his sense of helplessness as two equally valid loyalties tear him apart, and his sense of responsibility as a parent, all as excuses for doing what he wants to do anyway.

Both Créon and Créuse are made more calculating in their cruelty to Médée in this version, the latter by specifically asking for Médée's sumptuous wedding dress and the former by making it clear that he is retaining Médée's children (rather than exiling them with their mother) at the request of his daughter, who wishes to parent them alongside Jason. And in Corneille's play it is Créon's blind stupidity that prompts him to accord Médée a day for consideration of her options. She does not ask for this lease of time, so her own decisions seem less calculating. This Créon is indeed throughout patronizingly dismissive of Médée, which even in the seventeenth century might have further increased sympathy for her. A negative portrayal of Créon as tyrannical would also have helped to make his murder more tolerable in an age and context where regicide was second only to infanticide in its ability to evoke horror.[52] Corneille is also unique among the ancient and early modern dramatists of the story in turning Créuse into a flesh-and-blood character rather than an off-stage cipher.

---

52   Schweitzer, p. 10.

A particularly interesting attempt to confront the inherited story of Medea with the reality of a modern experience was the production of Corneille's play at the Studio Théâtre d'Asnières in 2016, directed by Nicolas Candoni. Despite retaining Corneille's classical and poetic diction, this production presented a twenty-first-century couple in a minimalist setting dominated by anachronisms: Médée takes to drink in order to alleviate her pain; Créuse attempts to win over the children's affection with presents of a skateboard and a basketball, leading to a game in which Créon participates; and one of the boys persistently films the actions of his intended step-mother on his mobile. This increased focus of attention on the boys themselves enabled the audience to enter fully into the pain of both Médée and Jason at the potential loss of them. The sense that Médée is a victim, abandoned and betrayed by Jason and cruelly treated by Créon, was underlined, so that the situation almost goes beyond the notion of excuse. This Médée is driven by Jason's cynical indifference to a pitch of righteous indignation in which, as director Nicolas Candoni put it, the audience was explicitly invited to 'questionner les raisons de l'infanticide: acte barbare intolérable ou reconquête de soi et affirmation de sa liberté dans un monde qu'elle refuse?' ('... call into question the motivation for the infanticide: is it an intolerably barbaric act or rather a reclamation of her identify and an affirmation of her liberty within a world that she refuses to accept?')[53] This production also brought out the complacent self-justification of Jason, who presents his 'choice' of Créuse as something close to a self-sacrifice: in an ultimate attitude of bad faith, he pretends that he is accepting the offer of marriage to the princess in order to assure for his sons a life-style that is worthy of their status.

Although Racine did not treat the subject of Medea, Corneille's was not the only version produced in seventeenth-century France. Marc-Antoine Charpentier wrote an operatic version of the story to a libretto by Thomas Corneille in 1693, which had a strong influence on the play by Longepierre mentioned above, which itself became the most performed *Médée* of the eighteenth century.[54] In keeping, perhaps, with the ethos of opera at that time, their Jason is less cynical and irresponsible than those of their predecessors, expressing both shame and love in tones which the text does not invite the actor to subvert or call into question. If Jason then takes responsibility for

53   Quoted by Solange Jambon at http://autreenjeu2016.over-blog.com/2016/02/medee-de
      -corneille-revisitee-aujourd-hui.html, accessed on 13 December 2017.
54   Benjamin Pintiaux, '*Médée* within the Repertory of the *tragédie en musique*: Intertextual
      Links and the "Posterity" of Charpentier's Opera', in Shirley Thompson (ed.), *New Perspectives on Marc-Antoine Charpentier* (Farnham: Ashgate, 2010), pp. 251–268 (pp. 262–3).

his conduct as a lover, Médée becomes more of a victim, suffering and hesitant, suspense arising out of her changes of intention. The opera takes advantage of the relative freedom of that genre as regards decorum to maximize the horror and brutality of the ending. Other operatic treatments, too, have allowed Jason to be portrayed in a more sympathetic light. When Jonathan Kent directed Cherubini's 1797 version for Opera North in 1996, the company's director Phyllida Lloyd (who had herself previously produced Euripides' play) expressed 'disappointment that Jason was comparatively the nice guy, as opposed to the pragmatic bastard of the Greek'.[55] In this version, Medea is spectacularly burned alive.

It was suggested at the start of this chapter that the only valid reason for presenting a play about the actions of Medea would be to make some attempt to understand those actions, make contact with her motivation and thus approach her with the sort of sympathy required for tragic catharsis. On the other hand it is most unlikely that even the most ardently feminist re-interpreter of her plight and her story would concede that they were seeking to justify infanticide. If we are lulled or seduced by a production into seeing her as an Everywoman, who loves her children but is driven by despair to destroy them, this might be tantamount to suggesting that any woman might do the same, so that the worst of crimes risks being trivialized.[56] On the other hand, the tendency of some modern interpretations of all plays about her to turn her act into a heroic gesture of defiance, where she makes a spectacle of herself (with herself as her most spellbound spectator, relishing the effect of her action with glee as well as horror) carries the different but equal danger of seeming to justify individual violence. Excusing violence, particularly in domestic situations, on the grounds that the ultimate victim was the initiator of a cycle of violence, points towards a special category of diminished responsibility, which we will consider in the next chapter.

---

55   Robert Hanks, 'Medea – the fatal attraction' in *The Independent*, 14 April, 1996, accessed at
       http://www.independent.co.uk/arts-entertainment/medea-the-fatal-attraction-1305049
       .html on 13 November 2017.
56   Schweitzer, p. 16.

CHAPTER 5

Provocation: The Defence of Clytemnestra

Agamemnon and his wife Clytemnestra lived violent lives in a bloodthirsty age. He obtained her hand by killing her former husband, his own cousin, Tantalus; he accepted the ritual sacrifice of their daughter Iphigenia as the price imposed by Artemis for the success of the Trojan expedition; during and since that expedition he had openly lived with concubines, Chryseis, Cassandra and others, treated exploitatively as the spoils of war. It is therefore scarcely surprising that his homecoming after the siege and sack of Troy was greeted by Clytemnestra – who had for a long time found consolation for her husband's absence in the arms of another of his cousins, Aegisthus – with bitter resentment rather than joy. Luring him with false expressions of relief and pleasure into a bath, she killed him.

In representations of her story in Classical Antiquity, Clytemnestra's guilt was seldom seriously questioned, although it was through her children, Orestes and Electra, rather than by judicial process, that she was punished. Her action was portrayed in *The Odyssey* as a straightforward crime: 'Who else could conceive so hideous a crime as her deliberate butchery of her husband and her lord?'[1] In tragedy, she sometimes sought to defend her action, as in Euripides' *Electra*:[2]

> (Agamemnon) lured my daughter with the hope of marriage to Achilles [...] Though I was wronged in this, I did not turn wild and would not have killed my husband. But he came back with his girlfriend, a mad prophetess, and brought her into our marriage bed, keeping two wives in the same house. [...] Was it not then right for him, the killer of my child, to die?
>
> 1011–46, pp. 109–10

Electra, however, scornfully dismissed such defences as mere 'pretexts':

---

1 Homer, *The Odyssey*, XI, 427–8, trans. E.V. Rieu (London: Methuen, 1952), p. 163.

2 Euripides, *Medea and Other Plays*, translated and edited by James Morwood (Oxford: Oxford University Press, 1998).

© KONINKLIJKE BRILL NV, LEIDEN, 2021 | DOI:10.1163/9789004442788_007

You destroyed the best man of Greece and hid behind the pretext that
you killed your husband for your daughter's sake. And some believe you,
for they do not know you as well as I do.

> 1066–8, pp. 110–111

Clytemnestra was generally condemned by choruses within the drama, and
by commentators on it, as well as by her children. Her action was depicted (by
men) as self-righteous, controlled and vindictive, attempts at extenuation were
rejected, and her punishment was seen as appropriate. Thus, in Aeschylus's
The Choephori,[3] Clytemnestra's guilt haunts her in terrible nightmares, and it
is taken for granted that Electra and Orestes will justifiably seek reparation for
the unlawful killing of their father. Clytemnestra herself, when challenged by
Orestes, produces rather pathetic pleas to diminish her responsibility:

> My child, Fate played a part; I was not all to blame.
>
> 910, p. 136

> Your father sinned too. Count his sins along with mine.
>
> 918, p. 137[4]

> A woman without her man suffers no less, my son.
>
> 920, p. 137

Then in the final part of Aeschylus's trilogy, *The Eumenides*, her ghost confirms
that she is shunned by the inhabitants of the underworld, as a guilty party
rather than as the outraged victim of a matricide.

Under twentieth-century judicial systems, however, female victims of
male bullies are given more sympathy if they retaliate in kind, and a modern
Clytemnestra might plausibly enter a plea of diminished responsibility or
provocation. Debate around such cases became a significant feminist issue
in Europe, Australia and America in the last decade of the century. Legal and
medical experts developed new terms, like 'battered woman syndrome' or
'learned helplessness', to deal with victims of domestic violence. In July, 1995,
for example, Emma Humphreys was released from a UK prison. Her conviction for murder had been overturned on appeal, and although she was guilty of
manslaughter, having killed her partner in 1985, the term of imprisonment she

---

3 Aeschylus, *The Oresteian Trilogy*, translated by Philip Vellacott (Harmondsworth: Penguin
   Classics, 1956).

4 The word translated 'sins' here by Vellacott is more commonly translated as 'follies'.

had already served was deemed a sufficient penalty. This was widely greeted as a 'landmark' ruling, because it was the first time an English court had accepted that a defence of provocation – as grounds for conviction for manslaughter rather than murder – could succeed if it were based not on a single explosive event triggering an impulsive reaction, but on a series of incidents over a period, which drove a female victim of bullying to turn on her male tormentor and kill him. Judges and juries could take account of the cumulative effects of long-term violent mistreatment. They could do so, moreover, even if those effects had included incidents in which the eventual killer had fantasized about revenge or publicly threatened to kill the bully, so that it became a very delicate judgment as to whether the act of killing resulted from a temporary loss of control or was the realization of a conscious plan. On the evening of his death, Humphreys' partner Trevor Armitage had incited two other men, including his own son, to rape her, threatening to beat her up if she resisted, and had then taunted her as she contemplated suicide. She stabbed him to death with a knife with which she had previously been attempting to slit her own wrists.[5]

What is the relationship between these two sordid stories of domestic violence? Should modern judges, considering cases like that of Humphreys, pay attention to the precedent – ethical if not legal – of Clytemnestra, as she has been presented in tragic literature? To what extent, on the other hand, should modern understandings of criminal behaviour point towards a reinterpretation of ancient myths and dramas? Is it inevitable or helpful that contemporary experience and debate affect the interpretation of plays composed in a different ethical and legal context?

Discussion of Humphreys and others was fuelled by the argument that the English legal system was inherently discriminatory: it was statistically easier for a male than for a female assailant to obtain (from a predominantly male judiciary) leniency or acquittal on grounds of provocation. Thomas Corlett in July 1987, Shirley Freeman in February 1989, Peter Lines in April 1990, Joseph McGrail in August 1991, Bisla Rajinder Singh in January 1992, were all convicted of manslaughter and given short or non-custodial sentences, because British juries or prosecuting authorities accepted that the women whom each of them admitted killing had shared some of the responsibility for their own deaths. These cases were contrasted with the initial fate of Humphreys, convicted of murder in 1985 and not released until 1995, of Sara Thornton, convicted of murder in 1990 and not released until 1995, and of Kiranjit Ahluwalia, convicted of

---

5 *The Times*, 30 June 1995, p. 8, article by Richard Duce, and 8 July 1995, p. 1, article by Tim Jones.

murder in 1989 and not released until 1992.[6] The sorts of behaviour deemed to constitute provocation also demonstrated sexual bias: a man who beat, abused or killed his wife could successfully claim that her nagging, or exhibitions of jealousy, or withholding of sex, was a contributory and extenuating factor, whereas after years of drunken brutality and abuse, a wife was not accorded much sympathy if she complained, let alone responded in kind.

To appeal to provocation as a defence for an admitted act of violence, you must establish that your life had been rendered so unbearable through torture that the killing of the torturer appeared to be the only alternative to suicide. The English law depended for over forty years on Lord Devlin's 1949 definition: if an individual acted in circumstances under which 'an ordinary and reasonable person would be expected to suffer a temporary and sudden loss of control', then the defence of provocation could be brought forward for a jury's consideration. If there was any cooling-off period, or sense that the crime involved planning or premeditation, this defence was ruled out. This aspect of the legal definition was challenged by feminist groups who saw it as the perpetuation of a built-in bias against female victims of domestic violence, who could never hope to win a purely physical confrontation.[7] In the most notorious and contentious case, that of Sara Thornton, the plea of provocation was rejected because she killed her husband with a kitchen knife which she had moved to another room for the purpose, and this involved an unacceptable degree of premeditation and calculation. The flaws in the argument seem obvious with hindsight. If a woman is consistently brutalized, then any attempt at physical retaliation must involve equipping herself with a weapon, or she is bound to be physically overwhelmed. If a woman (to use phrases which are often employed in the successful defence of male killers in provocation cases) sees red and lashes out, then she will simply be hurt all the more by the aggressive and stronger male. So if the use of a weapon is a disqualification, it is hard to see how any woman could ever use the defence: with few open fireplaces in modern homes, blunt instruments do not easily come to hand – only the most quick-witted murderess is likely to find a frozen joint of meat at the right time and place, as in Roald Dahl's bleak comic story *Lamb to the Slaughter*;[8]

---

6 Phil Cleary's campaign to change the law in Australia was based on a similar sense of outrage over inherent discrimination in the cases of Peter Keogh and James Ramage. See Phil Cleary, *Just Another Little Murder* (St Leonard's, NSW: Allen and Unwin, 2002).

7 See J. Horder, *Provocation and Responsibility* (Oxford: Clarendon Press, 1992). For additional details of the feminist debate, see S. Walklate, *Gender and Crime* (London: Harvester Wheatsheaf, 1995), pp. 145–147, and Mandy Burton, 'Sentencing Domestic Homicide Upon Provocation: Still "Getting Away with Murder"', *Feminist Legal Studies*, 11, 2003, pp. 279–289.

8 In *The Collected Short Stories of Roald Dahl* (Harmondsworth: Penguin Books, 1992).

and here, too, although there was a degree of provocation, it is not suggested
that the woman was innocent of murder. It is also essential that the male pro-
voker be caught off guard, and this is likely to enable a male prosecutor before
a male judge to cast doubt on the validity of the defence by alleging a degree
of premeditation.

When Thornton was released after a retrial, the judge made it clear that the
revised verdict of manslaughter was based on diminished responsibility, but
that the decision, and reduced sentence, would have been the same if based
on provocation. 'I take into account the difficulties of living with an alcoholic
but you nevertheless took a life.'[9] Mrs Thornton accepted the new verdict and
thought the punishment she had received was fair. She did not advocate violence which she said represented 'powerlessness, not power'. Although one
of Mr Thornton's sisters accepted the outcome, another said: 'We think the
jury bowed to feminist pressure. No one could stand up to that.' Gareth Peirce,
Thornton's solicitor, said: 'This case makes it clear that the law needs simplify-
ing. For a jury to have to resolve the many difficult stages involved with these
charges is something not even a PhD Law student would feel comfortable with.'

This scenario does not lend itself to interpretation within the perspective
of Aristotelian tragedy. For a defence of provocation or diminished responsibility to succeed, the bully must seem irremediably sadistic and evil, otherwise the defence that 'there was nothing else I could do' is seriously weakened.
Similarly, the accused party must be a passive and innocent victim, since any
significant contribution on her part to the tension which led to the explosion
of violence would reduce the plea's chance of success. So a black-and-white
moral framework, generally thought of as inimical to the operation of tragedy,
must be established: an innocent victim lashing out against an evil monster.
However, that pattern is perhaps commoner in successful tragedies, especially
in the French tradition, than Aristotle's strictures suggest. Innocent victims
are treated with suspicion by Aristotle, but their tendency to be haunted by
guilt is often a focus of attention in tragedy. Racine, although he presents himself as a faithful disciple of Aristotle, extracts tragic intensity from figures like
Andromaque, Iphigénie and Hippolyte for whom the term 'guilty' is extremely
problematic. In provocation cases, the experience of torture systematically undermines the self-esteem and confuses the value judgments of the victim, so
that even as he or she is driven to retaliate, self-doubt in many forms assails him
or her. The study of such a character, therefore, attempting self-justification before a judge or another moral or religious authority, or simply his or her own
bewildered conscience, while lacking any real confidence in the basis of the

9   *The Times*, 31 May 1996, p. 3, article by Tim Jones and Richard Ford.

justification, generates precisely the ambiguities over responsibility, freedom
and guilt which are central to the tragic tradition. It is in that context that it
might be appropriate to re-open the case of Clytemnestra, and to investigate
in particular how treatments of her story in modern drama have reflected
changes in attitude towards female victims of bullying husbands.

1   Racine

Curiously, one of the strongest dramatic images of Clytemnestre as a provoked
wife occurs in a play which does not depict her crime: Racine's *Iphigénie*, where
she confronts Agamemnon before the Greek armies leave for Troy. Physical
violence is strongly foreshadowed in Clytemnestre's verbal violence towards
her husband, and the play portrays actions and attitudes of Agamemnon
that could subsequently become the basis of a defence based on provocation. Their first meeting (III, 1) begins in an uneasy atmosphere of shiftiness
and suspicion. Agamemnon does nothing to alleviate the situation, first begging and finally commanding Clytemnestre to absent herself from the altar
whither Iphigénie is to be led. Her initial haughty anger suggests hostility towards Agamemnon: 'Qui? moi?' she begins (III, l, 795), and quickly asserts her
own authority:

> Dois-je donc de Calchas être moins près que vous ?
>> III, 1, 799

> [Should I then be less close to Calchas than you are?]

> Fier de son nouveau rang, m'ose-t-il méconnaître ?
> Me croit-il à sa suite indigne de paraître ?
>> III, 2, 821–22

> [With his new rank does he misprize his Queen,
> Think me unworthy of his retinue?]

When Arcas reveals the true reason for Agamemnon's summons – the sacrifice rather than the marriage of Iphigénie – Clytemnestre's reaction rapidly
explodes into outrage directed specifically against her husband:

> Les dieux ordonneraient un meurtre abominable ?
> [...]

Je ne m'étonne plus de cet ordre cruel
Qui m'avait interdit l'approche de l'autel.
    III, 5, 922–25

[So foul a murder's ordered by the gods?
...
His cruel order now I understand
That I should not approach the altar steps.]

This makes it more difficult for Agamemnon to hide behind *his* excuse, that the gods or his destiny are really to blame: Clytemnestre's refusal to countenance such an attitude on their part underlines the king's ultimate responsibility. In stirring up Achille's resentment, she reminds him of Agamemnon's role, not of the gods' iniquitous demands:

C'est vous que nous cherchions sur ce funeste bord,
Et votre nom, Seigneur, l'a conduite à la mort.
    III, 5, 935–36

['Twas you we sought upon this ill-starred shore,
And it's your name that leads her to her death.]

As she and Achille then seek to confront Agamemnon, their invective becomes ever more vigorous and personal, with no attempt to consider the hapless father's position:

Un barbare osera m'insulter ?
[...]
Cependant aujourd'hui, sanguinaire, parjure,
[...]
Il veut que ce soit moi qui vous mène au supplice !
    III, 6, 964–78

[A barbarian dares affront me so?
...
Yet he, bloodthirsty and forsworn ...
What's more, *I* am to take you to your death.]

Clytemnestre's most vigorous verbal assault on Agamemnon occurs in IV, 4. The king is determined to obey the oracle, and Iphigénie consents. The queen spells out all the reasons Agamemnon could have given for refusing to comply with the gods' demand: he could have expressed his feelings of paternal love much more vigorously, even violently; he could have argued that oracles are often ambiguous, or that the cost of the expedition should more appropriately be borne by Ménélas and his direct family, or that Hélène was in any case not worth this sacrifice. Since Agamemnon had manifestly not used such arguments, Clytemnestre insists that his reason for going through with the murder must be ambitious pride. This will (though not within Racine's play) give her the justification she needs for her spiteful rejection of Agamemnon, and thus ultimately for her own adultery and murder:

> L'orgueil de voir vingt rois vous servir et vous craindre,
> Tous les droits de l'empire en vos mains confiés,
> Cruel, c'est à ces dieux que vous sacrifiez.
> [...]
> De mes bras tout sanglants il faudra l'arracher,
> Aussi barbare époux qu'impitoyable père.
>
> IV, 4, 1286–1309

> [The thirst to reign that nothing can assuage,
> And empire over twenty kneeling kings –
> These are the gods to whom you sacrifice.
> ...
> You must uproot her from my bleeding arms,
> Pitiless father, barbarous husband!]

Clytemnestre sums up her case against her husband in the horrific charge with which this vitriolic speech opens:

> Vous ne démentez point une race funeste :
> Oui, vous êtes du sang d'Atrée et de Thyeste.
> Bourreau de votre fille, il ne vous reste enfin
> Que d'en faire à sa mère un horrible festin.
>
> IV, 4, 1245–48

> [Yes, you do not belie your baleful race,
> You are of Atreus', of Thyestes' blood.
> You kill your daughter; it remains for you
> To serve her to me in a hideous feast.]

Having rejected destiny or the gods as an excuse for Agamemnon's actions, she here allows him to argue genetic determinism as a cause; nevertheless she makes it clear that her personal resentment is unreasonable and boundless, and the audience does not need detailed knowledge of the story to interpret this outburst as a bitterly ironic foreshadowing of the assault on Agamemnon's person which will occur ten years later. The tragedy in Racine's play lies in the fact that Iphigénie herself is a silent, helpless and no doubt horrified witness of this verbal assault, so that the sparing of her life which Racine contrives is in no true sense a happy ending. Our final image is of Iphigénie weeping, surrounded by cheering soldiers off to battle, her friend Eriphile dead and all that gave her a basis for emotional security destroyed. Tragedy need not necessarily involve death, as Racine insisted in his *Préface* to *Bérénice*, but resides in the loss of what makes life worth living. At any rate Racine has provided us with a very powerful and striking portrayal of a Clytemnestre whom one can very easily imagine claiming self-righteous justification for her attacks on her husband on the basis of his provocative disregard of her needs.

2   **Twentieth-century France: Giraudoux and Sartre**

Many twentieth-century dramatists have adapted the story of Clytemnestra and Agamemnon, and several of these have re-interpreted the legal, ethical and moral responsibility of each character in the light of modern concepts. As early as 1937, Jean Giraudoux's *Electre* put an explicitly feminist slant on the discussion. His is essentially a humanist reinterpretation of the myth in which notions of providence are treated with cynicism, and both classical form and ethical discussion are subjected to parodic distortion. Although Giraudoux made no attempt to turn Clytemnestre into a sympathetic character (as he did in the case of Egisthe), he presented her perception that women are treated unfairly:[10]

CLYTEMNESTRE	Prends ma cause, elle est la tienne. Défends-toi en me défendant.
ELECTRE	Je ne suis pas inscrite à l'association des femmes. [...]
CLYTEMNESTRE	Nous sommes femmes, Electre, nous avons le droit d'aimer.
ELECTRE	Je sais qu'on a beaucoup de droits dans la confrérie des femmes. Si vous payez le droit d'entrée, qui est

---

10   Jean Giraudoux, *Electre*, II, 5, in his *Théâtre* (Paris: Grasset, 1959), pp. 75–76.

lourd, qui est d'admettre que les femmes sont faibles,
menteuses, basses, vous avez le droit général de faiblesse, de mensonge, de bassesse. Le malheur est que
les femmes sont fortes, loyales, nobles. Alors tu te
trompes.

[Take up my cause, it's your cause too. As you defend me, defend yourself. / I'm not a signed-up member of the sisterhood. / We are women,
Electra, we have the right to love. / I am aware that the feminist sorority
imparts many rights. If you pay the entry fee, a heavy one, by admitting
that women are weak, treacherous and vile, then you have the right to
weakness, treachery and vileness. Unfortunately, however, women are
actually strong, loyal and noble – so you are wrong.]

Electre, unaware of her mother's complicity in Agamemnon's death, conducts
an increasingly bitter inquisition into Clytemnestre's feelings for her dead father, challenging her mother's use of stereotyping as an excuse for personal
shortcomings. Clytemnestre's expressions of dissatisfaction with her married
state foreshadow the language of later feminist defendants of women provoked
to killing, even though her hatred of him preceded his sacrifice of Iphigénie or
his adultery with Cassandre, and his crime at one level seems simply to be
his gender:

Tout dans ma vie a été dur [...] Depuis mon mariage, jamais de solitude
[...] Pas de repos, même pour mon corps. Il était couvert toute la journée
par les robes d'or, et la nuit par un roi.
II, 5, p. 77

[Everything in my life has been hard ... Since I was married, I have never
known solitude. Not a moment's rest, even for my body. It was weighed
down all day by golden robes, and all night crushed beneath a king.]

Agamemnon is described explicitly as the man who wrecked and sullied her
childhood paradise:

Je passais mes journées dans la prairie derrière le palais. Il y avait tant
de fleurs que pour les cueillir je ne me courbais pas, je m'asseyais. Mon
chien se couchait à mes pieds, celui qui aboya quand Agamemnon vint
me prendre. [...] Oui, je le haïssais. Oui, tu vas savoir enfin ce qu'il était,
ce père admirable ! [...] Du jour où il est venu m'arracher à ma maison,

avec sa barbe bouclée, de cette main dont il relevait toujours le petit
doigt, je l'ai haï. Il le relevait pour boire, il le relevait pour conduire, le
cheval s'emballât-il, et quand il tenait son sceptre, ... et quand il me tenait
moi-même, je ne sentais sur mon dos que la pression de quatre doigts :
j'en étais folle, et quand dans l'aube il livra à la mort ta sœur Iphigénie,
horreur, je voyais aux deux mains le petit doigt se détacher au soleil ! Le
roi des rois, quelle dérision ! Il était pompeux, indécis, niais. C'était le fat
des fats, le crédule des crédules. Le roi des rois n'a jamais été que ce petit
doigt et cette barbe que rien ne rendait lisse. [...] Roi des rois, la seule
excuse de ce surnom est qu'il justifie la haine de la haine.

     II, 8, pp. 102–5

[I used to spend all my time in the meadow behind the palace. There
were so many flowers that I sat down to pick them rather than bending
over. My dog would sleep at my feet, until Agamemnon came to fetch me
and he'd start barking ... Yes, I hated him. Yes, I'm about to tell you what
he was like, this wonderful father of yours! ... From the day he first came
to rip me out of my home, with his curly beard and his hand with its little
finger always sticking up, I hated him. He'd stick it up when drinking, he'd
stick it up when riding – even if his horse was galloping out of control –
and when he was holding on to his sceptre ... and when he was holding
on to me, all I felt on my back was the pressure from four fingers; it drove
me mad, and when one day at dawn he handed your sister Iphigénie
over to be killed, the horror of it, I could see on each of his hands the
little fingers held up towards the sun! King of kings, what a joke! He was
a stuck-up, indecisive twit. He was the show-off of show-offs, the slob of
slobs. The king of kings has never amounted to more than his little finger
and his beard that could never be straightened out ... King of kings, the
title has no excuse except that it justifies the hatred of hatreds.]

This intense and intimate sequence, in which a generalized distaste has been
symbolized by a fixation with detail, is presented in counterpoint with a more
comic exposition by a character invented by Giraudoux, Agathe, who gives
more uninhibited expression – 'la chanson des épouses' or 'wives' chorus', she
calls it – to the effect of male possessiveness and domination:

Nous sommes toutes là, avec nos maris insuffisants [...] Et toutes nous
nous consumons à leur rendre la vie agréable. Et s'ils mangent de la laitue
cuite il leur faut le sel et un sourire. [...] Et vingt-quatre heures par jour,

nous nous tuons, nous nous suicidons pour la satisfaction d'un être dont
le mécontentement est notre seule joie !

II, 6, pp. 80–1

[We are all stuck here with our unsatisfactory husbands … and all of us
wear ourselves out making their lives pleasant. Just to eat cooked greens,
they demand salt and a smile … And twenty-four hours a day, we destroy
ourselves, we drive ourselves to death for the satisfaction of these beings
when nothing brings us more joy than their dissatisfaction!]

When Jean-Paul Sartre adapted the Electra story as *Les Mouches* in 1943, the
context of World War II and his own personal agenda led him to concentrate
on the exploration of different aspects of personal responsibility, and the silent majority in Argos is blamed almost as much as Clytemnestre and Egisthe
for the crimes committed by the latter with the connivance of the former and
expiated painfully by all. So far from being a crime of passion, the murder of
Agamemnon is described by Egisthe in cold and clinical terms as a matter
of politics:[11]

C'est pour l'ordre que j'ai séduit Clytemnestre, pour l'ordre que j'ai tué
mon roi; je voulais que l'ordre règne et qu'il règne par moi. J'ai vécu sans
désir, sans amour, sans espoir: j'ai fait de l'ordre. O terrible et divine
passion !

[It was for the sake of order that I seduced Clytemnestra, for the sake of
order that I killed my king. I wanted order to reign and I wanted to be the
one who brought it about. I've led my life without desire, without love,
without hope, but I have created order – my terrible and godlike passion!]

Clytemnestre herself appears in only two scenes, depicted as a passive accomplice to Egisthe, and although she shares in the communal remorse – 'moi qui
ai ruiné ma vie en un seul matin […] N'importe qui peut me cracher au visage,
en m'appelant criminelle et prostituée' ('I threw my life away in a morning …
anyone would be justified in spitting in my face and calling me a whore and a
criminal', I, 5, pp. 137–41) – she does not attempt self-justification.

---

11   Jean-Paul Sartre, *Les Mouches* (Paris: Gallimard, Folio, 1990), II-2, 5, p. 202.

3   Marguerite Yourcenar

The central focus of Marguerite Yourcenar's adaptation of the Electra story, written in 1944, is very different: her agenda is to explore what it would be like for Orestes to discover that he is in fact the son of the usurper Aegisthus rather than of Agamemnon.[12] Her choice of title – *Electre ou La Chute des masques*[13] – suggests an interest in identity and hidden motivation and hence in the relationship between genuine extenuation and mere excuse, an interest confirmed by her forensic analysis, in an *Avant-propos*, of the relationship between vengeance, justice, self-justification and pardon in the story of the Atrides from Antiquity to the present day. Her Clytemnestre, lured as in Euripides to the hut where Electre lives by the false news that the latter is pregnant, appears only in one central confrontation with her daughter. Her posture as the victim of a bully in a sour marriage, whose retaliation may implicitly be excused, is at first hinted at quite subtly, although she does foreshadow the legal definition of provocation as a situation in which murder appears to be the only alternative to suicide:

> Tu continues à prendre la mort de ton père pour une petite fête qu'Egisthe et moi nous nous serions offerte. Tu ignores de quelles nécessités naissent les haines, et quelles douleurs cuisinent les vengeances. Notre crime a été une amputation sanglante, et ton beau-père et moi deux malades qui n'avaient le choix qu'entre la mort et le couteau.
>
>   II, 1, p. 57

> [You keep on taking your father's death for a little celebration that Egisthe and I presented ourselves with. You have no idea what necessities give rise to hatred, what pains cause vengeance to be cooked up. Our crime was an amputation bathed in blood; your step-father and I were two invalids with no choice except that between death and the surgeon's knife.]

Goaded by an increasingly bitter and hysterical Electre, Clytemnestre becomes ever blunter in her self-justificatory attacks on Agamemnon:

---

12   See Victoria B. Korzeniowska, 'Feminine Justice and Morality in Giraudoux's *Electre* and Yourcenar's *Electre ou La Chute des Masques*', *Forum for Modern Language Studies*, 38 (2002), pp. 14–23.

13   In *Théâtre II* (Paris: Gallimard, 1971).

Ton père n'a pas toujours été cette brute dont les retours imprévus effrayaient les enfants et les servantes. [...] On peut tout craindre d'un homme abruti par dix ans de guerre, d'occupation coloniale et de rapines [...]. Nous savions que ses rêves d'ambitieux et ses projets d'homme d'affaires ont seuls prolongé de dix ans une guerre inutile. [Ses soldats morts] l'intéressaient moins que ses maîtresses vivantes, ramassées dans les bouges d'Asie. [...] Ton père n'était qu'un gros dégoûtant, un simple idiot, une sale brute, moins propre au sortir du bain qu'après une heure d'amour mon amant nu [...]. Ton père n'a eu que ce qu'il méritait, le vieux bourreau, le vieux pourri, le vieux vendu ...

II, 1, pp. 59–61

[Your father hasn't always been that brute who comes home unexpectedly to terrify the children and the servants. [...] Everything is terrifying about a man who has been brutalized by ten years of war, colonial occupation and pillaging [...]. We knew that it was just his dreams as a man of ambition and his projects as a man of business that kept that unnecessary war going for ten years. [His dead soldiers] were of less interest to him than the living mistresses he picked up in the low dens of Asia. [...] Your father was nothing but a disgusting lump, a stupid simpleton, a dirty beast, less clean at the end of his bath than my naked lover is after an hour of love-making [...]. Your father got what was coming to him, no more, the old butcher, the mercenary old crook ...]

This outburst triggers an explosive response in which Electre kills Clytemnestre in a paroxysm of rage.

Yourcenar had earlier depicted Clytemnestra in a prose-poem in the form of a dramatic monologue, entitled *Clytemnestre ou Le Crime*, within the collection *Feux*.[14] Written in 1935 in response to what Yourcenar referred to as a 'crise passionnelle' – an unreciprocated fixation on a homosexual man – this cycle of texts is a study of love as self-delusion, as sickness, and is built around a sequence of *récits* in the mouths of nine mythical figures, including Achilles, Mary Magdalene and Sappho as well as Clytemnestra. The latter is explicitly on trial and intent on self-justification: she admits the act of killing, so her defence is based entirely on extenuating circumstances.

Je vais vous expliquer, Messieurs les Juges ... [...] J'ai tué cet homme avec un couteau [...]. Je l'ai laissé sacrifier l'avenir de nos enfants à ses

14   First published Paris: Grasset, 1936.

ambitions d'homme : je n'ai même pas pleuré quand ma fille en est morte. [...] Messieurs les Juges, vous ne l'avez connu qu'épaissi par la gloire, vieilli par dix ans de guerre, espèce d'idole énorme usée par les caresses des femmes asiatiques [...]. Les hommes ne sont pas faits pour passer toute leur vie à se chauffer les mains au feu d'un même foyer.

pp. 174–7

[Let me explain, your Honour. I did kill that man with a knife. I had allowed him to sacrifice the future of our children to his human ambitions; I didn't even weep when this caused the death of my daughter. Your Honour, you've only known him since he was sort of fleshed out by his glory, matured by ten years of war, turned into a sort of idol and worn down by the embrace of his Asiatic women. Men are not designed to spend their lives warming their hands at a domestic fireside.]

But in enumerating thus the standard list of provocations which her inadequate husband had provided to justify her ultimate retaliation, this Clytemnestra is not seeking to convey an excuse for anger or violence but an explanation for longing: 'Je me substituais peu à peu à l'homme qui me manquait et dont j'étais hantée' ('Little by little I myself took the place of the man whom I missed and who haunted me', pp. 178–9). In that context, she argues, the consolation she sought from Egisthe, as though from a child rather than a lover, was not truly adulterous:

L'adultère n'est souvent qu'une forme désespérée de la fidélité. Si j'ai trompé quelqu'un, c'est sûrement ce pauvre Egisthe. J'avais besoin de lui pour savoir jusqu'à quel point celui que j'aimais était irremplaçable.

pp. 179–80

[Adultery is often nothing more than a desperate form of fidelity. If I betrayed anyone, it must have been poor Egisthe: I needed him to prove the extent to which the one I loved was irreplaceable.]

This inverted confession, therefore, concedes exploitation and even intent to kill, but she has convinced herself of her ultimate loyalty to her husband; Clytemnestre's perverted logic even suggests that her motive was to spare Agamemnon's feelings and to reassure him of her love:

Je voulais tuer Egisthe, faire laver le bois du lit et le pavement de la chambre, supprimer enfin ces dix ans comme un simple zéro dans le total

de mes jours. [...] Si j'en avais eu le cœur, je me serais tuée avant l'heure
de son retour, pour ne pas lire sur son visage sa déception de me retrouver
fanée. Mais je voulais au moins le revoir avant de mourir.

      p. 181–2

[I wanted to kill Egisthe, scrub the bedstead and the bedroom floor, oblit-
erate those ten years as though they counted for nothing in my life's span.
If I'd had the guts, I would then have killed myself before Agamemnon
got back, so that I didn't have to see in his eyes the disappointment in
finding me faded. But I did at least want to see him before I died.]

When her account reaches Agamemnon's homecoming, however, the tone
changes: her description of her husband with his 'sorcière turque' ('Turkish
witch') and of his cruelty at the celebratory feast is in line with an implicit
claim that her reaction in killing him was triggered inexorably by his own mistreatment of her:

Il l'aida à descendre de voiture ; il m'embrassa froidement, il me dit qu'il
compta sur ma générosité pour bien traiter cette jeune fille dont le père et
la mère étaient morts [...]. Il me regardait à peine; au dîner, il ne s'aperçut
pas que j'avais fait préparer tous ses plats favoris [...]. Il clignait de l'œil
du côté d'Egisthe ; il bredouilla au dessert des plaisanteries d'homme ivre
sur les femmes qui se font consoler. La soirée interminablement longue
se traîna sur la terrasse infestée de moustiques [...].

      pp. 184–5

[He helped her down from the carriage, he gave me a cold kiss, told me he
was counting on my generosity to look after this young girl whose parents
were dead. He scarcely glanced at me. At dinner, he did not notice that
I had ordered all his favourite dishes. He winked at Egisthe, muttering at
the end of the meal those jokes that drunk men make about women who
'need' to be comforted. An interminable evening drawn out for ever on a
terrace infested with mosquitoes.]

Thus in the end, she comes to believe that her murder of Agamemnon was an
act of despair, motivated by the need for attention rather than by revenge:

Un instant, j'eus envie de tout disposer pour un accident [...]. Mais je voulais au moins l'obliger en mourant à me regarder en face : je ne le tuais

que pour ça, pour le forcer à se rendre compte que je n'étais pas une chose sans importance.

p. 186

[For a moment I wanted to set it all up as an accident, but I wanted at least to force him to look right at me as he died. That's what I killed him for, to make him acknowledge that I was not something completely unimportant.]

Although the words provocation and excuse do not figure in this monologue, these are precisely the sorts of terms in which the defence of provocation and diminished responsibility are put forward in the modern law-court, in particular when the bullying behaviour of males is contrasted to that of females.

4   Jean Anouilh

Jean Anouilh, typically, treated the whole issue more whimsically.[15] In *Tu étais si gentil quand tu étais petit*,[16] a common-sense modern standpoint is represented by a quartet of stage musicians preparing for a performance of Aeschylus's *Choephori* and chatting about the events that are to be depicted as though they were gossipy items in the tabloid press:

LA VIOLONCELLISTE   Avoir tué son mari et se pavaner couronne sur la tête! Je ne comprends pas qu'on acquitte des créatures pareilles!

LA CONTREBASSISTE   Vous savez, avec un bon avocat, quand on plaide le passionnel ... Elle a pu prouver qu'elle vengeait sa fille. En vérité c'est parce qu'elle avait déjà son Egisthe dans la peau. Mais cela, ça n'a pas pu être établi aux Assises.

p. 17

[Kill your husband and then parade about with a crown on your head! It beats me how such monsters get acquitted!

Well, of course, if you get a good lawyer and call it a crime of passion ... She was able to establish that she was avenging her daughter. The truth

---

15   See *Avant-Scène Théâtre*, 499 (1972).
16   In *Pièces secrètes* (Paris: La Table Ronde, 1977), pp. 7–103.

is that she was already smitten by Aegisthus, but they couldn't prove that in court.]

The actress playing the part of Clytemnestre comes out of role to confirm this explicitly, in terms which evoke the disgust she felt towards the absentee husband who became her victim:

> Quand il est revenu avec cette putain qu'il avait ramenée de Troie, tout gonflé de gloire, ridicule, avec ses décorations, debout sur son char de vainqueur [...] Il m'avait un peu oubliée avec toutes les autres, à la guerre, et son gros œil vicieux s'attendrissait vaguement et me déshabillait déjà. Il a glissé sa main poilue entre mes jambes.
>
> p. 21

> [When he came back from Troy with that whore he'd brought with him, all puffed up in his glory, covered in his absurd medals, standing up in his victor's chariot [...] He'd pretty well forgotten me during the war, with all the other women he had, and his nasty big eyes went a bit misty as he mentally undressed me. He slipped his hairy hand between my legs.]

She admits that her defence with reference to Iphigénie was 'de la comédie' ('a joke'), but is still at pains to convey the more conventional complaints of a provoked wife, infidelity and sexual harassment as triggers for a violent response.

The confrontation between ancient and modern, and between regal and common, enables Anouilh in the same play to make suggestive comparisons between different conceptions of provocation and its relationship to the tragic. In one of the interludes during which the instrumentalists comment on the ancient tale from their down-to-earth perspective, the coarse double bass player suddenly – but in a strikingly matter-of-fact tone – reveals that she is herself a victim of domestic violence:

> Il était garde-chasse, papa, toujours armé, et le jour où il a compris que tout s'écroulait, parce que maman levait la jambe avec un dentiste ambulant, il n'a pas été long à mesurer la profondeur de la solitude humaine ... Et sans considérations superflues ... Tout y a passé! Maman, le dentiste, les trois petits frères et lui pour finir – après son chien. Il n'y a que moi qui y ai échappé parce que j'avais les oreillons et qu'une voisine m'avait emmenée au dispensaire à Guéret, ce jour-là. C'est pour vous dire que les Atrides, moi, leur histoire, ça ne m'épate pas !
>
> p. 42

[He was a game-keeper, my dad, always had a gun, and the day he discovered that everything was falling apart, because mum was having it off
with a travelling dentist, it didn't take him long to plumb the depths of
human solitude ... and without beating about the bush in an unhelpful
way ... he took out the lot: mum, the dentist, my three little brothers, his
dog and himself. I'm the only one who escaped because I had mumps and
a neighbour had taken me to the chemist's in Guéret that day. In short, as
far as I'm concerned, the house of Atreus and all its goings on is nothing
new!]

In a central confrontation between Clytemnestre and Egisthe, the usurping
king is made systematically to debunk any residual sense of nobility or romantic sensitivity underlying their motives:

> C'est dérisoire. Les crimes crapuleux ont au moins quelque décence, la
> décence des bêtes sauvages qui tuent pour se procurer ce qui est néces-
> saire à leur vie ... Mais les crimes passionnels doivent puer aux narines
> des dieux ... Notre amour ... Enfin je lui dirai « notre envie » s'il me laisse
> le temps de lui dire quelque chose.
>
>   p. 54

> [It's pathetic. Muggings and burglaries have at least a sort of a sense of
> decency, the integrity of wild animals who kill for what they need to live
> on ... But crimes of passion must turn the stomachs of the gods with
> their stench ... 'Our love ...' Rather, 'our lust', I'll tell him if he gives me the
> chance to say anything at all.]

As it happens, Oreste does give Egisthe the chance to speak, and it is this boor-
ish oaf who articulates the defence of Clytemnestre:

> Ta mère a peut-être des excuses ... Ta mère n'aimait plus ton père depuis
> longtemps, il s'éternisait à la guerre – il avait fait tuer ta sœur. [...] Tu
> étais très petit quand ton père est parti pour Troie. Tu n'as pas pu le juger.
> Crois-tu qu'il ait rendu ta mère heureuse? [...] Tu sais comment ta sœur
> a été sacrifiée? [...] Une brute qu'elle a subie, dix ans. [...]
>   pp. 74–6

> [Perhaps your mother has some excuses ... Your mother hadn't been
> in love with your father for ages, he was away at war for an eternity, he
> had had your sister killed. [...] You were very little when your father left

for Troy. You weren't in a position to judge. Do you think he made your mother happy? [...] Do you know how your sister was sacrificed? [...] A dirty beast he was, that she had to put up with for ten years.]

In the final confrontation between Clytemnestre and her children, the mother's appeal is brushed aside by Electre as a blatant excuse:

– Je le haïssais. Il avait tué ma fille !
– Ne l'écoute pas, petit frère ! Ce n'est pas pour ça. C'est pour pouvoir continuer à se frotter contre l'autre, comme une chienne, qu'elle l'a tué.

    p. 90

[I hated him. He had killed my daughter!
    Little brother, don't pay any attention, it wasn't for that. She wanted to go on rubbing up against the other one, like the bitch she is, that's why she killed him.]

This accusation provokes Clytemnestre not to a denial but to an extension of the defence she has outlined earlier:

Vous ne savez rien, petites larves ... Vous ne savez pas ce que c'est d'avoir un homme qui vous répugne dans son ventre, tous les soirs. Dix ans, j'ai subi cela !

    p. 91

[You know nothing about it, you little worms ... You don't know what it's like to have inside you, night after night, a man who disgusts you. For ten years I put up with that!]

This bitter-sweet version of the story ends with a grotesque scene in which the confrontation is made explicitly a battle of the sexes, as the female instrumentalists, representing the Erinyes, assault Oreste until he is defended by the male pianist.

5   Jean-Jacques Varoujean, Jean-Pierre Giraudoux

At about the same time as Anouilh wrote his play, a less well-known dramatist, Jean-Jacques Varoujean, was working on the same myth in response to a

commission from Madeleine Renaud. *La Ville en haut de la colline*,[17] designed
as a vehicle for Renaud, became a victim of the 1968 *événements*, the production being abandoned after she and Barrault were sacked from the Odéon. It
was presented as a television play in 1969, but not staged until 1988 when it was
produced in Périgueux.[18] Varoujean's Clytemnestre is an amnesiac who struggles, in rambling speeches by her sick daughter's bedside, to reconstruct both
what happened and why. Any resentment she felt about her husband's treatment of her – over Iphigénie or over Cassandre, neither of whom is named – is
hinted at rather than stated explicitly:

> Un homme occupé, rien ne l'irrite davantage que nos agaceries amou-
> reuses ... Et monsieur le général en chef était inflexible. C'est contre
> son avis que je suis allée au front, incognito, le surprendre. Il y avait là
> une jeune fille turque qui, visiblement, avait cessé d'être une simple
> prisonnière. [...]
>   Qui a trahi d'abord et pourquoi? N'avais-je pas pardonné la mort de
> mon enfant? Elle était fiancée ou mariée [...]. Sommée de renoncer à
> cette union qui faisait tort à la carrière de ton père, elle a préféré se suici-
> der [...]. De cela, oui, j'aurais pu chercher à me venger.
>   II, 1, p. 64–5

> [A busy man, always busy, nothing annoyed him more than our emo-
> tional upheavals ... And his lordship the general in chief didn't budge an
> inch. Against his commands I went incognito to take him by surprise at
> the front. There was a little Turkish girl there who had manifestly stopped
> being just a prisoner. [...]
>   Who betrayed whom first, and why? I'd already forgiven him for the
> death of my child, hadn't I? She was engaged, or married [...] Ordered to
> give up on that marriage because it would damage your father's career,
> she chose to let herself be killed [...]. That, sure enough, would have given
> me an excuse to take revenge.]

Only at the very end of the play does this feeling of resentment become crystal-
lized to an extent that conforms to the traditional depiction of the role:

---

17   Paris: Gallimard (Le Manteau d'Arlequin), 1969.
18   C. Turrettes, 'Une Electre moderne: *La Ville en haut de la colline* de Jean-Jacques Varoujean
      (1969)', *Revue d'Histoire du Théâtre*, 53 (2001), pp. 215–28 (pp. 216, 221–22).

Et pourtant, pendant des années, j'avais senti couver en moi un désir de vengeance, accru des rancunes accumulées par des infidélités continuelles ... J'étais une mère en furie, une épouse outragée, un animal rempli d'une jubilation sauvage lorsque la nouvelle de son retour me parvint ...

II, 11, p. 99

[And yet for years I had felt a thirst for vengeance growing within me, added to the endless grudges from his non-stop infidelity ... I was a mother in a frenzy, a wife in a state of outrage, an animal filled with wild jubilation when I heard he was back ...]

The only direct mention of provocation or other extenuating circumstances for an alleged crime is a playful one, and occurs when Egisthe rather than Clytemnestre is being accused. Confronted by Oreste, he runs through a sequence of scenarios which might have prompted *his* murder of Agamemnon:

Mes frères, jadis, avaient été tués par le père de la victime. Mon honneur exigeait réparation, criait vengeance. [...]
    Chassé par le mari, abandonné par celle que j'adorais et qui soudain faisait la volte-face en pardonnant aux infidélités du revenant ... Non, vous ne voulez pas non plus que je plaide le crime passionnel ?

II, 2, pp. 81–2

[The victim's father, a long time ago, had killed my brothers. I was honour bound to seek reparation, to call for vengeance. [...]
    Sent packing by the husband, abandoned by the woman I adored and who suddenly made a U-turn and forgave the infidelities of the one who came back to her ... So do you really think I shouldn't also claim it was a crime of passion?]

Finally, some fifty years after Jean Giraudoux had re-introduced Electra and her family onto the French stage, his son Jean-Pierre Giraudoux felt drawn to the same project. His *Electre*, performed at Strasbourg in 1985, also adopts the tone of a whodunit: Agatha Christie is cited as an inspiration, alongside the playwright's father and Euripides. Giraudoux invents an extra character, Agamemnon's sister Anaxobie, the mother of Pylade, so that the three standard male characters (Oreste, Egisthe and Pylade) are balanced by three females (Electre, Clytemnestre and Anaxobie), a sextet in turn balanced by a chorus of three men and three women, each of whom systematically supports one of the protagonists, spinning any information that emerges to further his or her cause. In effective *roman policier* style, many options are explored as to who took action, why, and whether a case for extenuation could be made for several private and public motives that might have given rise to the murder of Agamemnon; so although Clytemnestre is finally exonerated, due consideration is given to extenuating circumstances which might apply if she were identified as the culprit. Electre's early description of Clytemnestre is congruent with modern interpretations of battered woman syndrome:

> Tu ne choisis jamais, mère. Tu ne luttes jamais. Tu subis. La mort de Tantale, la mort d'Iphigénie, la mort d'Agamemnon, la mort d'Oreste. Tes noces avec Egisthe. Tes douzaines de noces anonymes et honteuses. Tout s'efface.
>
> I, 7, p. 31

> [You never choose, mother. You never fight. You just accept. The death of Tantalus, the death of Iphigeneia, the death of Agamemnon, the death of Orestes. Your marriage to Aegisthus. Your dozens of other marriages, anonymous and shameful. Everything seems faint.]

When suspicion subsequently falls on Clytemnestre, as instigator or accomplice, her supporter is quick to articulate the *crime passionnel* defence:

> PREMIÈRE FEMME   Cassandre, la Troyenne, n'était qu'un prétexte pour humilier la reine.
>
> DEUXIÈME HOMME   Clytemnestre l'avait trompé avec Egisthe.
>
> PREMIÈRE FEMME   Comme trompent tant de femmes. Pour se venger. Pour venger sa fille, Iphigénie. Cela ne comptait pas.
>
> II, 5, p. 53

> [FIRST WOMAN   Cassandra, the Trojan, was just a pretext to humiliate the queen.
>
> SECOND MAN   Clytemnestra had betrayed him with Aegisthus.
>
> FIRST WOMAN   As so many wives betray their husbands, for vengeance. To avenge her daughter, Iphigeneia. So that didn't count as betrayal.]

In November 2005, the specific issue of provocation in United Kingdom law was suddenly reopened, when the Lord Chief Justice announced his intention to revise the guidelines for judges in cases involving 'husbands who kill their wives in fits of jealous rage'. This time the acknowledged inequity between male and female defendants in such cases was to be addressed not by making it easier for women to be excused murder, but harder for men. Based on such cases over thirteen years – so including Humphreys, Ahluwalia and Thornton – new guidelines implicitly acknowledged that courts had been treating the victims of domestic violence, male and female, unduly leniently if their response was disproportionately violent and uncontrolled.[19] The argument about unequal treatment is repeated:

> Women who are forced to kill after provocation over a long period may not be treated the same as men who kill on impulse. Where the provocation is cumulative and 'battered woman syndrome' is found to exist, the required loss of self-control may not be as sudden, as sufferers display a slow-burn reaction and an outwardly calm appearance. It is in this respect that commentators have highlighted the apparent sexual bias of the provocation defence which favours men who kill in anger rather than women who kill out of fear.

But the law's response to this perceived bias has been to raise the threshold of the excuse of provocation for men, rather than to lower it for women.

During the same period the definition of 'provocation' itself was broadened by the emerging concept of 'coercive control' to encapsulate a wide range of insidious forms of bullying: the withholding of financial and social independence, the imposition of dress codes that were almost calculated to provide a future excuse for jealousy, subtle acts of humiliation or subordination. Such behaviour was established in the UK as a criminal offence in the Serious Crime Act 2015 and came into force on 29 December of the same year. The most significant legal illustration of this new approach to provocation was the case of Sally Challen, found guilty of murder and jailed for life in 2011. She had killed her husband in a hammer attack. In 2019, with the full support of her children, she successfully pleaded that she had suffered years of controlling and humiliating abuse and – as had been the case with Emma Humphreys – her plea of manslaughter on grounds of provocation was upheld, and the period she

---

19   *The Times*, 28 November 2005, pp. 1–2, article by Frances Gibb entitled 'Jealousy is no longer an excuse for murder'. The Lord Chief Justice's proposals are set out in the consultation paper (Law Commission, *A New Homicide Act for England and Wales?: A Consultation Paper* (London: Stationery Office), Law Commission Consultation Paper no. 177, 2006 (available online at www.lawcom.gov.uk/docs/cp177_web.pdf)) which incorporates a very full discussion of the state of the law as regards England and Wales in 2005.

had already spent in prison was deemed sufficient. Not innocent, therefore but guilty of a lesser charge by reason of exonerating circumstances.[20]

Each of these developments in social understanding of domestic abuse and in legal interpretation of reactions to it has the potential to reopen the ethical case against both Agamemnon and Clytemnestra. In a British court in 2006, Clytemnestra might still have been acquitted of murder, but she could expect a prison term of at least twelve years rather than the more nominal sentences imposed on provocation cases in the decade following 1995. But by 2019, if the broader definitions of control and humiliation (anticipated actually by Yourcenar and Giraudoux) were applied to Agamemnon's treatment of her, this new perspective might change both the verdict and the sentence yet again. At any rate, the case has once more demonstrated the ongoing power of tragic drama to interact with developments in moral thought in a fruitful and suggestive manner.

---

20   For one treatment of this case and outcome see *The Guardian*, 7 June 2019, article by Amelia Hill and Matthew Weaver, entitled 'Sally Challen walks free as court rules out retrial for killing abusive husband'. See also *The Independent*, 2 March 2019, article by Harriet Hall entitled 'The Sally Challen case isn't a cause for celebration', which explicitly links her case as a landmark to those of Kiranjit Ahluwalia and Sara Thornton.

CHAPTER 6

Saul, King of Israel, as Tragic Hero in French Drama

Pour être donc humain j'éprouve sa colère !¹

(God's wrath falls upon me for behaving humanely?)

∴

Most of the figures used by early modern and modern dramatists as vehicles for the exploration of tragic guilt and excuses have been characters from ancient Greek myths. The original plays of Aeschylus, Sophocles and Euripides have been reinterpreted for the modern stage, and contemporary dramatists have reworked their stories in the light of modern attitudes to blame and shame. The biblical figure of King Saul is one of the few from a different context to have appeared in French dramas from several periods. Saul, like Medea, Macbeth and Oedipus, behaves in ways which cause him to feel shame, but excuses can be made on his behalf. It is not surprising that scholars in Renaissance Europe, anxious to build on all that was best in the traditions of both Christian and Classical teaching, found in this story material of respectable lineage that lent itself to syncretic adaptation. It is more interesting that the same figure has recurred in plays from the Classical, Enlightenment, Romantic and modern periods, all of which probe the extent to which Saul was in control of his actions, and to which he can be held responsible and deserving of punishment. These plays provide an interesting counterpoint to the development of the theory of hamartia which was traced in chapter 2.

Saul's story is told in the First Book of Samuel.² Plucked from obscurity, he was anointed king by the prophet Samuel and led Israel through a tumultuous period of the 11th century BC. Although a successful military leader, Saul is portrayed as lacking in judgment and – at least in the eyes of Samuel – as persistently disobedient. Four actions in particular display his perceived failings. When commanded by Samuel to wait seven days before offering an

---

1 Jean de La Taille, *Dramatic Works*, ed. Kathleen Hall and Christopher Smith (London: Athlone, 1972), p. 33. *Saül le furieux*, Act II, line 313.
2 Particularly *1 Samuel*, 9:2; 10:1–9; 13:1–15; 15:2–25; 16:14; 22:11–23; 28; 31.

© KONINKLIJKE BRILL NV, LEIDEN, 2021 | DOI:10.1163/9789004442788_008

eve-of-battle sacrifice at Gilgal (*1 Samuel*, 10:8), he lost patience, taking on himself the priestly role and making the sacrifice on the seventh evening, moments before Samuel arrived to authorize him (13:8–14). When commanded to destroy every living thing in Amalek (15:2–3),[3] he spared the king, Agag, and the choicest cattle (15:7–23). In the course of his jealous disputes with his eventual successor David, he arranged for the massacre of a priestly community at Nob (22:11–23). Finally, he indulged in necromancy in an attempt to discern God's will (28:6–20). As a result of these moral shortcomings, he fell out of favour with God, witnessed the death of his own son Jonathan in battle, and died by suicide, defeated and disgraced (31).

The story, like many others in tragic drama, can be spun in various ways, depending precisely on the extent to which an observer sympathizes with the excuses put forward by Saul for his misdemeanours.

God's prophet instructed Saul regarding the timing of a sacrifice …	Saul received inscrutable and apparently vindictive instructions. He offered a sacrifice to allay his disenchanted troops' fear.
… and his behaviour in the event of victory at Amalek.	
Saul failed to obey these commands.	On achieving victory at Amalek, he magnanimously spared the life of the king out of respect for public opinion, and retained the best of the cattle and sheep, intending to make a sacrificial offering of them.
As a result he lived in fear and anxiety, to which he responded with violence.	Afflicted with depression as a punishment, Saul developed a paranoid persecution complex.
Despite the clear prohibition against necromancy, he used witchcraft to obtain advice from the spirit of the dead prophet Samuel.	In desperation bordering on insanity he sought to find out God's will by consulting the spirit of his recently dead prophet.

By either interpretation, a man of basic virtue is given humanly inexplicable tasks by a seemingly spiteful divine force. In response, he trusts human

---

3   The command to spare no life is explained with reference to an ancient feud recounted in *Exodus*, 17:8–16.

morality and public opinion above the letter of divine instructions. One, explicitly feminist and Christian, modern response to Saul and his fate is uncom-
promising in condemnation: 'Saul made himself miserable by turning his back
on God. [...] Saul had severed his relationship with God by intentionally disobeying the Lord's commands.'[4] This is an example of hamartia in both of its
generally accepted senses: a moral flaw, because it sets human reason above
divine dispensation, and a miscalculation, because Saul cannot fully take account of the basis for God's ordinance, namely a fitting punishment for an ancient wrong, and a safeguard for the future wellbeing of the chosen people. The
initial situation is thus almost tailor-made to illustrate that moral ambiguity
which is characteristic of tragedy on the Aristotelian model: Saul is guilty but
with extenuating circumstances.

It has long been recognized by biblical and literary scholars that parallels
can be drawn between Saul and a Classical tragic hero. The account of Saul's
life by the Jewish historian Josephus highlighted parallels between his career
and those of Achilles and Agamemnon.[5] Gerhard von Rad referred to an 'affinity' between the Bible's 'poetic production' of the story of Saul and 'the spirit of
Greek tragedy',[6] while Northrop Frye considered Saul 'the one great tragic hero
of the Bible'.[7] Like Oedipus, Saul thinks he can outwit the divine will, so he is
guilty of pride, but wins sympathy because he is kept in the dark about the implications of decisions he cannot avoid. Like Agamemnon, he is charged with
safeguarding the future of his people, but given inadequate guidance about
the extent of his actions. Agamemnon is punished for carrying out Zeus's command *too* zealously, destroying Troy root and branch, annihilating its gods and
all centres of their worship. Saul is punished for showing mercy to God's enemies, but later condemned for indiscriminate destruction at Nob. Both can
plead that in the context of a just war, such borderlines are almost impossible
to define, especially in the heat of battle.

Like both Oedipus and Agamemnon, Saul can be depicted as either ashamed
or defiant: if he complains too vehemently that his punishment is unfair or disproportionate, or that he has been put into an impossible position for which
he is unjustly being given total responsibility, observers (paradoxically) may
sympathize with him less – *qui s'excuse, s'accuse*. If he meekly accepts his fate,

---

4   Liz Curtis Higgs, *Really Bad Girls of the Bible* (Colorado Springs: Waterbrook Press, 2000),
    pp. 21–22.
5   Louis Feldman, 'Josephus' View of Saul' in Carl Ehrlich and Marsha White (eds.), *Saul in Story
    and Tradition* (Tübingen: Mohr Siebeck, 2006), pp. 214–44 (pp. 227 and 233).
6   *Old Testament Theology*, translated D. Stalker, 2 vols (Edinburgh: Oliver and Boyd, 1962–65),
    I, p. 325.
7   *The Great Code: The Bible and Literature* (New York: Harcourt Brace Jovanovich, 1982), p. 181.

the neutral observer may be more inclined to make excuses on his behalf, but he is liable to turn into a figure of pathos rather than a dignified hero. Saul has also been compared to Macbeth:[8] successful military leaders brought down through events which can be interpreted either as flaw (disobedience, ambition) or miscalculation based on misleading information (the weird sisters, Samuel's inscrutable commands) or on ignorance of the full picture. Both could be said to hover uneasily between genuine ignorance and culpable negligence, and it is open to debate how far their responsibility for their actions is diminished.

The form of punishment meted out to Saul is also appropriate to the worldview of both Ancient Greeks and Ancient Jews: a form of madness is inflicted on him, under the influence of which he commits further sins, for which in turn he is bound to be punished. Scholars have explored the nature of Saul's affliction in relation both to modern medical and legal concepts and to the context of his own society.[9] For our present purposes what matters is not so much what the real Saul's contemporaries thought of him, nor how modern doctors would diagnose him, nor even how modern lawyers would judge and exonerate him, but how far differing attitudes towards guilt, freedom, madness and necessity alter the ways in which the king's story is adapted in the plays we shall study, to generate tragic intensity for their intended audiences. Is Saul to be pitied as helpless in his madness, or blamed for falling short of his status as anointed king? Zeus sent Ate to take away Agamemnon's wits, so he could not resist the pressure to assent to the sacrifice of Iphigenia at Aulis, nor the temptation to steal Briseis from Achilles. God's apparent withdrawal of support from Saul appears as inscrutable as any whimsical decree of the Greek pantheon. In the biblical account, the madness inflicted on Saul is explicitly described as 'sent from God' (*1 Samuel*, 16:14) and is tantalizingly difficult to distinguish from prophetic ecstasy (Gunn, pp. 62–63). In drama, its source is various and sometimes ambiguous,[10] but it almost always turns him into a pathetic figure, sometimes verging on the comic, and presents a Greek image of tragic helplessness. The irony inherent in the appointment of David the harpist – Saul's future rival for the kingship – as the person most likely to alleviate Saul's affliction, is itself worthy of the most callous Greek divinity.

---

8   D. Gunn, *The Fate of King Saul* (Sheffield: JSOT, 1980), p. 31. Cf Frye, p. 182.

9   'The Madness of Saul, a Warrior-King', in Philip Esler, *Sex, Wives and Warriors: Reading Biblical Narrative with its Ancient Audience* (Eugene, OR: Wipf and Stock, 2011), pp. 159–79.

10   Sarah Nicholson, 'Catching the Poetic Eye: Saul Reconceived in Modern Literature' in Ehrlich and White, pp. 308–33 (pp. 326–27).

Dramatizations of the Saul story in tragic form must therefore negotiate a number of tightropes. Most have explored the nature of the king's frenzy or madness, but have taken care to ensure that he is not straightforwardly mad – his responsibility for the outcome of his acts may be diminished, but in Aristotelian terms must not be totally removed. Few have dwelt on the rather technical and scarcely dramatic issue of the sacrifice at Gilgal – if this is alluded to, it is generally used by playwrights seeking to win additional sympathy for Saul, by portraying Samuel as a pernickety stickler for the letter rather than the spirit of the law. Those who have sought to portray Saul as a victim stress his sparing of Agag, those who have sought to portray him as a flawed hero draw more attention to his murder of the priests at Nob. All have sought in various ways to strike the balance defined by Terry Eagleton[11] between dignity, justice and palatability.

1   Jean de la Taille

Jean de la Taille (c1533–c1607) was a Renaissance humanist scholar whose family had Calvinist sympathies and who studied law at Paris and Orléans, but devoted more energy to writing as a disciple of Ronsard, Du Bellay and Marc-Antoine Muret. His *Saül le furieux* (*The Madness of Saul*) was probably written by 1562. When it was published in 1572, it was accompanied by a prefatory treatise subtitled *De l'Art de la tragédie*, an important early adaptation in French of Aristotle's *Poetics*.[12] His paraphrase of the doctrine of hamartia does not shed any remarkable light on the concept (p. 20):

> Que le sujet aussi ne soit de Seigneurs extrêmement méchants, et que pour leurs crimes horribles ils méritassent punition; ni aussi par même raison de ceux qui sont du tout bons, gens de bien et de sainte vie.

> [Tragedy should not deal with extremely vicious lords, who deserve to be punished for their terrible crimes; nor yet, similarly, with altogether good men of virtuous and saintly life.]

---

11   See above, 'Hamartia', p. 50.
12   Jean de La Taille, edn. cit., pp. 19–65. References to this play will be to this edition, except that spelling has been modernized.

In practice, La Taille's treatment of Saul shows insight, remarkably percep-
tive for this early period, into the need to strike a fine balance in his portrayal
of the character between culpability and exoneration. In a further prefatory
Argument, La Taille summarized the plot in terms which stressed the moral
ambiguities he wished to explore (p. 24):

> Le prophète Samuel avait un jour commandé à Saül qu'il eût à mettre
> à sac, et à mort, non seulement les personnes, mais tout ce qui respire-
> rait dans une ville nommée Amalec [...]. Ce que n'ayant du tout exécuté
> Saül, mais ayant par mégarde, ou par quelque raison humaine, réservé
> le plus beau bétail (comme en intention d'en faire sacrifice à Dieu) et
> ayant par quelque respect sauvé vif d'un tel massacre Agag le Roi de ces
> Amaléchites : il ne cessa depuis d'être en la male-grâce de Dieu.

> [The prophet Samuel had commanded Saul to put to death not just the
> human inhabitants, but everything that had breath in a town named
> Amalec, and to destroy it. Saul did not do this, but – by negligence or for
> some human motive – retained the best of the cattle (as though he in-
> tended to sacrifice them to God) and out of respect spared the life of the
> king of the Amalechites, Agag, following the massacre. Since then God's
> grace was constantly withheld from him.]

None of this is invented, but it is loaded to draw attention to the mitigating
circumstances Saül could allege. La Taille ignored his disobedience over the
timing of the sacrifice, and the massacre at Nob, concentrating on an act of
humanity, his sparing of Agag. The extreme and inscrutable nature of the instruction is clear from the first sentence. Saül's disobedience is perhaps negligent but not culpably wilful, being caused either by inadvertence, or from
humane motives – mercy towards Agag and a desire to glorify God with a sacrificial offering of the spoils of a just war. These are not clear-cut defences: negligence over details in such a major enterprise is blameworthy, the priority given
to human reasoning over divine command smacks of hubris, and the claim
that the prize cattle were to be reserved for sacrifice sounds self-justificatory.
Nevertheless the thrust of this summary is to allow for extenuation, to make it
clear that the protagonist is not a straightforward villain.

This attitude is then borne out by La Taille's dramatic portrayal of the character himself. In the first act and a half he is portrayed in his frenzied state,
unable to recognize his sons, and furiously preparing for battle. It is clearly
significant that when there is explicit moral discussion of right and wrong,
of shame and guilt, it occurs during an episode in Act II in which Saül has

mentally 'returned to himself'.[13] This enables him to weigh up the pros and cons of past and future actions, and means he cannot subsequently fall back unequivocally on a plea of diminished responsibility: his decision to consult the necromancer from Endor is taken in full knowledge of the nature of that action and the divine proscription of it. During this lucid scene, Saül articulates most of the excuses for his behaviour listed above. He bemoans the fact that his mercy towards Agag and his cattle has been misunderstood and undervalued: 'Pour être donc humain j'éprouve sa colère!' (II, 313: 'God's wrath falls upon me for behaving humanely?'), and insists that he cannot be blamed for misguided decisions because God's instructions are unclear:

> Si j'étais aimé
> De lui comme devant, il m'eût or informé
> De ce que je ferais.
>   II, 423–5

[If God still loved me as he used to, he would have told me what to do.]

Saül's tone here is more one of perplexed sadness than of self-righteousness, although his *écuyer* does remind him that questioning God's judgment perpetuates a state of sin:

> On le provoque
> Au juste accroissement de sa punition,
> Quand on se justifie avec présomption.
>   II, 418–20

[God is provoked to a just increase in his punishment if we presumptuously seek to justify ourselves.]

But as he continues to hover between lucidity and frenzy, Saül suggests that he is in no position to make calculations or balanced moral decisions:

> J'ai l'esprit si confus d'horreur, de soin, d'effroi
> Que je ne puis résoudre aucun avis en moi.
>   II, 447–48

---

13   The stage direction 'revenant à soi' ('returning to his senses'), whose significance is quite easy to miss, occurs in Act II, between lines 262 and 263, p. 32.

[My spirit is so distressed by horror, anxiety and fear that I cannot form any coherent opinion in my mind.]

La Taille saw that if Saül was to remain a tragic hero at the end of his life, he should *not* be punished for crimes committed while he was mad – that would amount to innocent suffering – so his decision to visit the necromancer is made during this brief if rather insecure moment of lucidity.

Saül's confrontation with the Phytonisse[14] provided La Taille with a superbly melodramatic climax at the heart of his tragedy, where again the drama is allied to examination of the moral implications of the king's decisions and actions. The woman summons up a host of demons, devils and fallen angels to force the spirit of Samuel – against his own and God's will – to return to earth so that Saül may seek his advice. The names used (Satan, Beelzebub, Lucifer) have biblical authority, and are identified either as personified forces of evil and temptation hostile to the Jewish God, or as heathen gods worshipped by races hostile to Israel.[15] Whatever they represent in cosmological terms, the woman is clear that they have responsibility both for original sin and for the ongoing wickedness of humankind:

Et vous Diables lesquels fîtes au premier homme
Goûter à ses dépens de la fatale Pomme,
[…]
Qui faites aux humains commettre tant d'abus.
        III, 637–40

[And you, o devils who caused the first man to taste the fateful apple, to his loss […] and who still make men commit so many sins.]

Saül hears this speech and is so troubled by it that he considers abandoning his attempt to consult Samuel: 'Hélas! quelle horreur j'ai! […] Las! ôtez-moi d'ici' (III, 683–9: 'Alas! what horror grips me, take me away from this place'). With tragic irony, the necromancer returns at that precise moment of hesitation and

---

14   The woman from Endor 'that hath a familiar spirit' (*1 Samuel*, 28:7) is referred to thus in La Taille's text. In modern French the word has become 'Pythonisse' and derives not from any Judaeo-Christian source but from the Classical Greek world; Pytho was the original name of Delphi, where Apollo's oracle was situated. The precise nature of her role will be considered further in our final chapter on scapegoat characters, pp. 209–10.

15   Relevant biblical references are to *Job* 1, *Job* 41, *Deuteronomy* 13:13, *2 Kings* 1:2, *Numbers* 25:3, *Isaiah* 14:12. See the cited edition, p. 197, n. 39 for further details.

Saül takes the fateful step despite the *écuyer*'s further reminder that the action is sinful:

> Sire, que songez-vous ? Voulez-vous donc parfaire
> Ce que vous savez bien être à Dieu tout contraire ?
>   III, 691–2

> [My Lord, what are you thinking of? Will you undertake what you well know God has entirely forbidden?]

Any temptation to present this scene in a melodramatic manner, reflecting a black-and-white moral position such as is expressed by the Chorus of Levites and by Samuel himself, should be tempered by the dramatist's care to raise delicate moral questions about the extent of the king's responsibility at each stage. Saül is trapped in a vicious circle of sin, as Samuel reminds him:

> À la divine voix
> Obéi tu n'as point ainsi que tu devais.
>   III, 773–4

> [You have not obeyed God's voice as you should have.]

This play has provided the character with sufficient lines of extenuation for the actor to invite sympathy for his plight rather than outright condemnation. Driven by fear, perplexity and despair, he hovers between lucidity and madness, neither helpless victim nor wholly responsible for his decisions. An audience will note his condemnation by some characters but is not obliged to share their perspective unthinkingly. In this way, La Taille has successfully applied principles suggested by Aristotle to the biblical story in order to depict his character as a genuinely tragic figure whose downfall and death in the following two acts arouses cathartic pity as well as fear. To pick up again Eagleton's terms, his fate is not too undignified, his character is not too unpalatable, and his treatment by destiny is terrifying but not manifestly unfair.

2   Pierre du Ryer

Although Pierre du Ryer (1605–1658) has been largely forgotten, he was a successful and quite prolific playwright, whose works were performed by Molière's company and who was elected to the *Académie française* in preference to

Corneille in 1646. His tragedy *Saül*[16] was written around 1640, during the period that followed the *querelle du Cid*, and in that context he can be seen as a precursor of Racine in his rejection of the baroque complexity represented by the plays of Alexandre Hardy, and his pursuit of a much simpler and more classical form. Dramatic theory in that period was dominated by formal considerations and debates about the unities, but critics were also alert to the moral significance of theatrical performance, and the major treatise on tragedy from the decade, La Mesnardière's *Poétique* of 1639[17] contains a long chapter (pp. 107–235) on *Les Mœurs*. Although derived in essence from Aristotle, this chapter presents a predominantly moralistic view of tragedy, and La Mesnardière has great difficulty in accepting any interpretation of hamartia that risks being perceived as unjust (pp. 107–108):

> Le poème tragique, étant toujours obligé de récompenser les vertus et de châtier les vices, ne doit jamais introduire des personnes très vertueuses et absolument innocentes qui tombent en de grands malheurs, ni des hommes fort vicieux qui soient heureux parfaitement.

> [The tragic poem is always obliged to reward virtue and punish vice, so it should never deal with altogether virtuous and innocent individuals who fall into misfortune, nor highly vicious men who achieve total happiness.]

The tension between La Mesnardière's desire to prove his fidelity to Aristotelian principles and his sense that the best – and most socially useful – tragedy should be characterized by the fairness of its dénouement recurs elsewhere in the treatise (p. 141):

> Ce fruit [l'utilité merveilleuse de la tragédie] est attaché à deux rameaux opposés, à la punition des méchants, et plus encore aux bonnes mœurs des héros qui ne sont coupables que par quelque fragilité qui mérite d'être excusée.

> [The reason that tragedy is so marvellously beneficial to society springs from two opposing sources of moral nourishment: from the punishment of evil-doers, but even more from the virtuous behaviour of its heroes

---

16   Du Ryer, *Saül*, ed. Maria Miller (Toulouse: Société de littératures classiques, 1996). References to this play will be to this edition.

17   Hippolyte-Jules Pilet de La Mesnardière, *Poétique* (Paris: Sommaville, 1639).

whose guilt stems from a single weakness for which they deserve to be excused.]

This utilitarian attitude is reflected in du Ryer's *Préface*: the play (p. 3) is dedicated

> aux Profanes et aux Religieux, parce que les uns et les autres peuvent trouver dans son sujet une instruction sans aigreur et un divertissement sans scandale.

> [... to both secular and religious people, because both categories can find in the subject of this play instruction without harshness and entertainment without scandal.]

His is the play in which Saül comes closest to deserving his fate, undermining his reputation as a good and wise ruler when he disobeys God's commands as mediated by Samuel, becoming guilty at once of overweening pride and of negligent blindness.[18]

For the first half of the play, Saül is presented as perplexed, driven to despair by the silence of God's prophets:

> Je ne trouve en moi que de tristes auspices.
> Le signe du malheur où je suis destiné
> C'est moi, c'est mon esprit, c'est Saül étonné.
>
> I, 1, 66–68

> [I find within me nothing but inauspicious omens. The witness of the misfortune that awaits me is myself, my spirit, the perplexity of Saul.]

His anxiety increases when news arrives that David has apparently betrayed the Jewish camp: Saül 'se promène en rêvant' (I, 2, 136–7: 'walks around as though in a dream') and reacts with fearful indecision, reminiscent of his attitude towards Jonathas at the start of *Saül le furieux*:

---

18   Similarly in du Ryer's *Alcionée* (1639), the title character inspires admiration for his military valour but brings about his own downfall by injudiciously putting personal motivation before state interest.

> Va donc, va, Jonathas,
>
> [...]
>
> Va donc, non, non, demeure: Hélas que veux-je faire ?
> Es-tu mon ennemi ? suis-je ton adversaire ?
>
> I, 2, 139–42

[Away with you, Jonathan, away! No, no, stay! Alas what am I to do? Are you my enemy? Am I your adversary?]

Saül's summoning of the necromancer is presented as a crime, and not one committed when he is out of control: he has himself ordered the execution of 'Tous ceux de qui l'esprit et la noire science / Avecques les enfers ont de l'intelligence' (II, 1, 369–70: 'All those whose mind and devilish learning are in league with the underworld'), and on the point of meeting the necromancer, he is carefully reminded by Jonathas that he should not proceed – 'Mais c'est un sacrilège' (III, 2, 793: 'this is blasphemous') – so he cannot subsequently allege ignorance or forgetfulness. It is during his dramatic confrontation with the necromancer and *l'Ombre de Samuel* (the shade of Samuel) that the guilt on which his distress is based is spelled out for the first time, and it is a basis that reflects La Mesnardière's instinctive preference for justice:

> Le Ciel te commanda, tu te montras rebelle,
> Tu lui donnas ta foi, tu lui fus infidèle,
> Et ta rébellion, et ton manque de foi
> Ont allumé les feux qui vont choir dessus toi.
>
> III, 8, 997–1000

[Heaven gave you its command, and you revealed yourself to be a rebel. You gave your word and were then faithless. This rebellion of yours, this faithlessness of yours have lit the flames that will pour down upon you.]

Although 'ton manque de foi' may allude to Saül's sparing of Agag, the focus is on the more tangible crime, his murder of the priests of Nob for having sheltered David:

> Pense à ce peuple saint par tes lois égorgé
> Pour avoir contre toi l'innocent protégé.
>
> III, 8, 991–992

[Think of the holy men massacred by your command because they sheltered the innocent against you.]

On that basis, in a speech which combines prophecy with curse, Samuel con-
demns Saül to the fate that awaits him: the death of his children, the defeat of
his army and his own death in despair.

From a modern perspective, the ending of the play is something of an
anti-climax: Saül has been depicted as deserving a fate which is inflicted upon
him under the eye of a divine force whose motivation appears to be justice
rather than forgiveness, reconciliation or mercy. There is little ethical debate at
the end beyond a conventional reminder of the fallibility of human endeavour:
'de votre ruine / Mes forfaits seulement ont été l'origine' (v, 4, 1637–38: 'My sins
have been the sole cause of your downfall'). Unlike La Taille's Saül, who was
defiantly ready to express his outrage at the disproportion between his sin and
God's punishment, du Ryer's Saül has little defence beyond a rather pathetic
sense of helplessness:

Je reconnais mon mal, et ce qui m'en délivre,
Bref, je sais mon devoir, mais je ne puis le suivre.
    III, 2, 837-8

[I know the source of my evil-doing, and how to escape from it – in short,
I know my duty, but lack the strength to follow it.]

In a context where the predominantly elegiac tone of Renaissance tragedy had
been largely displaced by the Cornelian aesthetic of *admiration*, it is hard to
conceive how such lines could be delivered without an inappropriate hint of
comedy, even though Saül has been implicitly supported in this attitude by
his son:

Mais que pensons-nous faire, impuissants que nous sommes ?
Le Démon qui le pousse est plus fort que les hommes.
    III, 1, 709-10

[But what are we to do in our powerlessness? The demon that pushes him
on is stronger than mortals.]

Such 'worm theology' points to a fatalistic determinism that foreshadows that
of Racine's Oreste – 'Non, non, suivons la voie où mon malheur nous guide'

(III, 6, 922: 'No, no, we must follow the way that my misfortune directs us') –
and is linked to blatant political expediency:

> Ce dessein est un crime,
> Mais la nécessité le rendra légitime,
> C'est le dernier espoir d'un Prince malheureux.
>   II, 1, 357–9

[This plan is criminal but it will be legitimized by necessity, the last hope
of an ill-fated prince.]

Precisely because Du Ryer has sought to minimize the extent to which his universe was unfair, his hero is almost bound to come across as both less palatable
and more undignified than his equivalents elsewhere, and thus to pose a modern spectator with less penetrating insights into the nature of human guilt.

3   Augustin Nadal

L'abbé Augustin Nadal (1659–1741) was a diplomat, administrator and man of
letters whose notoriety was largely based on disputes with Voltaire, but who
achieved a certain reputation as a dramatist. Of his handful of tragedies on
biblical subjects, *Saül* was the most successful, being performed in 1705 and
1731.[19] By the time he wrote it, the notion of hamartia had significantly moved
away from La Mesnardière's conception of dramatic justice to the balance
which Racine encapsulated in his characterization of Phèdre as neither 'tout
à fait coupable' ('altogether guilty') nor 'tout à fait innocente' ('altogether innocent').[20] Racine did not leave an explicit treatise on tragic theory, but his
defensive *Préfaces* to individual plays demonstrate, as we have seen, his loyalty
to Aristotle's line of argument in several different formulae.[21] His tragic protagonists 'tombent dans le malheur par quelque faute qui les fasse plaindre sans
les faire détester' ('fall into misfortune through some fault that allows us to pity
them without disliking them'),[22] or 'méritent en quelque façon d'être punis,
sans être pourtant tout à fait indignes de compassion' ('deserve to some extent

---

19   L'abbé Augustin Nadal, *Saül* (Paris: Ribou, 1731). References to this play will be to this
      edition.
20   Racine, *Phèdre, Préface*, in his *Théâtre*, ed. Jean Morel and Alain Viala (Paris: Garnier,
      1980), p. 577.
21   See above, 'Hamartia', pp. 49–50, 64–5, 68.
22   Racine, *Andromaque, Première Préface*, edn. cit., p. 131.

to be punished, but without being altogether unworthy of pity').[23] Nadal's Saül could be seen as inviting comparison with these: in a play which dwells on the horrific aspects of the story, he is consistently compared unfavourably with David, but his decisions are well-meaning and his all-too-human helplessness is underlined.

This note is struck immediately in a *Préface* which interprets Saül in terms explicitly reminiscent of Aristotle and Racine (p. x):

> Saül ne nous paraît d'abord ni juste ni méchant dans un souverain degré, et à ne regarder que d'une première vue ce qui a donné lieu à sa réprobation, il serait difficile de le condamner jusqu'à lui refuser sa pitié. Il entre même dans sa désobéissance je ne sais quelle religion et quelle vertu ; et s'il tombe ensuite dans une infinité de crimes, c'est comme involontairement, et comme emporté par l'effet d'une justice terrible.

> [Saül at first appears to us as neither overwhelmingly good nor evil: if we consider those things in him that initially give rise to blame, it would be hard to condemn him to such an extent as to exclude an element of pity. Even his disobedience has a certain religious quality and a certain virtue; and if he subsequently falls into a deeper level of criminality he does so involuntarily, as though he is carried away by the impact of a terrible sense of justice.]

To maintain sympathy for Saül, Nadal emphasized those of his sins for which he can most readily be excused: his failure to wait for Samuel before undertaking the sacrifice at Gilgal, and the sparing of Agag and the cattle from Amalec. Nadal admitted that he had taken liberties with the story to show *David* in as good a light as possible – 'cette licence [...] m'a servi [...] à mettre dans un plus grand jour les mœurs et les sentiments de David' ('I have taken these liberties with a view to bringing out the morality and feelings of David', p. xiii). He nevertheless equally went out of his way to present Saül as less than villainous: when the king anticipated the sacrifice at Gilgal he was 'pressé par les Philistins, et même abandonné par les siens' ('under pressure from the Philistines, and even abandoned by his allies', p. x); and many of his subsequent actions, including the violence towards the priests of Nob (reduced to a passing mention), were defensible on the grounds of diminished responsibility (p. xi):

---

23   Racine, *Iphigénie*, *Préface*, edn. cit., p. 510.

[…] de là ce trouble dans son esprit, qui succéda à l'esprit de Dieu; de là le
meurtre de plus de quatre-vingts prêtres revêtus de leurs habits sacrés, la
désolation de toute la ville sacerdotale de Nobé, cette haine si injuste et si
cruelle dont Saül fut animé contre David.

[This is the source of his spiritual anguish, taking over from God's Holy
Spirit within him; this is the source of his murder of over eighty priests in
holy garb, of the ruin of the priestly house of Nob, of the cruel injustice of
the hatred against David that was inspired in Saül.]

This essentially defensive presentation of Saül in the *Préface* is reflected in the
characterization of the king on stage. A production can be envisaged in which
he is neither villainous nor pathetic: we are reminded of his past wisdom and
glory, contrasting starkly with his current lamentable condition, for which he
cannot be blamed:

> Dans les divers transports dont il est combattu,
> De ses malheurs, du moins, sépare sa vertu.
> J'en rougis comme toi.
> > I, 1

[In the midst of the rage which is besetting him, do at least distinguish his
misfortunes from his virtue. I am as ashamed as you of his current state.]

His troubles are explicitly linked to Agag and Amalec, and are presented in a
positive light:

> Mais depuis qu'épargnant une odieuse race,
> L'ennemi du Seigneur devant lui trouva grâce,
> Reste impur d'Amalec à nos coups échappé,
> D'une secrète horreur il est toujours frappé.
> > I, 1

[But ever since he showed pity on a hateful race, sparing God's enemy
and allowing the sullied remains of Amalec to escape our blows, he has
been struck by a mysterious sense of horror.]

Jonathas and Michol emphasize Saül's immediate danger, and his perplexity over the behaviour and attitudes of David, the army and the people of

Jerusalem, so that Saül, entering in I, 3, cuts a despairing but dignified figure, accepting his own responsibility but confident in an essentially just divinity:

> Pourquoi ne puis-je, hélas ! fuyant plus loin encore,
> Dérober à vos yeux l'ennui qui me dévore,
> Et du Ciel sur moi seul épuiser le courroux
> Qu'un noir pressentiment me fait craindre pour vous ?
>   I, 3

[Why, alas, can I not flee yet further off, to hide from your eyes the anguish which assails me, taking God's anger upon myself alone? I have a dark premonition that you are in danger.]

Michol, rather than Saül himself, depicts the sparing of Agag positively:

> Quel crime avez-vous fait ? [...]
> A vos genoux, Seigneur, un roi trouve un asile :
> Est-ce là le forfait qui vous trouble aujourd'hui ?
>   I, 3

[What crime have you committed? A king, my lord, found sanctuary by your side: is that the misdeed which fills you with such dread?]

whereas Saül refuses to blame God for injustice: 'Des jugements d'un Dieu qui peut percer l'abîme?' ('Who can plumb the mysterious depths of God's judgment?' I, 3). In this atmosphere of anxiety it would not be hard to portray Saül as justified in his distrust of David, in his attempts to divert danger from his children and in his desperation to discern God's will: 'De mon aveuglement telle est la violence' ('My blindness causes this violence' II, 7). Only when Asser reminds him that legitimate prophetic channels are apparently blocked to him – 'Quoi donc, ignorez-vous qu'aux cris de nos prophètes / Le Ciel est toujours sourd?' ('Come, my lord, you must be aware that Heaven remains deaf to the cries of our prophets', II, 7) – does Saül determine to consult 'l'artifice de l'Enfer' ('the devices of Hell'):

> Cherche un de ces mortels qui percent l'avenir :
> Je veux de Samuel interroger la cendre.
>   II, 7

[Seek out for me one of those mortals who can divine the future. I want to consult the ashes of Samuel.]

For Nadal's 1705 audience, the terms in which he brushes aside Asser's legal scruples to justify his action would have had powerful significance in relation to the rights of kings:

> Un Prince, de ses lois reconnaît-il l'empire ?
> Ce pouvoir souverain d'où partent tant de droits,
> En vous les imposant en affranchit les Rois.
>
> II, 7

[Does a prince acknowledge the sway of his own laws? The very sovereign power that bestows so many rights, even as it imposes them on you, makes him exempt from them.]

In dramatic terms, the logic of Saul's position does not inspire hostility or invite condemnation: Nadal has contrived a position in which Saül, as a true tragic hero, is coerced into actions which he acknowledges to be questionable but for which he can be excused.

This balanced position is maintained in Acts III and IV, when Saül faces the necromancer and recounts his confrontation with the spirit of Samuel. In Nadal's presentation, Saül is never defiant or self-justificatory; on the contrary, he is aware of the horror of his position, fearful of the outcome and ready to face the consequences. His professed helplessness can be depicted as genuinely perplexed rather than stupidly pathetic:

> De mon cœur tout à coup quel mouvement s'empare ?
> Mais quel ordre invincible, et quel arrêt funeste
> M'attache à des desseins que mon âme déteste ?
> Un pouvoir dont le mien ne peut me dégager
> M'entraîne dans l'abîme où je cours me plonger.
>
> III, 6

[What emotion suddenly takes a grip on my heart? By what unchallengeable command, by what fateful order, am I driven to ends which my soul finds detestable? Some power from which my strength cannot escape, is leading me to the abyss that I am plunging headlong into.]

There is a sense of dramatic irony in Nadal's staging of the sequence (as there had been in La Taille's), since Saül does seem to be on the very point of abandoning his sacrilegious plan when the necromancer enters, and from that point there is no going back:

> Non, non, retirons-nous de ces funestes lieux,
> Où bientôt tout l'Enfer va paraître à mes yeux.
> Fuyons la Pythonisse, éloignons-la de moi.
> Qu'entends-je ? on entre : O ciel ! elle vient. Je la vois.
>
>   III, 6

[No, no, let us escape from this dreadful place, where I am soon to be faced with all the visions of Hell. We must flee the Pythonisse, keep her away from me. But what is this I hear? Someone's coming ... it's her, o God, I can see her arriving.]

In the climactic confrontation between Samuel and Saül, the prophet adopts a condemnatory mode, which Saül accepts, but this does not mean that an objective audience would share their perspective. It is often the very point of tragedy that the protagonist blames himself more than the audience does, and Nadal has so arranged the sequence that his actor has every opportunity to win the sympathy of the spectator for his plight even as he quotes the words that hold him responsible for it:

> Ce n'est point un fantôme, ou des chimères vaines ;
> C'était lui. Tout mon sang s'est glacé dans mes veines.
> *Pourquoi m'appelles-tu ?* [...]
> *Dans la nuit du tombeau quelle fureur me trouble ?*
> A-t-il dit. A ces mots ma frayeur se redouble.
> *Le Sceptre va bientôt sortir de Benjamin,*
> *Et de ton ennemi le règne enfin s'approche.*
> *Par toi de tous les Juifs la race est criminelle.*
> Il dit, et soudain rentre en la nuit éternelle.
>
>   IV, 2

[It was no phantom, no empty simulacrum, it was Samuel in person. My blood froze in my veins. 'Why do you summon me?' he demanded. 'What frenzy disturbs me in the darkness of the tomb?' At these words my terror is redoubled. 'The crown will soon fall from the line of Benjamin, and the reign of your enemy is approaching at last. Through your action the whole race of Jewry is made criminal.' Having said this he returns abruptly to everlasting darkness.]

Whether this constitutes threat, curse or prophesy, Saül's reaction is clear: to save his children and his race, he must destroy David. Although violent, this can be justified by the reminder that it is not just he that is imminently at risk. For Jonathas, tasked by Saül with David's murder, this is a further sign of his father's helpless madness:

> Sauvons David: d'un père arrêtons la furie.
> Tout est à redouter de sa fureur extrême.
>   IV, 3

> [We must save David and nullify my father's madness. Everything is to be feared from this extreme fury of his.]

By the end of Act IV, each individual is desperately clinging to suicidal hopes of saving all the others – David ready to sacrifice his safety for Jonathas, Michol rushing towards danger to save David, and all determined despite everything to save Saül from himself. Ultimately their human efforts are negated by the sudden news that the Philistines are on the point of attacking, and the act ends with Saül's moralistic reflection on the futility of human decision-making:

> Des efforts des mortels ainsi le Ciel se joue,
> A ses propres desseins fait servir nos forfaits,
> Et qui veut les combattre en presse les effets.
>   IV, 12

> [See how Heaven mocks the efforts of humankind! Our crimes are turned to serve God's own ends, and if we fight against these ends we bring about their effects even more quickly.]

Act V presents Saül's downfall and reconciliation with David as a fitting climax to the moral dilemmas explored in the previous four acts. Neither a horrific act of despair as in La Taille, nor a fitting punishment for wrong-doing as in du Ryer, Saül's suicide is here presented as a logical and appropriate response to his fate: worthy of reproof, but not of outright condemnation, he accepts responsibility, reconciles himself with his daughter and enemy, and faces death and judgment with dignity:

> Ainsi le Ciel l'ordonne.
> Vaincus et renversés, tout fuit, tout m'abandonne.
> Le Ciel de mes desseins jusqu'au bout s'est joué.
>   V, 3

[Such is Heaven's command. My allies, defeated and destroyed, abandon me in flight. Heaven has mocked my plans to the very end.]

He hands the throne over to David, begging him to rule justly and to provide Michol with 'un frère, un père, et son époux' ('a brother, a father and a husband'). He describes himself as 'des desseins du Ciel déplorable victime' ('the pitiable victim of Heaven's designs') but assures David that 'dans mes plus grands transports vous eûtes mon estime' ('in the very depths of my madness I never lost my respect for you').

4   Voltaire

When Voltaire dramatized the story of Saul and the witch of Endor in 1763,[24] any attempt to invite sympathy for Saul, Samuel or David had been submerged in Enlightenment rage at the abuses of religious and political authority. Voltaire's *Saül* comes over, frankly, as little more than a melodramatic demonstration of the evils of monarchy, clericalism and privilege, in which human misdemeanours reflect what Sarah Nicholson characterizes as the deity's 'unwavering wickedness'.[25] Act I reveals Samuel's fanatical brutality, Act II David's self-centred absolutism and Saül's superstitious fear, heartlessly exploited by the cynical witch, while the final three acts concentrate on David's callous treatment of his political enemies and on his financial and sexual corruption. Despite the play's title, Saül is in fact killed between Acts II and III, and most of the attention is given to David and his women.

The play begins with Voltaire's interpretation of the sequence surrounding the sparing of Agag and Saül's consultation of the witch at Endor. Insofar as it explores the extent to which Saül can be excused for disobedience, this is not so much to make Saül more attractive, as to make Samuel appear even more unreasonable. When the first act begins, Saül is at the height of his military triumph, and there is no question of madness, although he appears subdued and oppressed, explaining to Baza that Samuel is jealously turning David against him and seeking to displace him. Agag praises Saül's clemency, but Samuel insists that Saül has sinned in disobeying God's command, and brutally slaughters Agag, to the horror of Saül and Baza. When Samuel had lambasted Saül for his disobedience, outrage was expressed both by Saül and by Agag:

24 Voltaire, *Saül*, in his *Œuvres complètes* (Paris: Garnier, 1877), vol. V, pp. 569–611. References to this play will be to this edition.
25 Nicholson in Ehrlich and White, p. 329.

SAÜL   Parlez, de quoi suis-je coupable ?

SAMUEL   D'avoir pardonné à un roi.

AGAG   Comment ! la plus belle des vertus serait regardée chez vous
            comme un crime ?

SAÜL   Je n'ai pas cru qu'un tel ordre fût positif; j'ai pensé que la bonté
            était le premier attribut de l'Être suprême.

   I, 3

[SAUL   Tell me, where lies my guilt?

SAMUEL   You spared a king.

AGAG   What? You consider the greatest virtue as a crime?

SAUL   I did not believe that such an order was a positive thing, con-
            sidering that goodness was the first attribute of the supreme
            Being.]

Saül had already defended his decision to spare Agag's life:

> Illustre prince, que le malheur rend encore plus grand, je n'ai fait que
> mon devoir en sauvant vos jours: les rois doivent respecter leurs sem-
> blables; qui se venge après la victoire est indigne de vaincre.
>
>   I, 2

> [Illustrious monarch, misfortune has made you even greater; in saving
> your life I have merely done my duty. Kings must respect their equals: he
> who seeks revenge in victory does not deserve to conquer.]

Samuel's cold-blooded insistence that Agag be hacked to pieces is as barbaric
as anything Voltaire could have witnessed in a production of Shakespeare. The
scene has the potential to convey a picture of Saül as tragic in the way that
Macbeth is tragic, his descent into irrationality triggered by what we might
now call post-traumatic stress, but Voltaire does not dwell on ethical analysis
so much as on his depiction of humanity as misguided and badly led:

> AGAG   Hélas ! Saül, que je te plains, d'être soumis à de pareils monstres !
>   I, 3

> [Alas, how sorry I am for you, Saül, to be under the sway of monsters like
> this.]

Saül's madness is portrayed in such a way that it would be hard in performance
to avoid the grotesque: he is clearly disfigured by fear and anxiety:

ABIGAÏL   Ah! Madame, comme il roule les yeux, comme il grince les
           dents! Fuyons au plus vite; votre père est fou, ou je me trompe.
MICHOL   Il est quelquefois possédé du diable. [...] C'est cette mal-
           heureuse boucherie d'Agag qui lui a donné des vapeurs;
           dérobons-nous à sa furie.

           II, 6

[Ah, Madame, how he rolls his eyes and grinds his teeth! Let us flee as
quickly as we can, your father is clearly mad!

   The devil does sometimes take possession of him: he's clearly overcome by the violent murder of Agag, let us escape from his frenzy.]

It is while Saül is in this disturbed state that he confirms his decision to consult
the Pythonisse d'Endor, who cons him for money and plays on his pre-existing
fears, filling him with dread by her account of Samuel's enmity (Act II). This
makes his defeat in the ensuing battle almost inevitable, and Voltaire's play
then switches focus to concentrate on David's equally bleak descent into
debauchery, cynicism and death – the last to the evident relief of all his entou-
rage, particularly the women.

5   Alphonse de Lamartine

Both Lamartine[26] and Gide[27] explored the story of Saul in a post-Enlightenment
period when one would have expected dramatists to have less compunction
in portraying the universe as unfair or flawed; yet both go out of their way to
make Saul appear more violent and villainous than their predecessors. In the
most extreme departures from the biblical story, Lamartine exposes Saül as
the murderer of Samuel and of the high priest Achimélec, while Gide's Saül
violently kills his own wife and the necromancer from Endor on stage; all of
these acts of violence are inventions superimposed onto the biblical story. As
Nicholson comments, 'it is probably easier for a modern reader to understand
God's displeasure at the murder of a prophet (or priests), than at Saul's failure
to butcher a foreign king'.[28] In these plays, Saul's fall into madness – amounting to paranoia – and disgrace becomes a reflection on the vicious cycle of

---

26   Alphonse de Lamartine, *Saül*, in his *Œuvres complètes* (Paris: chez l'auteur, 1860), vol. 3,
     pp. 333–437. References to this play will be to this edition.
27   André Gide, *Saül*, in his *Théâtre* (Paris: Gallimard, 1942), pp. 7–151. References to this play
     will be to this edition.
28   *Ibid.* (see above, n. 10, p. 158), p. 318.

violence, bringing out strongly the parallels between Saul and Macbeth. Lamartine's version in particular is a meditation on decline: the old age of his Saül is stressed several times[29] and this is coupled to insistence on his unreliable self-control – 'Crains d'éveiller en lui cette fureur soudaine' (I, 1: 'Be careful not to awaken in him the sudden outbursts of madness to which he is prone'). This is depicted explicitly as caused by 'le ciel' ('heaven'), and ascribed by him to God's withholding of earlier support: 'depuis longtemps Dieu ne m'éclaire plus' (I, 4: 'for some time now, God has given me no guidance'). In this version, as in La Taille's, the decision to consult the woman from Endor is made during a period of lucidity following the reconciliation with David that ends Act I, but here it is not portrayed as sinful in itself, even though it is suggested by Abner, who in this as in other versions is presented as a trouble-maker. The consultation occurs early in Act II, so establishes from the start not only that Saül is sinful – 'Saül, pour tes forfaits ton fils est rejeté' ('Saül, your son will be rejected because of your crimes', II, 3) – but also that his disgrace forms part of a providential God's plan, since the birth of the Messiah to the line of David is explicitly mentioned. After this scene, Saül is predominantly portrayed as frenzied if not mad: jealous and suspicious of David, and of Jonathas for defending the latter, beset by nightmares, and given to sporadic outbursts of physical violence. A momentary respite in his condition brought about by the soothing influence of his daughter Michol in Act III is undone by the sound of the crowds hailing David as victor and saviour. A relatively lucid statement by Saül in Act IV, insisting that his suspicions of David are entirely well founded, gives way to a more Racinian sense of his own insecurity:

> Depuis ce temps, sans cesse à moi-même contraire,
> Je me cherche, et je suis pour moi-même un mystère.
> [...]
> Sais-je ce que je veux ? sais-je ce que j'ordonne ?
> Puis-je percer jamais la nuit qui m'environne ?
>
>   IV, 2–3

[Since then, I have been divided against myself, seeking to know myself but remaining a mystery to myself. Can I tell what I want, can I tell what commands I give? Shall I ever see clearly in the darkness that surrounds me?]

---

29   I, 2; III, 1 and later in Act III.

This again gives way to violent rage when he recognizes Goliath's sword –
reserved for his own use – in David's hand:

> Ton crime t'a jugé. Va, ce trait odieux
> Fait tomber à la fin le bandeau de mes yeux.
>   IV, 3

> [You are judged by your crime. At last, with this horrible action the scales
> have fallen from my eyes.]

The act ends with Saül in another paroxysm of self-justification, having as-
saulted David and arranged the execution of Achimélec:

>   Justice ou crime
> Que m'importe ? Et que font aux aveugles destins
> Les malheurs, les vertus, les crimes des humains ?
> De trente ans de vertus quelle est la récompense ?
>   IV, 5

> [What does it matter to me whether this is an act of justice or a crime?
> What difference do the misfortunes, the virtues and the crimes of mor-
> tals make to the blind fates? What reward am I receiving for thirty years
> of virtue?]

Despite the lapse into pagan language here, all this builds on the kernel of the
biblical story, but Saul's violence is highlighted here more than in earlier dramatizations. It lays the foundation for a bleak conclusion in which Saül rejects
any possibility of reconciliation with David, and ultimately exults in the evil
personality which his madness represents and which he embraces in the face
of death:

> Dieu cruel, Dieu de sang, je te brave et t'outrage !
> Tout ton pouvoir ne peut avilir mon courage.
> [...]
> Je ne me repens pas des crimes de ma vie :
> C'est toi que les commis, et qui les justifie.
>   IV, 6

[Cruel God, God of bloodshed, I defy you, I willingly offend you! All of your power cannot diminish my courage. I do not repent of the crimes of my life – it is you who committed them and you who excuses them.]

Although Jonathas sees these blasphemous and defiant lines as proof that Saül is not in control of himself, and begs for God's mercy on his father, his own death sours Saül's response and removes any possibility of reconciliation not just with David, but with God, and Saül kills himself in despair, surviving just long enough to witness the triumph of David, who is still his 'exécrable rival'.

6   André Gide

Gide's Saül comes across more as tortured than as frenzied or villainous. His play, written in 1896–98 and published in 1903, but not performed on stage until Jacques Copeau produced it in 1922, has recently come to be seen as 'one of the first modern gay dramas'[30] and portrays the disintegration of Saül's personality, under the pressure of his obsessive attraction to David, who, as he knows, will destroy and displace him. This is coupled to his strong jealousy towards his own son Jonathan, whose relationship with David is intimate and reciprocal. To that extent the play demonstrates the abhorrent and destructive nature of shame, rather than analyzing issues of guilt and ethics from a more detached perspective. However justified Saül may be in despising the values of a society which blocks his self-fulfilment, his own violence towards his wife, his priest and his sickly son is neither explained nor exonerated by the structure of the play: it is hard to be sure whether his loss of control, like Hamlet's, is madness or masquerade.[31] There is a degree of poetic justice in the fact that the demons who increasingly haunt Saül and represent his repressed and destructive desires are there only because he has killed all the sorcerers, soothsayers and witches who, he fears, might otherwise reveal his guilty secret, but in other respects the play does not seek to balance fault with punishment.

   This play incorporates or alludes to several events in the biblical story which are overlooked by other dramatizations, although it takes liberties with the time-line in order to do so. Events from David's defeat of Goliath to the death of Saül are compressed, the arrival of David at Saül's court as both music therapist and military saviour is presented as the work of spies employed by Saül's

---

30   http://www.glbtq.com/literature/modern_drama.html, p. 2, accessed on 19 June 2012.

31   Cf. Germaine Brée, *Gide* (New Brunswick, NJ: Rutgers University Press, 1963), p. 103.

queen and the high priest, and the characterization of Jonathan as a neurotic and fragile invalid is Gide's own invention. Neither David nor Jonathan have any political ambition of their own, but seek to triumph only to restore power to Saül. Saül himself cuts a pathetic figure in many ways, becoming obsessed with his quest for lost donkeys,[32] setting up elaborate charades to spy on his court and family, shaving his beard off – ostensibly as a disguise to visit the woman at Endor, but also to make himself appear younger and more seductive – and exuding childish righteous indignation when he demands an explanation from the high priest for God's ongoing silence:

> C'est pourtant un peu fort ! Qu'est-ce que je lui ai fait ? Voyons, parle, toi, prêtre ! Pourquoi se tait-il maintenant ? Il faudrait s'expliquer à la fin ... Ah ! je voulais me justifier devant lui.
>
>   III, 5

> [This really is a bit much! What have I ever done to him? Come on, priest, tell me! Why does he hold his tongue now? Ah, I needed to be able to put my case before him myself.]

This is the closest Saül comes to considering whether he is himself guilty of wrong-doing or responsible for his alienation from God and for the suffering of himself and others. His tone is similarly childish when, confronted by the shade of Samuel, he has to accept the rather cryptic advice that it was his own action in admitting David to court that had brought about his downfall:

> SAMUEL   C'est maintenant ton ennemi que Dieu protège. Avant qu'il fût conçu dans le sein de sa mère, Dieu se l'était déjà choisi. C'est pour t'y préparer que tu l'accueilles.
> SAÜL   Mais quelle était ma faute alors ?
> SAMUEL   De l'accueillir.
> SAÜL   Mais puisque Dieu l'avait choisi.
> SAMUEL   Crois-tu que Dieu, pour t'en punir, n'ait pas déjà connu de loin les derniers chancellements de ton âme ?
>
>   III, 7

---

32   In *1 Samuel*, 9, it was while out in search of his father's straying donkeys that Saul had first come into contact with the prophet Samuel, and been identified as the future ruler of Israel. Earlier dramatists had ignored this picturesque but distracting detail, whereas Gide makes it a source of comedy, indicating his Saül's obsessive character.

[SAMUEL Now it's your enemy that God is protecting. Before he was
        conceived in his mother's womb, God had already chosen
        him. You only invited him into your court to prepare you for
        this.
SAUL   So what did I do wrong?
SAMUEL You invited him.
SAUL   But God had already chosen him!
SAMUEL Do you believe that God did not know far in advance how
        your spirit would falter as it has recently, and punish you for
        that?]

Insofar as this portrait represents the God of any religion, it is one that invites some sympathy with Saül, but Gide considered Copeau's portrayal of the
king as a 'senile, dirty old man' to be symptomatic of an interpretation which
'missed the moral side' of his play.[33] This may explain why the twentieth century had more problems with hamartia than earlier periods: we expect the
universe to be unjust, but still do not want our heroes to be either undignified or unpalatable. In Germaine Brée's view, Saül does 'preserve tragic dignity'
through 'the pathetic shame with which he witnesses and lucidly judges his
own moral downfall'.[34]

    It was argued at the end of chapter 2 that the tension between 'tragic flaw'
and 'tragic error' in our interpretation of hamartia could be resolved if we see
that a character imperfection might be relevant to the audience's response to
the tragic hero without necessarily having to be implicated as a cause of his
downfall: 'The tragic hero should not fall through wickedness; but his being
less than perfectly good is important to our pity and fear'.[35] As we argued more
generally then, even if we were able to prove that Saul's disgrace and suffering
were the result of some specific (or indeed general) stupidity or sinfulness on
his part, it would scarcely allay our uncomfortable sense that he got a raw deal,
and his son an even worse one. But the fact that he was liable to stupidities and
weaknesses is what enables us to avoid thinking of him as a superman whose
fate is of no concern to us, and – in most of the dramatizations we have been
considering – to try to grapple alongside him with the perplexities generated
by his misfortune.

33   Alan Sheridan, *André Gide: A Life in the Present* (Harmondsworth: Penguin, 1998), p. 355.
34   Brée, p. 116.
35   Martha Nussbaum, *The Fragility of Goodness: Luck and Ethics in Greek Tragedy and
     Philosophy* (Cambridge: Cambridge University Press, first published 1986, revised edition
     2001), p. 387.

The appeal of King Saul to dramatists wishing to explore the spectacular – power struggles, battles, witchcraft and sorcery – is obvious. Any of the plays we have studied – even those from the seventeenth and early eighteenth centuries, which reflect a baroque rather than a classical aesthetic in their exploration of violence and in their depiction of the woman from Endor – would challenge a modern director to deploy current resources for the atmospheric, the eye-catching and the histrionic. More subtle, I think, is the extent to which the subject has enabled these playwrights to combine their overtly dramatic aims with ethical ones, to open up to debate the extent to which Saul deserves his fate, and thereby, from the perspectives of their own times, to generate works which have the potential to deliver a fresh understanding of the contemporary predicament to new audiences. That Saul, as he emerges from these very different works, is sometimes less palatable than we feel comfortable with, that God is sometimes less slow to anger than we would like, and that the logical connection between decisions and their results is sometimes more haphazard than we feel would be the case in a well-ordered universe, should all help to show that a sense of the tragic can still be made relevant to us by the re-appraisal of an old story. Echoing across the centuries, La Taille's 'Pour être donc humain j'éprouve sa colère!' is surprisingly close to Voltaire's 'La plus belle des vertus serait regardée chez vous comme un crime?' and Gide's 'C'est pourtant un peu fort!'

CHAPTER 7

Scapegoats: Passing the Buck to Snakes, Partners, Parents and Others

It is, of course, quite literally, the oldest excuse in the book. 'The woman whom thou gavest to be with me, she gave me of the tree, and I did eat.' 'The serpent beguiled me, and I did eat.'[1] Characters accused of wrong-doing have always been liable to claim that other people committed the acts for which they are unfairly being blamed, or that other people subjected them to irresistible temptation or pressure, or that for some other reason they themselves are carrying a disproportionate share of responsibility or punishment and should be allowed to share it with – or even off-load it onto – somebody else. It may even seem a moot point whether Adam and Eve were banished from Eden for the original sin of eating a fruit which Adam had been told not to eat, or rather for the evasion, subterfuge and buck-passing that followed their discovery. Lady Macbeth leads her husband astray when he hesitates, but which of them is the more fundamentally to blame for his descent and disintegration? Should Iago carry the whole can for Desdemona's suffering and death, or does Othello – or Emilia, or anyone else – deserve some of the blame? To what extent is Thésée to blame for the outcome of *Phèdre* on the grounds that he set Hippolyte an unhealthy example – and does Théramène then have to shoulder some blame too, as an ineffectual tutor? Could Willie Loman or Stanley Kowalski have done anything, or at least more than they did, to escape from the peer pressure that led them inexorably from the American dream into the American nightmare? All of these attempts to divert attention from the obvious primary agent to others acting as external triggers for deviant behaviour relate to the all-embracing question of the nature of evil in the universe. Is the Devil the *cause* of bad behaviour or an *excuse* for it? Sophocles implicitly believed in devilish spirits; Marlowe presumably believed in the force of Satan – so what happens when their tragedies are presented, let us imagine, on successive evenings before an audience largely made up of spectators who believe in neither? In all these sorts of instances, if a dramatist can suggestively blur the edges of guilt and extenuation in distributing the responsibility for a disastrous outcome between a number of parties, a fruitful source of moral ambiguity will be created.

---

1   *Genesis*, 3:12–13.

The overall cop-out of blaming 'forces beyond our control' has been dealt with in the chapters on helplessness and on ignorance,[2] and will not be returned to here, except insofar as one of the ways in which the gods can be seen as partly responsible for human failures is that they set a bad example:[3]

> Les dieux mêmes, les dieux, de l'Olympe habitants,
> Qui d'un bruit si terrible épouvantent les crimes,
> Ont brûlé quelquefois de feux illégitimes.

> [The gods themselves that in Olympus dwell,
> Who smite the evildoer with their bolt,
> Have sometimes felt unlawful passions' fire.]

Œnone, in insisting that Phèdre's 'erreur' is 'excusable' (1296),[4] here reminds her not just that all mortals are subject to the laws of their feeble nature or the characteristics inherited from their parents, but that the role models that they emulate, human and divine, are in part responsible for their character and thus their acts. Corneille's Créuse puts forward a similar view:[5]

> Ainsi nous avons vu le souverain des dieux,
> Au mépris de Junon, aimer en ces bas lieux,
> Vénus quitter son Mars et négliger sa prise,
> Tantôt pour Adonis, et tantôt pour Anchise [...]

> [Thus we have seen the lord of all the gods,
> despising his Juno, come down to earth to love,
> Venus leave her Mars, discounting his right,
> and turn first to Adonis and then to Anchises.]

---

2 See particularly pp. 28–31, 35–8, 90–91.

3 Racine, *Phèdre*, IV, 6, 1304–06.

4 Line 1296, translated by Cairncross as 'And of your error take a different view', reads 'Regardez d'un autre œil une excusable erreur', so more literally 'Take a different view of this excusable mistake'. The whole speech would provide Phèdre with an anthology of excuses: destiny is inescapable, a spell was cast on you, all mortals are subject to human frailty, and the gods themselves are not above similar misconduct.

5 Corneille, *Médée*, II, 5, 639–42.

Such a view can of course be challenged: in Du Ryer's *Lucrèce*, the malicious slave Libane articulates this excuse for infidelity:[6]

> Les dieux plus forts que nous ne le portent qu'à peine,
> Ses liens sont pour eux une espèce de gêne,
> Et pour les rendre aussi plus doux et plus légers,
> Ils cherchent comme moi des plaisirs étrangers.
>> III, 3, 735–8

> [Even the gods, stronger than we are, scarcely support (the bonds of marriage), consider them to be a hindrance, and to make them lighter and sweeter they, like me, seek delight outside these bonds.]

but Lucrèce's response is virtuous and vigorous:

> Quel excès de blasphème et d'extrême artifice,
> De faire de nos dieux les excuses du vice !
>> III, 3, 739–40

> [What a blasphemous and tortuous claim,
> To turn our gods into excuses for our sins!]

1   Parents

The bad example set by the gods is not commonly put forward in extenuation of human evil, but inadequate human role models – parents, teachers – can often seem to blur the extent of their protégé's responsibility. We have already looked at the influence of inherited characteristics, but as well as providing our genes, our parents also shape our upbringing, which is why the balance between nature and nurture is so hard to determine. At a purely human level, without reference to supernatural forces, individuals can feel both crushed by their parents' force and tempted by their example.

Phèdre is haunted by the influence of her mother: her shame over her lust for Hippolyte derives partly from the parallel she draws between her own 'monstrous' feelings for her stepson and those of her mother for the bull which begat the Minotaur. 'Dans quels égarements l'amour jeta ma mère!' (I, 3, 250: 'Into what dark abyss love hurled my mother!'). When she has blurted out to

6   1638. Eds. James F. Gaines and Perry Gethner (Genève: Droz, 1994).

Hippolyte the nature of her feelings for him, images of monstrosity dominate her discourse: 'ce monstre affreux ne doit point t'échapper' (II, 5, 703: 'This frightful monster [i.e. myself] must not now escape'[7]). This enhances the ironic intensity of her anxiety when she envisages the fate of her own sons after her death: 'Je tremble qu'un discours, hélas! trop véritable, / Un jour leur reproche une mère coupable' (III, 3, 865–6: 'I tremble lest reports, alas, too true, One day upbraid them with a mother's guilt'). Insofar as she is drawing a parallel between herself and Pasiphaé, she here projects on her ashamed sons a feeling which she is acknowledging in herself: 'Le crime d'une mère est un pesant fardeau' (III, 3, 864: 'A mother's crime lies heavy on her [children]'). Although it is not made explicit, the shameful shadow of Pasiphaé also haunts Phèdre's final hallucinatory self-image when jealousy of Aricie is added to her catalogue of destructive feelings:

> Moi jalouse ! Et Thésée est celui que j'implore !
> Mon époux est vivant, et moi je brûle encore !
> Pour qui ? Quel est le cœur où prétendent mes vœux ?
> IV, 6, 1265–7

> [*I*, jealous? and 'tis Theseus I implore!
> My husband is alive and yet I pine.
> For whom? Whose heart have I been coveting?]

Each of these reproaches is in fact more valid as applied to Pasiphaé's infatuation with the bull, on which she calculatedly acted, than to Phèdre's long-concealed and actively opposed desire for Hippolyte in the context of a political marriage to an unsatisfactory husband.

In a universe governed naturally by genetics and the impact of early influences, the effect of Pasiphaé's shame and disgrace on her daughter would and should be balanced by the moral strength and justice embodied in her father Minos. From the very start of the play she is almost defined as the product of this split inheritance, 'la fille de Minos et de Pasiphaé' (I, 1, 36: 'the child of Minos and Pasiphae'). When Œnone is striving to steer her mistress into a moral path, she formulates her advice in terms that directly reflect the dichotomy, without explicitly naming the mother:

---

7 The French text makes it clearer than the translation that Phèdre views herself as the monster, and Hippolyte as responsible for ridding the world of her, in emulation of his father. Cf. line 701.

Vous nourrissez un feu qu'il vous faudrait éteindre.
Ne vaudrait-il pas mieux, digne sang de Minos,
Dans de plus nobles soins chercher votre repos.

    III, 1, 754–6

[(Your misfortunes) inflame a fire you ought to quench.
Daughter of Minos, should you not aspire
To seek your peace of mind in nobler cares?][8]

In practice, however, any awareness that Phèdre has of her father's excellent
example is distorted into a harsh conviction that she has manifestly failed to
follow it and live up to his expectations. This thread reaches its climax in the
hallucinatory vision she has of Minos, transformed into a judge in the underworld, finding her wanting and greeting her in condemnation:

Minos juge aux enfers tous les pâles humains.
Ah ! combien frémira son ombre épouvantée,
Lorsqu'il verra sa fille à ses yeux présentée,
Contrainte d'avouer tant de forfaits divers,
Et des crimes peut-être inconnus aux enfers !

    IV, 6, 1280–4

[Minos judges in hell the trembling dead.
Ah! how his horror-struck shade will start
To see before him his own daughter stand,
Forced to admit to such a host of sins
And some, perhaps, unknown even in hell!]

It takes but a moment's reflection to confirm that this is a mad hallucination
since it is simply untrue. Phèdre's crimes, both real and imaginary, are entirely
familiar ones: lustful desire, spiteful jealousy leading to murderous impulses,
infidelity but only in the mind. Even if she had gone ahead as a widow and married her stepson it is only by the strictest interpretation of Levitican law that
she would be condemned. Such a relationship would no doubt be subjected to

---

8   The translation here loses the word 'digne' ('worthy'), implying a moral obligation on Phèdre's
part to reject the nefarious influence of Pasiphaé, and live up to the example and teaching
of Minos. Cairncross's insertion of the word 'aspire' does reflect that implication. Either way,
Phèdre's furious rejection of this *good* advice from Œnone is an important factor in deciding
the balance of responsibility between the two women.

prurient scrutiny by popular journalism,[9] but such stories would be more likely to produce fascination than condemnation or disgust. Even if Phèdre had gone so far as to desire the death of her husband, this is scarcely a 'sin unknown in hell'. Indeed, another potentially shameful role model in the background of her own family is that of Medea, her cousin.[10] We do not discover it until the very end of the play, but Phèdre must at some level of consciousness know that she has in her possession 'un poison que Médée apporta dans Athènes' (v, 7, 1638: 'A poison that Medea brought to Greece'). Racine does not encourage us to dwell on this, but we can legitimately ask both why he mentions Medea at all, and why Phèdre had made the decision to bring this poison with her from Athens to Troezen.

Thus in addition to her overwhelming sense of helplessness, of responsibility submerged by passion, and her retrospective awareness that she had been misled in her decision-making processes by the false news of Thésée's death, an excuse-seeking Phèdre could and occasionally does call on the inadequacies of her genetic inheritance and upbringing in exoneration of her actions: she is imbued with her mother's character; and has been overawed by an idealized but distant father.

Hippolyte can scarcely be less confused about his parents and the examples they set him. To have a mother with a reputation like Antiope's – dedicated to Artemis, hunting, warfare and chastity – and a father with a reputation like Thésée's – good works of brutal violence allied to excessive philandering – is calculated to produce in him a division of instincts and impulses that must go some way to excuse his inability to act decisively and appropriately when faced with delicate emotional situations. How could he help it if his wooing of Aricie was inept, or if his response to Phèdre's ill-judged avowal of love was hopelessly tongue-tied, or if he gave a grotesquely misleading impression before the ranting Thésée? His inheritance on his mother's side gave him no chance. He attributes his uneasiness about sexual activity in part to the personality of his mother, and its influence on either his genetic make-up or his infantile upbringing:

---

9   Indeed, it has been: here are three examples, all accessed on 22 October 2019: https://trove
     .nla.gov.au/newspaper/article/58589458; https://www.mirror.co.uk/news/world-news/i
     -fell-in-love-with-my-stepson-now-were-1662498; https://metro.co.uk/2019/05/27/widow
     -46-disowned-children-sex-stepson-21-9697783/.

10   Both Phaedra and Medea were granddaughters of the sun-god Helios. Madeline Miller's
     Circe (first published 2018, London: Bloomsbury, 2019) points very suggestively towards
     radical reinterpretations of the characters of Medea, Pasiphaë and Minos and the rela-
     tionship between them.

> [...] avec son lait une mère amazone
> M'a fait sucer encor cet orgueil qui t'étonne.
>   I, 1, 69–70

> [The Amazon, my mother, with her milk
> Suckled me on that pride you wonder at.]

When at last he does stumblingly blurt out his feelings for Aricie, he introduces the confession by a *reductio ad absurdum* of his own reputation:

> Avec quelques couleurs qu'on ait peint ma fierté,
> Croit-on que dans ses flancs un monstre m'ait porté ?
>   II, 2, 519–20

> [However my aloofness be decried
> Do you believe a monster gave me birth?]

to which the most honest answer is 'yes': the people around Hippolyte do generally ascribe to Thésée's Amazon bride a degree of austerity which removes her from human sympathy, and go on to assume that her son takes naturally to a similarly self-abnegating lifestyle which most see not as an avoidance of sin but as an indulgence in superheroism. Other characters in the play frequently associate Hippolyte closely with his mother, often defining him in terms of his relationship with her:

> Ce fils qu'une Amazone a porté dans son flanc
>   I, 3, 204
> [...] le fils d'une Scythe
>   I, 3, 210
> [...] fils de l'étrangère
>   I, 4, 328
> Songez qu'une barbare en son sein l'a formé
>   III, 1, 787

> [That youth whose mother was an Amazon ...
> A Scythian's son ... the foreign woman's son ...
> An Amazon, forget not, gave him birth.]

Nevertheless, although Antiope is scarcely mentioned within the play *except* in connection with her reputation for icily rejecting the blandishments of Venus, neither she nor Hippolyte fully live up to this reputation for chastity and purity. The hope Phèdre clings to of wooing Hippolyte is partly based on the fact that even Antiope had deserted her vows of chastity in marrying Thésée: 'Quoique Scythe et barbare, elle a pourtant aimé' (III, 1, 788: 'Though a barbarian, yet she did love'). This echoes Théramène's statement that she had 'brûlé pour Thésée [...] d'une pudique amour' (I, 1, 126: 'Had [...] been consumed by legitimate love for Thésée'), on which Hippolyte's very existence depended.[11] Even when Hippolyte makes the claim to Thésée that he is innocence personified –

> Elevé dans le sein d'une chaste héroïne,
> Je n'ai point de mon sang démenti l'origine.
>
> IV, 2, 1101–2

> [Reared by a virtuous Amazon from birth,
> I never have belied my mother's blood.]

– he is all too well aware that this is scarcely true, and within a few lines he has replaced it with a more just admission: 'Ce cœur [...] n'a point d'un chaste amour dédaigné de brûler' (IV, 2, 1119–20: 'I have not scorned to glow with virtuous love').

If the influence which Antiope had over her son was thus confusing – sexual impulses should be suppressed but it is not the end of the world if they are not – the example of his father was even more perplexing. Hippolyte longs to emulate his father in his heroic exploits, but vigorously resists embracing his reputation as a philanderer:

> Tu sais combien mon âme, attentive à ta voix,
> S'échauffait aux récits de ses nobles exploits [...]
> Mais quand tu récitais des faits moins glorieux [...]
> Je te pressais souvent d'en abréger le cours.
>
> I, 1, 75–6, 83, 92

> [You know how, as I hung upon your words,
> My heart would glow at tales of his exploits,

---

11   The slightly awkward use here of the word 'pudique' (either discreet or modest) probably reflects Théramène's delicacy in broaching the subject with Hippolyte, rather than any real characteristic of the feisty woman Antiope was. Racine takes pains to establish that Thésée was lawfully married to Hippolyte's mother: Phèdre's position is 'un second hymen' (II, 5, 612: 'a second marriage'), and Hippolyte is the 'fils d'une autre épouse' (II, 5, 610: 'the son of another bride').

But when you told me of less glorious deeds,
I often urged you quickly to conclude.]

It is possible to argue that this is another example of a reputation that is somewhat distorted by exaggeration. By the standards set by the Greek pantheon
and heroes, the list of Thésée's shameful amorous exploits is not particularly
outstanding, and many if not all were consensual rather than exploitative – he
is blamed more for abandoning loving mistresses than for rape.[12] Hippolyte
(I, 1, 85–90) mentions by name only Helen of Troy, Péribée (Periboea, consort
of Telamon, king of Salamis) and Ariadne, adding rather tamely 'Tant d'autres,
dont les noms lui sont même échappés' (I, 1, 87: 'Others, whose very names
he has forgot'). These could include Perigenia, the daughter of Sinis, one of
Theseus's monstrous victims; and Aegle, the daughter of Panopeus for whom
in some versions of his story Theseus abandoned Ariadne.[13] As we have seen,
Hippolyte does not consider his own mother as a victim in that sense: Thésée
married her and remained faithful to her in her lifetime. Phèdre, too was 'en-
levée sous de meilleurs auspices' (II, 1, 90: 'abducted, though for lawful ends')
and 'depuis longtemps ne craint plus de rivale' (I, 1, 26: 'Phèdre has in his heart
long reigned alone'). Théramène lacks confidence in this: Hippolyte had to
prevent him from hinting at the start of the play that Thésée's long and unex-
plained absence was probably caused by another amorous dalliance:

Qui sait même [si ...]
        Nous cachant de nouvelles amours,
Ce héros n'attend point qu'une amante abusée ...
        I, 1, 17–21

[Who knows indeed ... whether ...
He is not tasting all the joys of love
And soon the outraged victim of his wiles ...]

In any event what matters here is not so much the reality of Thésée's past, nor
our judgment on his moral character, but Hippolyte's own conviction that this
part of his father's story is shameful. His father was a hero badly flawed by sexual transgressions and he himself is groping for a way to emulate the heroism

---

12   Reading this sentence causes greater discomfort in 2020 than it did when the paragraph
      was first drafted! There was always a significant power imbalance in Thésée's relationships.
13   Both of these are mentioned by Oberon in Shakespeare's *A Midsummer Night's Dream*, II, 2.

whilst remaining immune in the sexual sphere to any propensity within himself to follow either innate influence or the example.

Another egregious case of poor parenting from the tragic canon is Agrippine, in Racine's *Britannicus*. If Néron is to be allowed to pass any of the responsibility for his wicked acts on to a third party, the more obvious candidate is Narcisse, his almost caricatural wicked counsellor who uses flattery and guile both to steer the young emperor towards evil and to facilitate its accomplishment in practice. We will return to him in a moment, but Néron's mother Agrippine is also presented as someone who could be targeted as a scapegoat, sharing the blame for the monster her son is turning into. From the very start of the play she is defined as 'la mère de César' (I, 1, 4: 'Caesar's mother') and her confidante Albine reminds us of the debt of gratitude Néron should owe her:

> [...] vous à qui Néron doit le jour qu'il respire,
> Qui l'avez appelé de si loin à l'empire ?
>
> I, 1, 15–16

> [You whom Nero owes his very life?
> You who have raised him from so low to power?]

Agrippine herself comes close to admitting the effect of inherited characteristics on Néron's personality: he combines 'la fierté des Nérons qu'il puisa dans mon flanc' (I, 1, 38: 'the fierceness of the Neroes drawn from me') with 'Des fiers Domitius l'humeur triste et sauvage' (I, 1, 36: 'The fierce Domitians' wild and sombre mood'). She also makes it clear that she has calculatedly attempted to steer her son's development, demanding of Burrhus: 'Vous l'ai-je confié pour en faire un ingrat?' (I, 2, 149: 'Was it for that [to efface me from his memory, or from a few lines earlier "to put a bar between my son and me"] I gave you Nero?'), although Burrhus insists he did not accept this charge to make the emperor a puppet. Both by her example and by direct intervention in his fortune she has demonstrated the attraction of power and the means to obtain it, and although she may be outraged, she can scarcely be surprised if he imitates the model she has provided.

Néron also has, like Hippolyte, a model of masculine authority that links power to sexual gratification. He tells Junie:

> Vous-même, consultez vos premières années :
> Claudius à son fils les avait destinées,

Mais c'était en un temps où de l'empire entier
Il croyait quelque jour le nommer héritier [...]
    II, 3, 583–86

[Yourself look backward to your earlier years.
Claudius had destined you, then, to his son,
But that was at a time when he had planned
To make him heir to the whole empire.]

Having witnessed this behaviour in his role models, Néron is then reminded of
it by his mother in the crucial confrontation between them (IV, 2). Although
Burrhus has just pointed out to her that Néron is not only her son but 'votre
ouvrage' (IV, 1, 1108: 'your handiwork'), she nevertheless has the maladdress to
demonstrate to her son that crime often does pay, and that what she herself
fears most is the loss of personal power and prestige. Can he then be blamed
for following her example, and for doing so in a violent manner couched in deceit and subterfuge? His immediate response is sarcastic: pretending to quote
the general view at court, he chides:

Est-ce pour obéir qu'elle l'a couronné ?
N'est-il de son pouvoir que le dépositaire ?
    IV, 2, 1234–5

[And has she crowned him only to obey?
Is then his power only held in trust?]

There is a delicious if excruciating irony in the relish with which Agrippine describes her apparent reconciliation with Néron in the final act: blinded by relief
and confidence that her sway over him has been restored, she is clearly oblivious of the extent to which he has learned her own lessons in double-dealing
and flattery:

Mes soins à vos soupçons ne laissent point de place.
[...]
Ah ! si vous aviez vu par combien de caresses
Il m'a renouvelé la foi de ses promesses !
Par quels embrassements il vient de m'arrêter !
Ses bras, dans nos adieux, ne pouvaient me quitter.
    V, 3, 1584, 1586–90

[There is no room for your suspicions now.
Ah! Had you seen him when, caressing me,
He reaffirmed to me his promises!
By what embraces did he keep me here!
His loving arms could not take leave of me.]

2   Teachers, Advisors, Counsellors

Whatever core characteristics they have retained from emulation of their parents, Phèdre, Hippolyte and Néron are more directly influenced by the figures
with whom they are in daily contact as adults: the 'gouverneurs' Théramène
and Narcisse and (in practice despite her lower status) the 'nourrice' Œnone.
A sympathetic onlooker is bound at least to consider that these characters
have some responsibility for the actions of the tragic figures they influence,
whether by directly advising or encouraging inappropriate actions, or by failing to exert sufficient moral pressure to resist them. Œnone will be directly
blamed by Phèdre for having 'directed' the bulk of her operation (v, 7, 1626:
'conduit'). Narcisse will be directly blamed by Agrippine (v, 6, 1658: 'Narcisse a
fait le coup'/'Narcissus did the deed') and torn apart by an angry crowd. Even
Théramène is unfairly reproached by Thésée: 'Théramène, est-ce toi? Qu'as-tu
fait de mon fils?' (v, 6, 1488: 'What have you done with him, Theramenes?').[14] In
the context of an exploration of the balance in tragedy between responsibility
and extenuation, it is pertinent to ask how far these accessories before or after
the act share the blame of the protagonist, but also how far they are treated as
scapegoats and made to carry an unfair burden of responsibility.

Narcisse is widely perceived as the evil influence on a suggestible Néron,
'l'accoucheur du "monstre naissant" [...] un double de Néron, lui soufflant
les actions qu'il n'ose accomplir'.[15] Or again, 'Néron's resistance yields rapidly
under the insinuating pressure of the villainous Narcisse'.[16] Narcisse consistently eggs his master on to resist the more virtuous advice of Burrhus, and

---

14   Literally, 'Theramenes, is that you? What have you done with my son?'
15   Laurence Lévy-Delpla (ed.), *Racine: Britannicus* (Paris: Hatier, 1988), p. 29: 'the midwife
    who delivers the emerging monster [...] Néron's *alter ego*, prompting him to take actions
    he dares not undertake'. The label 'monstre naissant' ('emerging monster', or 'monster
    in process of formation') forms part of the argument by which Racine defends himself
    against the accusation that, with reference to Aristotle's theory of hamartia, Néron is too
    wicked a character to arouse catharsis. See above, p. 67.
16   John Cairncross, edn. cit., p. 117.

pursue his selfish interests at the expense of his family, the court and moral
rectitude. This interpretation turns the play into something closer to a morality play than a tragedy: the forces of good and evil fighting over the soul of a
blank canvas. Racine himself points us in this direction in his *Seconde Préface*
by defining Narcisse as Néron's 'confident' and Burrhus as 'un honnête homme'
who is opposed to that 'peste de cour' ('I have chosen Burrus as an upright man
in opposition to this court pest').[17] However, this will not be the first or the
last time that Racine, in polemical mode, prioritizes a moralistic interpretation
of his own work over a purely theatrical one. At any rate, it has been argued
that the idea of Narcisse as an effective agent of evil is largely the invention of
Néron himself, who manipulates his relationship with the 'gouverneur' precisely to deflect attention from his own calculated acts and decisions. Antoine
Soare has demonstrated how Narcisse's relationship with Néron is complicated
if not problematic.[18] Even in private, the emperor addresses the tutor sometimes as 'tu' (II, 2, 391 – a moment of intimate confession) and sometimes as
'vous' (IV, 4, 1398 – a moment where he distances himself from the suggestions of Narcisse, although within the same scene he does revert to the more
complicit 'tu' form by line 1423). That in itself might suggest a degree of independence in Néron's spirit: it is he who decides, and if he follows Narcisse's suggestions he expresses complicity with him, but if not he stands up to him with
the more formal address. He certainly limits the extent to which he confides in
Narcisse, in contrast to Britannicus who consistently reveals his intentions and
motivations. Furthermore, Néron cannot convincingly blame Narcisse for the
bad advice he has given him, when at the same time he consciously upbraids
Burrhus for giving him good advice:

> Mais depuis quelques jours, tout ce que je désire
> Trouve en vous un censeur prêt à me contredire.
>
> III, 9, 1094–95

> [But, for these last few days, my every wish
> Has found you thwarting me censoriously]

It is simply not true that Narcisse proposes, instigates or facilitates many of
Néron's actions. The banishment of Pallas, the abduction of Junie, the mental torture imposed on her and Britannicus and the restrictions placed on the

17   P. 258, translation p. 136.
18   Antoine Soare, 'Néron et Narcisse: ou le mauvais mauvais conseiller', *Seventeenth-century
      French Studies*, 18, 1996, pp. 145–157 (p. 149).

movements of Agrippine are all undertaken by Néron quite independently of any suggestion made by Narcisse. Even the poisoning of Britannicus, although carried out by Narcisse, was conceived and decided by the emperor, who makes Narcisse both instrument and fall guy. It is a role, curiously, which Narcisse accepts with some relish – he longs to think of himself as a unique influence on Néron, as a special confident and advisor, and Néron cultivates that false image by flattery and manipulation, until his immediate ends are achieved, after which Narcisse can be brutally and peremptorily disposed of. The contrasting reactions of Néron and Narcisse to the death of Britannicus are striking and consistent.[19] Néron pretends it is a recurrence of a long-standing medical condition, whereas Narcisse cannot conceal 'sa perfide joie' (v, 5, 1642: 'his false joy'). Néron responds sarcastically to Agrippine's reproach: 'Voilà les soupçons dont vous êtes capable' (v, 6, 1651: 'How can you harbour such suspicions?'[20]), whereas Narcisse is defiant: 'Hé, Seigneur! ce soupçon vous fait-il tant d'outrage?' (v, 6, 1660: 'My lord, does this suspicion wound you so?'). In short, as Soare sums it up: 'Néron mure dans le rôle du mauvais conseiller un Narcisse qui n'en a point l'étoffe, lui refilant ainsi une bonne moitié de la culpabilité qu'exsude la tragédie' ('Néron walls Narcisse up in the role of evil counsellor that he is really not up to, thereby burdening him with at least half of the guilty responsibility that oozes from the tragedy').[21] Burrhus is left, with Agrippine, to describe the monster perceptively not as 'emerging' or 'new-born' but as 'un tyran dans le crime endurci dès l'enfance' (v, 7, 1712: '[One of those] tyrants who're inured to crime since childhood'). Agrippine and Néron's male ancestors may share some responsibility for the way he has turned out, but Narcisse has been little more than a pawn in the process.

If Narcisse is then in some sense a victim who gets an unfair share of blame, Théramène may be considered the opposite. Very few observers would seriously considering him even marginally responsible for the tragic outcome of *Phèdre*, yet Hippolyte's world view, which clearly does contribute to that outcome, must have been partly formed by interventions or negligences on the part of his 'gouverneur', the more so since he has been raised in isolation from his parents and step-mother. We have already noted the moment when Théramène fails to take advantage of an opportunity to correct an exploitative

---

19   Soare, p. 155.
20   The sarcasm is slightly more obvious in the original than in this translation but becomes
      evident in the next few lines.
21   Soare, p. 154.

sexual bias in his pupil.[22] Comparing himself to his father, Hippolyte explicitly draws a connection between heroic exploits and sexual gratification:

> [...] Qu'un long amas d'honneurs rend Thésée excusable,
> Qu'aucuns monstres par moi domptés jusqu'aujourd'hui
> Ne m'ont acquis le droit de faillir comme lui !
>
>   I, 1, 98–100

> [Since countless exploits plead on his behalf,
> Whereas no monsters overcome by me
> Have given me the right to err like him.]

This whole speech is an evasion: Hippolyte is reacting with indignation to Théramène's justified suggestion that he might be in love, even in love with Aricie. That is the logic of the sequence from line 50 to line 65. Yet when Hippolyte defiantly denies that he is capable of love (66–72), insists that he has not yet earned the 'right to err' in that way (73–100), and that in any case the last person he could start a relationship with is Aricie (101–113), the tutor makes no serious effort to challenge his pupil's spurious arguments and equivocations. The lines just quoted mark the end of an argument, so could plausibly be followed by a pause as Hippolyte reflects on what to say next. I would like the actor playing Théramène to find some way of conveying during this pause at least some disquiet with his pupil's glib assumption that there is an equivalence between violence and the right to sex. At the end of Hippolyte's long speech, Théramène does return to his perception that the prince is attracted to Aricie, but he does so in bland and fatalistic terms rather than with any probing of Hippolyte's moral sense. 'Le ciel de nos raisons ne sait point s'informer' (I, 1, 115: 'Heaven of our reasons takes but little heed'), and 'Quels courages Vénus n'a-t-elle pas domptés?' (I, 1, 123: 'What hearts has Venus' power not subdued?'), he says, almost anticipating Œnone's equally tendentious 'Votre flamme devient une flamme ordinaire' (I, 5, 350: 'Your love becomes like any other love'). In practice there is probably little that Théramène can do at this stage to change Hippolyte's attitudes or actions. In effect he offers to Hippolyte several excuses which he does not really want to rely on, and the prince responds with an icy concision which more or less forces Théramène to change the subject. In any event, the conversation is not brought to a satisfactory conclusion since the scene is abruptly interrupted by the arrival of Œnone. A performance that left a slight feeling that the tutor had been somewhat ineffectual

---

22   See above, 'Hamartia', p. 77.

in responding to his pupil's very real anxiety and confusion would add some psychological interest to what might otherwise seem a long-winded and contrived exposition.

The extent to which Œnone can be blamed for the attitudes and actions of Phèdre is more tangible, but still problematic. The default position seems to be to regard Œnone at best as 'an obtuse do-gooder [...], amoral, meddling, misconceived, morally purblind'.[23] Or again, 'Œnone incarne un esprit de compromission, qui ne respecte ni les lois ni les valeurs. [...] Elle n'est qu'un objet d'horreur, une image des « détestables flatteurs » qui poussent les puissants vers des forfaits'.[24] This view is apparently supported by Phèdre herself, whose two damning accusations of Œnone we have already seen:[25] 'Voilà comme tu m'as perdu' (IV, 6, 1309: 'Thus it is that you have caused my doom') and 'La détestable Œnone a conduit tout le reste' (V, 7, 1626: 'Detestable Œnone did the rest'). It is also supported to a certain extent by Racine in his *Préface*: 'Cette bassesse m'a paru plus convenable à une nourrice, qui pouvait avoir des inclinations plus serviles' (p. 577: 'This baseness seemed to me more appropriate to a nurse, who could well have more slave-like inclinations', p. 145). This leads her sometimes to be portrayed as a sort of witch figure, Phèdre's 'evil genius', egging her mistress on at every turn to take the next step in the implacable journey towards disaster. I think it makes the play more powerful in its investigation of moral dilemmas if you do not push that interpretation of Œnone too far. She does not have to be an aged crone – she is after all of an age to have suckled Phèdre, who herself is the mother of a young boy. Already in the *Préface* Racine had hinted at a defence of Œnone: 'qui néanmoins n'entreprend cette fausse accusation que pour sauver la vie et l'honneur de sa maîtresse' ('who nevertheless launches this false accusation only in order to save the life and honour of her mistress'). That defence has been taken up much more fully and effectively by Louis-Léonard Naneix and his arguments were rehearsed in the chapter on hamartia.[26] In much of her role she acts as wise counsellor – encouraging Phèdre to articulate her grief instead of bottling it up; pointing out the need to sort out the political situation when Thésée is reported dead; saving Phèdre

---

23   Donald Norman Levin, 'Phèdre and Œnone', *Rice University Studies*, 51 (1965), pp. 51–68 (p. 56 and p. 62).

24   Alain Viala, 'Commentaires', in Racine, *Phèdre* (Paris: Livre de Poche, 1985), pp. 100–101: 'Œnone embodies a spirit of compromise, respecting neither laws nor values. She is but an object of horror, a portrait of those "vile flatterers" who urge the powerful on to evildoing' (see IV, 6, 1323–35).

25   See Introduction, pp. 5, 10–11, 17–20.

26   L.-L. Naneix, *Phèdre l'incomprise* (Paris: La Pensée universelle, 1977), pp. 165–175. Cf. above p. 19 and pp. 74–5.

from brutal suicide at the end of act II; giving her perfectly good advice in
III, 3, 825–826:

> Il faut d'un vain amour étouffer la pensée,
> Madame. Rappelez votre vertu passée.

> [Your love is vain and you must stifle it,
> O Queen, and summon up your former strength.]

Only when that good advice is violently rejected by Phèdre and when she re-
affirms her intention to commit suicide, does Œnone, driven to despair, come
up with the ultimately immoral plan to lie about Hippolyte. In doing that she
is only following the example set by Phèdre herself in the play's 'back story',
when Phèdre had arranged for Hippolyte to be exiled from Athens by 'playing
the evil step-mother' – see I, 3, 291–296.

So I would give serious consideration to portraying Œnone as a much more
sympathetic figure – more like the nurses who accompany Shakespearean her-
oines (Juliet's Nurse, Desdemona's Emilia) – who is unfairly scapegoated by
Phèdre. Where we described Narcisse as a fall guy, Œnone is perhaps more
literally a scapegoat, one who truly assumes the responsibility which should
belong to another. This interpretation is effectively conveyed in a number of
modern productions. That by Pierre Jourdan, starring Marie Bell at the age of
68 in the title role, has the 73-year-old Mary Marquet as a dignified and compassionate Œnone.[27] A production by Christophe Rauck for the Théâtre du
Nord, performed at the Théâtre Gérard-Philipe in April 2014, did not shy away
from violent melodramatic effects but according to one anonymous online
reviewer achieved a certain intimacy in the relationship between Phèdre
and Œnone:

> La façon dont Phèdre traite la nourrice Œnone, lui reprochant régulière-
> ment et *a posteriori* toutes les idées qu'elle a pourtant suivies vaillam-
> ment, fait sourire, et cela interroge. La nourrice est-elle vraiment le
> personnage machiavélique et immoral dont Phèdre brosse le portrait ou
> n'est-elle que la victime des grands de ce monde, cruellement remerciée
> après les avoir servis de toute son âme ?[28]

---

27   It is available on DVD, OCLC number 946973669, and can sometimes be seen on Youtube.
     On 7 April 2020 it was available at https://www.youtube.com/watch?v=FIxUPxYNz5M.
28   https://lamaisonenverre.com/2014/03/10/phedre-de-christophe-rauck-une-belle-lecture
     -de-racine/, accessed 7 April 2020.

[Phèdre persistently reproaches her nurse Œnone, *a posteriori*, for all the ideas which she herself has intrepidly followed, and this treatment provokes a smile and a question. Is the nurse really the immoral Machiavellian character as depicted by Phèdre, or is she not the victim of secular authority, cruelly dismissed after whole-hearted service?]

3   Spouses and Other Partners

Considering the chord which the trope of the woman as temptress seems to strike in popular culture, it is perhaps surprising how rare are the examples in tragedy of wives who lead their husbands into wrongdoing. Even Lady Macbeth, who after Eve is the most obvious example, is a problematic case, and may turn out to be more scapegoat than villain. As with Œnone, it is not hard to build up a case against her. During the first third of Shakespeare's play, Macbeth is hesitant, confused, horrified at his own reaction to the suggestion by the weird sisters that he shall be king. It is Lady Macbeth who stiffens his resolve, by a caricaturally feminine combination of wile, seduction and manipulation, into going ahead with a plan which emerges rather cryptically, but which clearly the couple have had time to work out in some detail off stage, and it is she who overcomes his last-minute nerves. The deed done, it is she who takes control of the situation, ensuring that her shattered husband can appear clean and in nightclothes when the early visitors Macduff and Lennox arrive. And in most interpretations she diverts attention from the actions and mental condition of her husband by pretending to faint, thereby winning some time when they will be able to be private together before the post mortem proposed by Banquo. In at least one modern adaptation (the film directed by Geoffrey Wright)[29] the contrast between them at that point is underlined still further: it is she rather than Macbeth who speaks the lines beginning 'Who can be wise, amaz'd, temperate and furious, loyal and neutral, in a moment? No man'. He dwells helplessly on the horror of what has happened – the brutal execution of the chamberlains as well as the regicide itself – while she retains control and reason, albeit fraudulently. Those wishing to fix a major share of responsibility on her will further stress how her own descent into madness, her compulsive hand-washing and hallucinatory memories of the fatal night, all point to a guilty conscience. This is sometimes underlined still further by the presentation (or in filmic adaptations the portrayal) of her death as a suicide.

---

29   2006. Available as DVD REVD2532.

There have been adaptations of the play which take to an extreme this negative portrayal of the woman as primarily responsible for the outcome, most
clearly Akira Kurosawa's 1957 film *Throne of Blood*, where the equivalent character to Lady Macbeth is chillingly malevolent in her detached ambition. This
is reinforced by the use of Noh traditions, stylized action and facial expressions
suggestive of masks. Ionesco's Absurdist comedy *Macbett*, although it confuses
the issue by depicting an evil Lady Duncan as well as Lady Macbett, similarly
presents the aristocratic women as stylized personifications of evil. And yet,
as with Œnone, the situation and moral responsibility is not clearcut. Lady
Macbeth is not blamed or scapegoated by Macbeth to anything like the extent Œnone is by Phèdre, although *Macbeth* ends with a reference to the 'dead
butcher and his fiend-like queen' (v, 7, 99),[30] underlined by Malcolm's suggestion that her death was indeed a suicide. Although she supports Macbeth when
he falters, he himself is consistently the instigator of the actions. The idea of
murdering Duncan may come to them both independently, but it is initially
presented to her by him. His use in the letter of the phrase 'what greatness is
promised thee' could be seen as an invitation to her to become an accessory
and accomplice. It has been suggested that the reproach in I, 7, 47–8, 'What
beast was't then / That made you break this enterprise to me' must indicate
some conversation if not planning (at his instigation) between Macbeth and
his wife *prior* to the encounter with the weird sisters, since he had proposed it
at a time when 'Nor time nor place did adhere' (51–2) whereas they do now.[31]
He it is who actually murders Duncan, contributes to the faking of the evidence against the chamberlains and then kills them to prevent any possibility of counter-accusation. Above all, the actions against Banquo and Fleance,
and subsequently against Macduff's family, are carried out by Macbeth independently – indeed he explicitly excludes Lady Macbeth from involvement
in them: 'Be innocent of the knowledge, dearest chuck, till thou applaud the
deed' (III, 1, 48–9).

Detailed readings emphasize rather than resolve the tension. Lady Macbeth's
first instinct on reading her husband's letter is to feel and say that he will need
persuading, by 'my spirits in thine ear' (I, 5, 25) to 'catch the nearest way' (17),
and when she asserts that she is the more actively ambitious of the two, she
explicitly refers to what is lacking in him as an 'illness' (19). She calls on 'spirits'
and 'murdering ministers' to strengthen her own 'fell purpose' (39–47). Her
Adam needs his Eve, and she needs the support of the serpent. The similarities

---

30   All line references are to the Oxford World Classics edition by Nicholas Brooke (Oxford:
        Oxford University Press, 1990).

31   John Bayley, *Shakespeare* (London: Longman, 1929), p. 184.

and precise parallels between her language and that of the weird sisters points in the direction of her as another agent of Fate, and her intention is clearly to control her husband's mind and actions if she has to. She articulates this quite precisely: 'fate and metaphysical aid' might seem to offer him advancement, but she anticipates the need to overcome 'all that impedes' him from that end (27–8). Yet when Macbeth enters, the impression given by their quick-fire exchanges is more one of complicity and mutual understanding than of contrast. A director who wished to cling to the tradition of pinning the blame on Lady Macbeth could allow these comments to pass almost unnoticed, but Shakespeare did include them. If they are allowed their full potential significance they can set up a dynamic between the two characters that would make it harder for Macbeth to hide behind his wife's influence and pressure as an excuse for his actions. *Why* does he instantly mention the arrival of Duncan, before he has even expressed joy to be home with her? It could be done in a tone of urgency – we've got a royal visitor coming, get the housekeeper on the case. But it can also be made portentous, a response to Lady Macbeth's 'greater than both by the all-hail hereafter' (54). His delivery of the words 'Tomorrow – as he purposes' (59) is even more critical. Is there a dash there, or just a comma? At least one commentator is very precise:[32]

> 'As he purposes' says all that is needed for Lady Macbeth to know that he thinks of murdering his king, and her indirect answer communicates both her understanding and complicity in this.

Nevertheless, the dominant impression left by the scene is of a Lady Macbeth who is taking control. She insists (and thinks it necessary to point out) that Macbeth should disguise his true feelings, she implants in his mind the idea that he has to be braced for evil ('be the serpent under't', I, 5, 65), and she assumes responsibility for what is to happen: 'Put this night's great business under my despatch [...] Leave all the rest to me' (I, 5, 67–72). The last line is eerily reminiscent to us of Phèdre's 'Je m'abandonne à toi' (III, 3, 911: 'My fate is in your hands'). Although the roles are reversed, the situations are parallel: responsibility is transferred from the eventual agent to a second figure or accomplice, who will come to appear implicated in guilt for the act, fairly or unfairly.

The next confrontation between the Macbeths is even more critical, since it begins with Macbeth's strongest statement of refusal: 'We will proceed no further in this business' (I, 7, 31) – a firm, prosaic utterance which will be transformed less than fifty lines later (of which he has spoken barely a fifth) into

---

32   John Russell Brown, *Shakespeare: The Tragedies* (Basingstoke: Palgrave, 2001), p. 300.

'I am settled' (I, 7, 80). So the case against Lady Macbeth surely hinges on this scene: do we really believe that he would not have killed Duncan if she had not overcome his scruples with her mixture of mockery, taunting and encouragement? It is hard not to take it in that way at face value: a genuine moral scruple is dismissed as cowardice; a desire to hold onto a recently acquired 'golden' reputation (I, 7, 33) is mocked as fastidiousness; above all, his desire not to go beyond what is fitting for a 'man' (human) is twisted into a taunting challenge to his sense of 'manhood' (I, 7, 46–9). Not for the first time, we can be struck here by the contrast between the general view of Macbeth as a valiant and indeed ruthless warrior ('he unseam'd him from the nave to the chaps, and fix'd his head upon our battlements', I, 2, 22–3) and Lady Macbeth's picture of him as 'too full o' the milk of human kindness' (I, 5, 16). The argument is finely balanced. Does she persuade him so swiftly because he is really keen to proceed, or because she is amazingly persuasive?

In the end, the analysis of such nice distinctions and almost unanswerable questions may begin to seem fatuous. Whatever the shifting balance of blame and responsibility between the two protagonists at any one moment, it is quite clear that they are both guilty in a joint enterprise. It would almost be more interesting, at least legalistically, if we genuinely did not know which of the two had done the act of murder, since then the prosecution would be obliged to prove beyond reasonable doubt that party A, or separately party B, was guilty of murder rather than complicity. The UK law on 'joint enterprise' caused controversy in both 2016 and 2018, with sometimes bitter stand-offs between the relatives of murder victims on the one hand, and the families of those who had been convicted by association on the other.[33] Ideas like this are whimsically explored by the American humourist James Thurber in his short story, *The Macbeth Murder Mystery*.[34] In this wacky analysis, neither Macbeth nor Lady Macbeth did the deed, but each thinks that the other did so. The scenes of madness (Macbeth at the banquet, and the sleep-walking scene) are mere play-acting to shield the partner. But again, although fun, this is distracting, and the very fact that it seemed necessary to include this example in a chapter on scapegoating may reflect nothing more than the inherent tendency of patriarchy to seek to victimize the female as responsible for the ill-deeds of the male.

---

33   See for example http://www.bbc.co.uk/news/uk-35598896 and https://www.theguardian .com/law/ 2018/jan/25/senior-tories-urge-government-to-review-joint-enterprise-laws.

34   First published in *The New Yorker* in 1937, then included in *My World and Welcome to it* in 1942. See James Thurber, *The Thurber Carnival* (Harmondsworth: Penguin, 1945, reprinted 1976), pp. 83–86.

One way in which some modern adaptations of *Macbeth* have sought to explain if not exculpate the violence of Lady Macbeth's reactions is to make her
explicitly mourn the death of a child. This is not a random invention: it is as
plausible an explanation as any of the surface discrepancy between her claim
to have 'given suck' (I, 7, 54) and Macbeth's persistent bewailing the lack of a
male heir, and Macduff's claim that no response to the murder of his own children can be adequate because Macbeth has no children to kill in revenge (one
interpretation of IV, 3, 226). The film adaptation by Geoffrey Wright, set in the
drug subculture of Melbourne, opens in a cemetery where the Macbeth couple
are distractedly tending a child's grave, disturbingly surrounded by a trio of
rebellious convent schoolgirls violently desecrating as many religious monu-
ments as they can. These real girls return as figments of Macbeth's drug-fuelled
fancies to take on the role of the weird sisters in Shakespeare's play, which helps
to suggest that despite his more stoic attitude in the opening scene, he is no
less haunted than his distraught wife by the death of their son and everything
associated with that. The same device is used in Justin Kurzel's film adaptation
of 2015, which begins with the actual burial of a child, and this grief shared
between the Macbeths provides a context for the shared violence that follows.

Another married couple who indulge in extravagant mutual recriminations
in many versions of their story is Agamemnon and Clytemnestra. We have already explored their relationship,[35] but one peculiar sequence in Aeschylus'
Agamemnon invites consideration in connection with the theme of scapegoating. On his return from the Trojan War, Clytemnestra entices Agamemnon
to enter the palace along a carpet of expensive tapestries. Her motive in doing
so is hard to explain except as a means of putting her husband in the wrong –
making him guilty of pride, extravagance or even blasphemy – in order to give
herself an additional excuse for the murder which she has already decided
to commit. She has plenty of personal reasons for killing him: spite over his
connivance in the sacrifice of Iphigenia, jealous rage over his reputation as
womanizer, culminating in the presence of Cassandra at his side on his return, her own allegiance to Aegisthus and the power she shares with him in
practice. Perhaps she is aware that these do not provide sufficient justification.
If Agamemnon can be perceived by Argos as arrogant, vain and insufficiently
reverential, she might consciously (or more plausibly, unconsciously) feel that
her defence will be stronger.

Her initial welcome, effusive rather than warm, can be presented as setting a context for a degree of deviousness: the expected, but conventional,

---

35   'Provocation', pp. 130–154.

expression of joy at his homecoming turns into a scarcely veiled complaint about the cost for her of his long absence:[36]

> [...] that a woman should sit forlorn at home, unmanned,
> Is a crying grief,
> [...] and my sleepless eyes are sore
> With weeping by the lamp long lit for you in vain.

She then has her servants place crimson tapestries and silks before their master's feet. He must be aware that to walk on them would be an extravagant act, perhaps even blasphemous, since the tapestries were reserved for the use of gods, and would be destroyed by this action. If we are to attach any importance to the action in our analysis of Agamemnon's own guilt, however, it is important to stress his extreme reluctance to agree to Clytemnestra's bidding. His initial reaction is more than a little dismissive:

> Do not with these soft attentions woman me,
> [...] nor with your spread cloths invite
> Envy of gods, for honours due to gods alone.
> I count it dangerous, being mortal, to set foot
> On rich embroidered silks. I would be reverenced
> As man, not god.
>   918–924

This incenses Clytemnestra even further. Agamemnon seems to be aware of each of her motives for tempting him: he does not want to commit blasphemy, and he does not want to alienate observers within the palace. But Clytemnestra is merciless in her unrelenting browbeating. In a sequence of stichomythia she applies argument after argument:
- there is no shortage of such material in his home
- he should not oppose what is her first and only request on his return
- in the heat of battle he might have vowed to do such a thing as an offering in return for the gods' protection
- his enemy would not share his scruples
- he has no need to fear gossip or public reproach
- if he did have critics, they would be betraying their own cheap envy
- the victor ought in any case to grant favours.

---

36   Aeschylus, *Agamemnon*, 860–61 and 888–89. Translated by Philip Vellacott in Aeschylus, *The Oresteian Trilogy* (Harmondsworth: Penguin Books, 1959), pp. 72–3.

Agamemnon has plenty of rational answers to these points:
- he will not act against his own judgment
- there is no question of his having made a vow to behave in this way
- he has a healthy respect for the power and opinions of the people
- he would not wish to follow an enemy's bad example.

But in the end he rather lamely realizes the strength of her desire, and capitulates to that:

> Why, here's a battle! What would you not give to win?
> [...]
> Since you're resolved [...]
>
> 942–44

But still, returning to his starting point, he insists that he is doing this reluctantly and against his calculated better judgment:

> And as I tread
> This deep-sea treasure, may no watchful envious god
> Glance from afar. It offends modesty, that I
> Should dare with unwashed feet to soil these costly rugs.
>
> 945–48

It does seem very odd that anyone could argue that this sequence does anything at all to justify Clytemnestra later. It is certainly a curious scene, perhaps one that muddies the moral water a little, and dramatically effective in its symbolism although not to be given undue importance. It has been pointed out that Aeschylus' Clytemnestra is the most intelligent and manipulative portrayal of her in antiquity – less monstrous than Sophocles' bully but all the more chilling for that in her subversive evil – and this sequence may be a sophisticated manifestation of that intention.[37] Hugh Lloyd-Jones sums up the situation thus (edn, p. 67n):

> The scene's effect is truly tragic, for Agamemnon knows that what his wife proposes is wrong, and yet she persuades him to act against his better judgment. Would it be possible for her to persuade him if he were

[37] See Rachel M.E. Wolfe, 'Woman, Tyrant, Mother, Murderess: An Exploration of the Mythic Character of Clytemnestra in all her Forms', *Women's Studies: An Inter-disciplinary Journal*, 38 (2009), pp. 692–719 (p. 698), DOI: 10.1080/00497870903021554. Accessed 28 April 2020 at http://dx.doi.org/10.1080/00497870903021554.

not under a curse, so that (in the phraseology common to Aeschylus and
Homer) Zeus has sent Ate to take away his wits?

Note that of course the moral weighting of the arguments within the stichomythia sequence itself depends on how they are interpreted: the translator, the
director and the actors cannot but steer the spectator towards sympathy or disapproval for each argument, attitude and action. Scholars have taken different
views. E. Fraenkel defended Agamemnon as chivalrous and weary.[38] T.E. Page
saw the king as vain and arrogant, happily relieved to latch onto his wife's so-
phistic arguments, while H. Gundert argued that Agamemnon behaved badly
because he had been outwitted by Clytemnestra, after his wits had in the first
place been weakened by Zeus: this is associated with his dilemma at Aulis.[39]
Hugh Lloyd-Jones summarized these and other reactions to the scene, concluding that the truly tragic effect depends on a degree of balance between
them: Agamemnon as a tragic hero needs to be a figure of light and shade.[40]

4   Devils and Demons

Returning finally to the question with which this chapter began and which
has in a sense been underlying the whole book: what if anything is the role of
the Devil in human misjudgment or evil? Is he a *cause* of bad behaviour, an
excuse for it, or a *scapegoat*? The distinction between tragic agents and tragic
victims which was mentioned in passing in the chapter on hamartia (p. 55) has
not been a significant concern throughout this book, because we are looking
explicitly at decisions and actions for which extenuating circumstances might
be found: if the character has done nothing wrong there is no need for mitigation. However, there is an underlying paradox: if we find too many significant
mitigating factors for any given agents then by definition they become victims.
If it is a flaw in the universe that is ultimately responsible for misfortune, then
we are all off the hook. Since this was an unacceptable conclusion for western
religious orthodoxy in the early modern world, most dramatists reflected opposition to it by following biblical texts, selectively no doubt, in ascribing the

38   Eduard Fraenkel (ed.), *Aeschylus: Agamemnon* (Oxford: Oxford University Press, 2004),
        Volume II (Commentary).
39   H. Gundert, 'Agamemnon' in F. Eckstein (ed.), *ΘΕΩΡΙΑ, Festschrift für W.H. Schuchhardt*
        (Baden-Baden: Grimm, 1960), pp. 69–78.
40   H. Lloyd-Jones, 'The Guilt of Agamemnon', in *Classical Quarterly*, n.s. 12, 1962, pp. 187–199
        (p. 199).

blame for bad outcomes either directly to malevolent forces or indirectly to the effect of those forces on weak and fallen humanity.

Renaissance tragedy in France remained close to its roots in morality plays and devils are taken very seriously. In Jean de la Taille's *Saül le furieux*,[41] the biblical king Saul visits a woman at Endor to seek inspiration, specifically to ask her to summon up by sorcery the spirit of the dead prophet Samuel from whom he hopes to acquire enlightenment. She is described in the text as a 'Phytonisse'[42] or 'negromantienne', words which, as we have found before, cannot be translated until we have interpreted the reality they might represent. In the Authorized Version of the Bible she is described in English as a 'woman that hath a familiar spirit' (*1 Samuel*, 28:7), so in modern terms she would more properly be called a 'medium' than a 'witch' although the latter is the label most frequently attached to her, and it is used in some editions of the Authorized Version as a heading to the chapter or page. In La Taille's play she summons up a host of named demons and devils to force the spirit of Samuel – against his will and the will of his God – to return to earth so that Saul may seek his advice. There appear to be three categories: fallen angels, demons and devils. The first includes Lucifer:

> Vous anges encore
> Que l'arrogance fit avecques Lucifer
> Culbuter de l'Olympe au parfond de l'enfer.
> III, 642–4

[and also you angels whose arrogance set you tumbling with Lucifer from Olympus to the depths of Hell.]

Amongst devils she names Satan, Beelzebub, Leviathan, Belial and Belfegore. All these names have biblical authority,[43] and are identified either as personified forces of temptation or evil hostile to the Jewish God, or as heathen gods worshipped by races hostile to Israel. Whatever they represent in cosmological

---

41   Jean de La Taille, *Dramatic Works*, ed. Kathleen Hall and Christopher Smith (London: Athlone, 1972), pp. 19–65. References to this play will be to this edition, except that spelling has been modernized.

42   To add to the confusion, this word in modern French has become 'Pythonisse' and derives not from any Judaeo-Christian source but from the Classical Greek world; Pytho was the original name of Delphi, where Apollo's oracle was situated.

43   See above, 'Saul' (p. 162, note 15). Relevant biblical references are to *Job* 1, *Job* 41, *Deuteronomy* 13:13, *2 Kings* 1:2, *Numbers* 25:3, *Isaiah* 14:12. See the cited edition, p. 197, n. 39 for further details.

terms, the woman is clear that they have responsibility both for original sin
and for the ongoing wickedness of humankind:

> Et vous Diables lesquels fîtes au premier homme
> Goûter à ses dépens de la fatale Pomme,
> [...]
> Qui faites aux humains commettre tant d'abus.
>   III, 637–640

> [And you Devils, who made the first man taste the fatal apple, to his cost,
> and who make humans commit so many evils.]

King Saul of course, hears this speech and is subsequently deeply troubled by
it, since he is aware, and reminded in the course of the play, that it is against
the laws of God to use necromancy to seek guidance. So the woman blames
the devils for human misdemeanours but nevertheless blames Saul for forc-
ing her to use her powers in this way, while Saul effectively blames God for
making him lose his self-control (as a punishment for a different sin). This
vicious circle appears to present scapegoating in this play as an almost universal process.

An even earlier play, one which has some claim to be the first original
French text to be given the label 'tragedy', depicted the devil directly on stage.
Théodore de Bèze was a Burgundian scholar who as an ardent Protestant took
refuge in Lausanne (1549–58) and later settled in Geneva. As Professor of Greek
in Lausanne, alongside his learned work in theology and poetry, he wrote his
Abraham sacrifiant apparently in a whimsical spirit as light relief for a student
performance.[44] The character of Satan appears in the guise of a caricatured
Catholic monk, and is a pathetic and impotent figure rather than a threat to
the probity of Abraham. He claims responsibility for any doubt that Abraham
feels, much of which derives from objections, voiced by his wife Sara, to his carrying out God's inexplicable command to offer up his son Isaac as a sacrifice.
From his first entry, Satan expresses his frustration:

> Moi qui renverse et trouble tout,
> Ne puis pourtant venir à bout
> De ce faux vieillard obstiné.
> Quelque assaut qu'on lui ait donné,

---

44   Critical edition by Keith Cameron, Kathleen M. Hall and Francis Higman (Genève: Droz,
      1967). Line references are to this edition, but spelling has been modernized.

Le voilà parti de ce lieu,
Et tout prêt d'obéir à Dieu.
    501–6

[I who disrupt and overthrow everything, still can't get round this obsti-
nate and perverse old man. Despite my attacks on him, he's on his way,
quite determined to obey God.]

This Satan however never interacts directly with the characters on stage – he
is visible in his monk's vestments to the audience but is merely eavesdropping
on the characters' thoughts and speeches, and making it clear that his temptation to disobedience is having no impact. He manages to articulate a rather
Machiavellian interpretation of the situation as a 'win win' for himself – either
Abraham will disobey God's command, or he will suffer eternally for the loss
of his son:

[...] soit que son cœur change
Ou qu'il sacrifie en effet,
Ce que je prétends sera fait.
    508–10

[whether he changes his mind or actually carries out the sacrifice, I will
gain what I intend.]

Of greater interest are the thought-processes of Abraham himself about the
source of the divine command. His dilemma is not just that of a father faced
with the loss of his son, it is equally that of a believer to whom the words of
God are contradictory: God has promised to populate the world with his descendants, and now demands that the sole descendant be killed. On that basis,
Abraham speculates that the command itself may emanate not from God but
from the Devil as a temptation:

[...] car tant plus j'examine
Ce cas ici, plus je le trouve étrange.
C'est quelque songe, ou bien quelque faux ange
Qui m'a planté ceci en la cervelle.
    728–31

[for the more I examine this whole affair, the stranger I find it. It's a dream,
or some impostor angel has planted this idea in my head.]

Hamlet will similarly consider the possibility that the ghost of his father is a
demon sent to mislead him:

> The Spirit that I have seen
> May be the devil.
>
> *Hamlet*, II, 2, 594–5

Neither Catholic nor Protestant orthodoxy could contemplate a ghost operat-
ing in this way (apparently suffering the conventional punishment of purga-
tory by day, but wandering the surface of the physical earth by night), and in
general it is the inscrutability of supernatural operations that provide humankind with a blanket excuse in such cases. This is the sort of manipulative behaviour ascribed wittily to the devil in C.S. Lewis's *Screwtape Letters*,[45] where
all that the followers of Satan on earth have to do is sow seeds of doubt and
confusion in God's servants to undermine their confidence. Evil is a very sur-
reptitious force, which is scarcely designed to generate high drama.

In any case, as tragedy moved further away from its local roots in morality
plays and rediscovered the power of the ancients, and as Europe approached
the Enlightenment, there was a corresponding rejection of drama as a confrontation of supra-human forces for good and evil. Even in Racine's biblical plays,
Esther and *Athalie*, where belief systems are pitted against each other (and
there is no doubt as to which the viewer is intended to support), the dramatist
is at pains to ensure that the good/evil dichotomy is not too simplistic and
clearcut. Assuérus and even Athalie have redeeming characteristics, and Joad
has unattractive qualities and moments of weakness. To be sure, there are examples of characters even in great tragedy who appear to be vehicles of pure
and gratuitous evil – Iago is perhaps the clearest example. But in general, it is
necessary for the operation of tragedy that the forces opposing the human protagonist are not overwhelming: as the cosmology approaches Manichaeism,
the drama approaches pantomime.

Returning finally to *Macbeth*, we meet the figures who raise the most tantalizing questions about the nature of evil and its existence external to the human
character committing it. The identity of the weird sisters and the power which
they represent – whether to cause action or simply to predict it, and in the
latter case with what degree of self-fulfilling inevitability – remain ambiguous
and unclear. They are never referred to in the play itself as 'witches': indeed the
most obvious reading of the opening section of I, 3 suggests that they consider

---

45   First published by Geoffrey Bles in 1942. London: Collins, Fontana Books, 1955.

this to be an extreme insult.[46] They are not mere figments of Macbeth's imagi-
nation, as Banquo both sees and hears them, but they give both witnesses the
impression of appearing and disappearing at will. Every one of their cryptic
predictions does come true, and the only one which appears to depend on
Macbeth's intervention is his inheritance of the throne by regicide. Could he
therefore with any justification claim that they represent an irresistible force,
whether of temptation, of suggestion or even of compulsion?

Their responses and activities in I, 1 and I, 3 appear random and direction-
less, but they are aware (I, 1, 7) that they are going to meet Macbeth, and in
I, 3 before the arrival of Macbeth and Banquo, they hint at deliberate planning – 'Peace, the charm's wound up' (I, 3, 37). We never discover how they
have gained the inside information that Macbeth is already Thane of Cawdor,
or the logic by which they extrapolate his possible ambition to be king hereafter (whether or not there had been prior private discussion of this possibility
between Macbeth and his wife). As soon as the news of the first promotion is
confirmed, Banquo exclaims 'What, can the devil speak true?' (I, 3, 107); later
'oftentimes, to win us to our harm, / The instruments of darkness tell us truths'
(I, 3, 124–25) – so he at least is aware of a potential pressure on Macbeth to
bring the prophecies to reality.

In practice, Macbeth does not claim for himself the degree of helplessness
associated with Greek or Racinian tragic figures: on the contrary he knows in
the first act that he has a decision to make, and almost makes the right and
moral one. Nevertheless, there is a sense in which the sisters represent Fate or
the Fates – that is what the word weyward or Weïrd meant in Anglo-Saxon mythology – and so we cannot altogether dismiss the possibility that they inflict
on Macbeth an inescapable urge to act. Apart from a passing mention in his
penultimate speech of the 'juggling fiends' who have 'paltered' with him 'in a
double sense' (V, 7, 49–50, p. 208), he does not articulate this as an excuse on
his own behalf, and in some circumstances this might make an observer more
rather than less sympathetic towards him. Whether his evil acts are triggered
by forces internal or external to him, his acceptance of responsibility for them
is at one level admirable despite his desperate defiance at the end.

The sisters may be conceived as incarnations of devilish forces, as agents of
the devil, or as mischievous humans with some mysterious insight into forces
beyond normal comprehension. Whatever the original serpent in the Garden
of Eden was, it was not literally a serpent – it had the power of human speech
and of logical argument, and the human characteristic of subtlety. Yet the Bible
does posit elsewhere the existence of the Devil, for whom that serpent 'whose

---

46   *Macbeth*, edn. cit., p. 100.

guile, stirred up with envy and revenge, deceived the mother of mankind'[47] becomes an allegory or a direct agent: 'And the great dragon was cast out, that old
serpent called the Devil, and Satan, which deceiveth the whole world'.[48] It is
plausible that the historic name of Macbeth's armour-bearer Seton or Seaton,
was changed by Shakespeare to Seyton to hint at a devilish presence, visually
reinforced by the possibility that the actor had previously played the part of
one of the sisters, or that of Lady Macbeth herself.[49]

   What is blamed for humankind's sinful self-consciousness in the Garden of
Eden story is an external force, explicitly opposed to God, humanity and good,
which achieves its object by deceitful manipulation. It is easy enough – indeed
manifestly too easy – to argue that Eve should have resisted his blandishments.
Although the woman, when tempted, instantly repeats the words of the com-
mandment, the narrative does not tell us that she received it direct from God:
it was delivered by God to Adam before Eve was created, and it may have been
Adam rather than God who transmitted it to Eve herself. The fact remains,
within the logic of this story, that Eve and Adam both knew that it was wrong
to eat the fruit. Eve has the excuse that she was lied to about the nature of the
fruit, and implicitly the nature of God. Adam, on the face of it, is less easily
excusable: he is simply seduced by the attractiveness of what is offered. Each
of them is deeply conscious of the shame attached to their action and tries to
pass the responsibility for it to someone else. The judge involved within the
story rejects the adequacy of their excuse and metes out harsh punishments
on all three and their offspring. Where does the impartial observer stand, and
what impact if any might this familiar example of scapegoating have on our
reactions to the other excuses for shameful action we have been observing?

   In the end, like so much else, it is a matter of perspective. If characters in a
play feel they are in the grip of a malevolent force which cannot be resisted,
then they will believe themselves to be victims rather than agents of evil. If the
theatre audience, in its now familiar role of jury, share the characters' perspective and accept their excuses, then their fate seems unjust, the universe flawed,
and we are outraged rather than healthily cleansed by the experience. On the
other hand, if the audience dismisses the characters too peremptorily as superstitious fools, then a sympathetic connection is unlikely to be forged; the characters are unpalatable, and our witnessing of their experience can scarcely
transform us. Only the intermediate case generates the special experience for

---

John Milton, *Paradise Lost*, I, 34–36.
48 *Revelation*, 12.9.
49 See Brooke's edition pp. 85 and 199. However, Kenneth Muir, in his edition of the play
    (London: Routledge, 1951), p. 146, had dismissed this as a 'wild suggestion'.

which I would wish to reserve the term 'tragedy': the audience does not glibly share the characters' experience of outraged helplessness, but it does concede that under the circumstances represented, a reasonable man or woman might genuinely suffer that experience. Then we can pity them, because we accept that sufficient extenuation exists for their disastrous actions; we can empathize fearfully with them because it is not too implausible that similar circumstances could impinge on us and suck us into similarly uncomfortable decisions; and this realization, when it works at its best, can lead to remarkable discoveries about our own intrinsic worth. In the end, no-one can expect a life verdict of innocent, but we would be reasonably happy with 'guilty but with mitigating features'. If tragic drama can help us to believe that about ourselves and our neighbours, then not only will it have given pleasure, it will also have served a noble social purpose.

Bibliography

All web links included in the footnotes and bibliography have been rechecked in June 2020.

Primary Sources

Aeschylus, *The Complete Plays of Aeschylus*, ed. Gilbert Murray (London: George Allen & Unwin, 1952).

Aeschylus, *The Oresteian Trilogy*, trans. P. Vellacott (Harmondsworth: Penguin, 1965).

Aeschylus, *The Oresteia*, trans. Robert Fagles (London: Wildwood House, 1976).

Aeschylus, *Agamemnon*, trans. Hugh Lloyd-Jones (Englewood Cliffs, NJ: Prentice-Hall, 1970).

Aeschylus, *Agamemnon*, ed. Eduard Fraenkel (Oxford: Oxford University Press, 2004).

Anouilh, Jean, *Tu étais si gentil quand tu étais petit*, in his *Pièces secrètes* (Paris: La Table Ronde, 1977).

Aristotle, *The Poetics*, trans. J. Hutton (New York/London: WW Norton, 1982).

Aristotle, *The Poetics*, trans. Stephen Halliwell (Cambridge MA/London: Harvard University Press, Loeb Classical Library, 1995).

Aristotle, *Nicomachean Ethics*, ed. Sarah Broadie and Christopher Rowe (Oxford: Oxford University Press, 2002).

Bèze, Théodore de, *Abraham sacrifiant*, ed. Keith Cameron, Kathleen M. Hall and Francis Higman (Genève: Droz, 1967).

Cocteau, Jean, *La Machine infernale*, ed. W.M. Landers (London: Harrap, 1957).

Corneille, P., *Théâtre complet*, ed. G. Couton (Paris: Garnier, 3 vols., 1971).

Du Ryer, Pierre, *Lucrèce*, eds. James F. Gaines and Perry Gethner (Genève: Droz, 1994).

Du Ryer, Pierre, *Saül*, ed. Maria Miller (Toulouse: Société de littératures classiques, 1996).

Euripides, *Plays: One*, ed. J. Michael Walton (London: Methuen, 1988).

Euripides, *Plays: I*, ed. David Kovacs (Cambridge, MA: Harvard University Press, Loeb Classical Library, 1994).

Euripides, *Medea and Other Plays*, trans. James Morwood (Oxford: Oxford University Press, Oxford World Classics, 1998).

Euripides, *Medea*, ed. Donald J. Mastronarde (Cambridge: Cambridge University Press, 2002).

Euripides, *Medea*, trans. Michael Collier and Georgia Machemer (Oxford: Oxford University Press, 2006).

Euripides, *Suppliant Women, Electra, Heracles*, trans. D Kovacs (Cambridge, MA: Harvard University Press, 1998).

Euripides, *Hippolytos*, trans. Michael Halleran (Oxford: Aris and Phillips, 1995).

Euripides, *Alcestis and Other Plays* ed. Richard Rutherford, trans. John Davie (London: Penguin Books, 1996).

Gide, André, *Œdipe*, in his *Théâtre* (Paris: Gallimard, 1942), pp. 249–304.

Gide, André, *Saül,* in his *Théâtre* (Paris: Gallimard, 1942), pp. 7–151.

Giraudoux, Jean, *Electre*, in his *Théâtre* (Paris: Grasset, 1959).

Grillparzer, Franz, *Medea*, ed. Friedrich Schreyvogl (Salzburg: Bergland-Buch, 1984).

Harrison, Tony, *The Oresteia* (London: Rex Collings, 1981).

Harrison, Tony, *Dramatic Verse 1973-1985* (Newcastle upon Tyne: Bloodaxe Books, 1985).

Kennelly, Brendan, *Medea* (Newcastle-upon-Tyne: Bloodaxe Books, 1991).

La Mesnardière, Hippolyte-Jules Pilet de, *Poétique* (Paris: Sommaville, 1639).

La Taille, Jean de, *Dramatic Works*, ed. Kathleen M. Hall and C.N. Smith (London: Athlone, 1972).

Lamartine, Alphonse de, *Saül*, in his *Œuvres complètes* (Paris: chez l'auteur, 1860), vol. 3, pp. 333–437.

Lochhead, Liz, *Medea* (London: Nick Hern Books, 2000).

Longepierre, Hilaire-Bernard de Requeleyne, baron de, *Médée*, ed. T. Tobari (Paris: Nizet, 1967).

Nadal, l'abbé Augustin, *Saül* (Paris: Ribou, 1731).

Pascal, Blaise, *Les Provinciales*, ed. L. Cognet and G. Ferreyrolles (Paris: Bordas, 1992).

Racine, Jean, *Théâtre complet*, ed. J. Morel and A. Viala (Paris: Garnier, 1980).

Racine, Jean, *Athalie*, ed. Peter France (Oxford: Oxford University Press, 1966).

Racine, Jean, *Andromache/Britannicus/Berenice*, trans. J. Cairncross (Harmondsworth: Penguin, 1967).

Racine, Jean, *Iphigenia/Phaedra/Athaliah*, trans. J. Cairncross (Harmondsworth: Penguin, 1963).

Raine, Craig, *1953* (London: Faber & Faber, 1990).

Rotrou, Jean, *Hercule mourant*, ed. D.A. Watts (Exeter: University of Exeter, 1971).

Sartre, Jean-Paul, *Les Mouches* (Paris: Gallimard, Folio, 1990).

Seneca, *Tragedies*, trans. J.G. Fitch (Cambridge, MA: Harvard University Press, 2004).

Seneca, *Six Tragedies*, trans. E. Wilson (Oxford: Oxford World's Classics, 2010).

Seneca, *Medea*, ed. A.J. Boyle (Oxford: Oxford University Press, 2014).

Seneca, *Hercules furens: A Critical Text with Introduction and Commentary* by J.G. Fitch (Ithaca, NY: Cornell University Press, 1987).

Shakespeare, William, *Macbeth*, ed. Nicholas Brooke (Oxford: Oxford University Press, 1990).

Six Greek Tragedies, ed. J.M. Walton (London: Methuen Drama, 2002).

Sophocles, *Oedipus the King, Oedipus at Colonus* and *Antigone*, trans F. Storr (Cambridge, MA: Harvard University Press, 1912).

Sophocles, *The Theban Plays*, trans. E.F. Watling (Harmondsworth: Penguin, 1947).

Sophocles, *The Three Theban Plays*, trans. Robert Fagles (Harmondsworth: Penguin, 1984).

Sophocles, *The Theban Plays*, ed. and trans. Ruth Fainlight and Robert J. Littman (Baltimore: Johns Hopkins University Press, 2009).

Sophocles, *Oedipus Rex*, ed. R.D. Dawe (Cambridge: CUP, Cambridge Greek and Latin Classics, 1982).

Sophocles, *Electra and other plays*, trans. E.F. Watling (Harmondsworth: Penguin Classics, 1953).

Sophocles, *Antigone, Women of Trachis, Philoctetes, Oedipus at Colonus*, trans. Hugh Lloyd-Jones (Cambridge, MA: Harvard University Press, 1994).

Sophocles, *Ajax, Electra, Oedipus tyrannus*, ed. and trans. Hugh Lloyd-Jones (Cambridge, MA: Harvard UP, 1994).

Sophocles, *Women of Trachis*, trans. C.K. Williams and Gregory W. Dickerson (New York: Oxford University Press, 1978).

Tabori, George, *M: nach Euripides* (*M: after Euripides*) (Berlin: Kiepenheuer, 1995).

Teevan, Colin, *Alcmaeon in Corinth* (London: Oberon Books, 2004).

Varoujean, Jean-Jacques, *La Ville en haut de la colline* (Paris: Gallimard, Le Manteau d'Arlequin, 1969).

Voltaire, *Œdipe*, in his *Œuvres complètes* (Paris: Garnier, 1877), vol. 2.

Voltaire, *Saül*, in his *Œuvres complètes* (Paris: Garnier, 1877), vol. 5.

Yourcenar, Marguerite, *Clytemnestre ou Le Crime*, in the collection *Feux* (Paris: Grasset, 1936).

Yourcenar, Marguerite, *Electre ou La Chute des masques* in her *Théâtre II* (Paris: Gallimard, 1971).

Secondary Sources

Ahl, Frederick M., *Two Faces of Oedipus: Sophocles' Oedipus Tyrannus and Seneca's Oedipus* (Ithaca, NY: Cornell University Press, 2008).

Allen, A.L., *The New Ethics: A Guided Tour of the 21st-century Moral Landscape* (New York: Hyperion, Miramax Books, 2004).

Austin, J.L., 'A plea for excuses', in J.L. Austin, *Philosophical Papers*, ed. J.O. Urmson and G.J. Warnock (Oxford: Clarendon Press, 1961, 3rd edition, 1979), pp. 175–204.

Avant-Scène Théâtre, 499, 1972 (issue on Anouilh's *Tu étais si gentil quand tu étais petit*).

Barnes, Annie, 'La Prophétie de Joad', in W.G. Moore (ed.), *The French Mind* (Oxford: Oxford University Press, 1952), pp. 90–108.

Bates, Alfred, *The Drama: Its History, Literature and Influence on Civilization* (London: Historical Publishing Company, 1906), vol. 1.

Bates, W.N., *Euripides: A Student of Human Nature* (New York: Russell and Russell, 1930, reissued 1969).

Bayley, John, *Shakespeare* (London: Longman, 1929).

Beauvoir, Simone de, *Le Deuxième Sexe* (Paris: Gallimard, 1949).

Berger, A., *Encyclopedic Dictionary of Roman Law* (Philadelphia: The American Philosophical Society, 1953).

Bigel, J.-P., 'L'expression de la passion : Etude stylistique et dramaturgique de *Phèdre*', in P.L. Assoun (ed.) *Analyses et Réflexions sur Phèdre de Racine : La passion* (Paris: Marketing, Ellipses, 1983), pp. 34–43.

Booth, K., T. Dunne and M. Cox (eds.), *How Might We Live? Global Ethics in a New Century* (Cambridge: Cambridge University Press, 2001).

Bradley, A.C., *Shakespearean Tragedy: Lectures on Hamlet, Othello, King Lear, Macbeth* (London: Macmillan, 1905/London: Penguin, 1991/3rd edition Basingstoke: Macmillan, 1992).

Brée, Germaine, *Gide* (New Brunswick, NJ: Rutgers University Press, 1963).

Bremer, J.M., *Hamartia: Tragic Error in the Poetics of Aristotle and in Greek Tragedy* (Amsterdam: Hakkert, 1969).

Brereton, G., *Principles of Tragedy* (London: RKP/Florida: University of Miami Press, 1968).

Brooks, P., *Troubling Confessions: Speaking Guilt in Law and Literature* (Chicago/London: UCP, 2000).

Brown, John Russell, *Shakespeare: The Tragedies* (Basingstoke: Palgrave, 2001).

Burton, Mandy, 'Sentencing Domestic Homicide upon Provocation: Still "Getting Away with Murder"', *Feminist Legal Studies*, 11, 2003, pp. 279–289.

Butcher, S.H., *Aristotle's Theory of Poetry and Fine Art with a Critical Text of the Poetics* (London: Macmillan, 1895, fourth edition 1907, reissued 1951).

Butler, Judith, *Precarious Life* (London/New York: Verso, 2004).

Buxton, R.G.A., 'Blindness and Limits: Sophocles and the Logic of Myth', in Harold Bloom (ed.), *Sophocles: Modern Critical Views* (New York: Chelsea House Publishers, 1990), pp. 105–126.

Bywater, I., *Aristotle on the Art of Poetry* (Oxford: Clarendon Press, 1909).

Bywater, I., *Aristotle on the Art of Poetry*, with a Preface by Gilbert Murray (Oxford: Oxford University Press, 1920).

Calder, Ruth, '"La seule pensée du crime ...": the Question of Moral Rigour in *Phèdre*', *Seventeenth-century French Studies*, 20, 1998, pp. 45–56.

Calder, Ruth, 'Contrition, Casuistry and Phèdre's Sense of Sin', *Seventeenth-century French Studies*, 21, 1999, pp. 113–122.

Campbell, John, 'Racine and the Augustinian inheritance: the case of *Andromaque*', *French Studies*, 53, 1999, pp. 279–91.

Campbell, John, *Questioning Racinian Tragedy* (Chapel Hill: North Carolina Studies in the Romance Languages and Literatures, 281, 2005).

Cleary, Phil, *Just Another Little Murder* (St Leonard's, NSW: Allen and Unwin, 2002).

Cooper, Lane, *The Poetics of Aristotle: its Meaning and Influence* (first published 1923; Westport, Conn.: Greenwood Press, 1972).

Dalla Valle, D., 'Inceste et mythe dans le théâtre français du XVIIᵉ siècle', in J. Morel (ed.), *Littératures classiques*, 16, 1992: *La Tragédie*, pp. 181–197.

Dixon, W. MacNeile, *Tragedy* (London: Edward Arnold, 1924).

Domon, Hélène, '*Médée ou l'Autre*', *Cahiers du Dix-Septième. An Interdisciplinary Journal*, 1987, pp. 88–93.

Duchêne, Roger, 'Punition et compassion: tragédie et morale chez Racine', in Madeleine Bertaud (ed.), *Travaux et Littérature: offerts en hommage à Noémi Hepp* (Paris: Adirel, 1990), pp. 85–93.

Eagleton, Terry, *Sweet Violence: The Idea of the Tragic* (Oxford: Blackwell, 2003).

Esler, Philip, *Sex, Wives and Warriors: Reading Biblical Narrative with its Ancient Audience* (Eugene, OR: Wipf and Stock, 2011).

Evans, C.F., *Saint Luke* (London: SCM Press, 2008).

Fagan, S., S.M., *Has Sin Changed?: A Book on Forgiveness* (Dublin: Gill & Macmillan, 1977).

Feldman, Louis, 'Josephus' View of Saul' in Carl Ehrlich and Marsha White (eds.), *Saul in Story and Tradition* (Tübingen: Mohr Siebeck, 2006).

Fischer, John Martin, *The Metaphysics of Free Will* (Oxford: Blackwell, 1994).

Forman, Edward, 'Lyrisme et tragique dans l'*Athalie* de Racine', in Martine de Rougement et al. (eds.), *Dramaturgies/Langages dramatiques* (Paris: Nizet, 1986), pp. 307–313.

Forman, Edward, '"Je commence à rougir": Shame, Self-esteem and Guilt in the Presentation of Racine's Hippolyte', in K. Cameron & E. Woodrough (eds.), *Ethics and Politics in Seventeenth-century France* (University of Exeter Press, 1996), pp. 233–243.

Forman, Edward, 'Spirit, will and autonomy in Racine's later tragedies', in *Biblio 17* (supplements to *Papers on French Seventeenth-century Literature*), 101, 1997, pp. 273–281.

Frye, Northrop, *The Great Code: The Bible and Literature* (New York: Harcourt Brace Jovanovich, 1982).

Gil, Isabela Capeloa, 'Femininity as Trauma in R. Jeffers' *Medea* and G. Tabori's *M*', in Pascual Nieves, *Witness to Pain: Essays on the Translation of Pain into Art* (Bern: Peter Lang, 2005), pp. 186–208.

Gilbert, A.H., *Literary Criticism, Plato to Dryden* (Detroit: Wayne State University Press, 1962).

Grégoire, Vincent, 'Bruits et rumeurs dans les tragédies de Racine', *Papers in French Seventeenth-century Literature*, 24, 1997, pp. 383–94.

Gundert, H., 'Agamemnon' in F. Eckstein (ed.), *ΘΕΩΡΙΑ, Festschrift für W.H. Schuchhardt* (Baden-Baden: Grimm, 1960), pp. 69–78.

Gunn, D, *The Fate of King Saul* (Sheffield: JSOT, 1980).

Hall, Edith, 'Medea and the Mind of the Murderer' in Heike Bartel and Anne Simon (eds.), *Unbinding Medea* (London: MHRA, 2010), pp. 16–24.

Hammond, Nicholas, 'Educating Joas: The Power of Memory in *Athalie*', *Seventeenth-century French Studies*, 22, 2000, pp. 107–14.

Hammond, Paul, *The Strangeness of Tragedy* (Oxford: Oxford University Press, 2009).

Hanks, Robert, 'Medea – the fatal attraction' in *The Independent*, 14 April, 1996, accessed at http://www.independent.co.uk/arts-entertainment/medea-the-fatal-attraction-1305049.html.

Haynes, Natalie, *The Amber Fury* (London: Corvus, 2014).

Henn, T.R., *The Harvest of Tragedy* (London: Methuen, 1956).

Higgs, Liz Curtis, *Really Bad Girls of the Bible* (Colorado Springs, CO: Waterbrook Press, 2000).

Hillman, Richard, *Self-speaking in Medieval and Early Modern English Drama* (Basingstoke: Macmillan, 1997).

Horder, J., *Provocation and Responsibility* (Oxford: Clarendon Press, 1992).

House, H., *Aristotle's Poetics: A Course of Eight Lectures, Revised with Preface by C. Hardie* (London: Rupert Hart-Davis, 1956).

Howarth, W.D., '"A Hero like ourselves": A Theoretical Commonplace Re-examined', in U. Horstmann and W. Zach (eds.), *Kunstgriffe: Festschrift für Herbert Mainusch* (Frankfurt am Main: Peter Lang, n.d., c. 1990), pp. 152–162.

Hyde, I., 'The Tragic Flaw: is it a Tragic Error?', *The Modern Language Review*, 58, 1963, pp. 321–25.

Iglesias, I., 'Vergüenza ajena', in R. Harré & G. Parrott (eds.), *The Emotions* (London: Sage, 1996), pp. 122–131.

Jaquier, Véronique and Joëlle Vuille, *Les femmes et la question criminelle : Délits commis, expériences de victimisation et professions judiciaires* (Zurich/Genève: Editions Seismo, 2017).

Knight, R.C., 'A Minimal Definition of 17th-century Tragedy', *French Studies*, 10, 1956, pp. 297–308.

Korzeniowska, Victoria B., 'Feminine Justice and Morality in Giraudoux's *Electre* and Yourcenar's *Electre ou la Chute des Masques*', *Forum for Modern Language Studies*, 38, 2002, pp. 14–23.

Law Commission, *A New Homicide Act for England and Wales?: A Consultation Paper*. London: Stationery Office, Law Commission Consultation Paper no. 177, 2006.

Lee, Cynthia, *Murder and the Reasonable Man: Passion and Fear in the Criminal Courtroom* (New York/London: New York University Press, 2003).

Levin, Donald Norman, 'Phèdre and Œnone', *Rice University Studies*, 51, 1965, pp. 51–68.

Lewis, C.S., *The Screwtape Letters* (first published Geoffrey Bles, 1942, London: Collins, Fontana Books, 1955).

Lewis, H.B., *Shame and Guilt in Neurosis* (New York: International Universities Press, 1971).

Lloyd-Jones, H., 'The Guilt of Agamemnon', *Classical Quarterly*, n.s. 12, 1962, pp. 187–199.

March, Jennifer R., *The Creative Poet: Studies on the Treatment of Myths in Greek Poetry* (London: Institute of Classical Studies, Bulletin Supplement 49, 1987, pp. 47–77).

McDonald, Marianne, 'Medea as Politician and Diva: Riding the Dragon into the Future', in J.J. Clauss and S.I. Johnston (eds), *Medea: Essays on Medea in Myth, Literature, Philosophy and Art* (Princeton NJ: Princeton UP, 1997), pp. 297–324.

McEachern, Claire Elizabeth, 'Two Loves I Have: Of Comfort and Despair in Shakespearean Genre', *British Journal of Aesthetics*, 54, 2014, pp. 191–211.

Miller, Madeline, *Circe* (first published 2018, London: Bloomsbury, 2019).

Naneix, L.-L., *Phèdre l'incomprise* (Paris: La Pensée universelle, 1977).

Nciko, Arnold, 'Ignorance of the Law is no Defence', *Strathmore Law Review*, 3, 2018, pp. 25–47.

Nicholson, Sarah, 'Catching the Poetic Eye: Saul Reconceived in Modern Literature', in Carl Ehrlich and Marsha White (eds.), *Saul in Story and Tradition* (Tübingen: Mohr Siebeck, 2006), pp. 308–33.

Nussbaum, Martha, 'Serpents in the Soul: A Reading of Seneca's *Medea*', in James Clauss and Sarah Johnston, eds., *Medea: Essays on Medea in Myth, Literature, Philosophy, and Art* (Princeton, N.J.: Princeton University Press, 1997), pp. 219–250.

Nussbaum, Martha, *The Fragility of Goodness: Luck and Ethics in Greek Tragedy and Philosophy* (Cambridge: Cambridge University Press, first published 1986, revised edition 2001).

Nuttall, A.D., *Why Does Tragedy Give Pleasure?* (Oxford: Clarendon Press, 1996).

O'Donovan, Katherine, 'Defences for Battered Women Who Kill', *Journal of Law and Society*, 18, 1991, pp. 219–240.

Omesco, Ion, *La Métamorphose de la tragédie* (Paris: Presses Universitaires de France, 1978).

Pattison, S., *Shame: Theory, Therapy, Theology* (Cambridge: CUP, 2000).

Pintiaux, Benjamin, '*Médée* within the Repertory of the *tragédie en musique*: Intertextual Links and the "Posterity" of Charpentier's Opera', in Shirley Thompson (ed.), *New Perspectives on Marc-Antoine Charpentier* (Farnham: Ashgate, 2010), pp. 251–268.

Poole, A., *Tragedy, Shakespeare and the Greek Example* (Oxford: Blackwell, 1988).

Poole, A., *Tragedy: A Very Short Introduction* (Oxford: OUP, 2005).

Rouch, Dominique, *Amour à mort : enquête sur les crimes passionnels* (Paris: Hachette/ Carrère, 1992).

Sayer, John, *Jean Racine: Life and Legend* (Bern: Peter Lang, 2006).

Schneider, C., *Shame, Exposure and Privacy* (New York: W.W. Norton, 1987).

Schweitzer, Zoé, '"Si vous ne craignez rien que je vous trouve à plaindre." Violence et pouvoirs dans la *Médée* de Corneille', *Comparatismes en Sorbonne*, 2, 2011, pp. 5–18.

Sheridan, Alan, *André Gide: A Life in the Present* (Harmondsworth: Penguin, 1998).

Short, J.P., 'The Concept of Fate in the Tragedy of Racine', in J.C. Ireson et al. (eds.), *Studies in French Literature presented to H.W. Lawton* (Manchester/New York: Manchester UP, 1968), pp. 315–29.

Silverman, Paul H., 'Rethinking genetic determinism: with only 30,000 genes, what is it that makes humans human?', *The Scientist*, 24 May 2004, pp. 32ff.

Slovenko, Ralph, *Psychiatry and Criminal Culpability* (New York: Wiley, 1995).

Snaith, Guy, 'Andromache, Annette and Andromaque: A Look at Two Recent Translations', *Seventeenth-century French Studies*, 13, 1991, pp. 139–152.

Snaith, Guy, '*1953*: An *Andromaque* for our Times', *French Studies Bulletin*, 59, 1996, pp. 15–16.

Snell, Bruno, *The Discovery of the Mind in Greek Philosophy and Literature* (New York: Dover, 1982).

Snyder, C.R., R.L. Higgins and R.J. Stucky, *Excuses: Masquerades in Search of Grace* (New York: Wiley, 1983).

Soare, Antoine, 'Néron et Narcisse ; ou le mauvais mauvais conseiller', *Seventeenth-century French Studies*, 18, 1996, pp. 145–157.

Stalloni, Y., 'Hippolyte ou la passion impossible', in P.L. Assoun (ed.), *Analyses et Réflexions sur Phèdre de Racine : La passion* (Paris: Marketing, Ellipses, 1983), pp. 72–76.

Stinton, T.C.W., 'Hamartia in Aristotle and Greek Tragedy', *Classical Quarterly*, 25, 1975, pp. 221–254.

Sylvester, Joy, 'Will the Real Médée Please Step Forward ?', *Didaskalia: The Journal For Ancient Performance*, 1, 1994, available online: http://www.didaskalia.net/issues/ supplement1/sylvester.html.

Tarnopolsky, Christina H., *Prudes, Perverts, and Tyrants: Plato's Gorgias and the Politics of Shame* (Princeton, NJ: Princeton University Press, 2010).

Tennant, Edward E., *The Future of the Diminished Responsibility Defence to Murder* (Chichester: Barry Rose Law Publishers, 2001).

Tomotani, Tomoki, 'La faute tragique dans le théâtre classique français : La Mesnardière, Corneille, Racine', available online: http://www.waseda.jp/bun-france/pdfs/Vol18/ Tomotani.pdf.

Torrance, Isabelle, 'The Infanticidal Mother in Alejandro Amenábar's film *The Others*', in Heike Bartel and Anne Simon, eds., *Unbinding Medea* (London: MHRA, 2010), pp. 126–27.

Tumlirz, Karl, *Die tragischen Affecte Mitleid und Furcht nach Aristoteles* (first published 1885; facsimile edition, Charleston, SC: Nabu Press, 2009).

Turrettes, C., 'Une Electre moderne : *La Ville en haut de la colline* de Jean-Jacques Varoujean (1969)', *Revue d'Histoire du Théâtre*, 53, 2001, pp. 215–28.

von Rad, Gerhard, trans. D. Stalker, *Old Testament Theology*, 2 vols (Edinburgh: Oliver and Boyd, 1962–65).

Walklate, S., *Gender and Crime* (London: Harvester Wheatsheaf, 1995).

Walsh, A., *Love: The Biology behind the Heart* (New Brunswick, NJ: Transaction Publishers, 2016).

Webster, T.B.L., 'The Classical Background to Racine's *Phèdre*', in T.E. Lawrenson et al. (eds.), *Modern Miscellany presented to Eugène Vinaver* (Manchester: Manchester University Press, 1969), pp. 298–311.

Williams, Bernard, *Shame and Necessity* (Berkeley, Los Angeles and Oxford: California UP, 1993).

Wolf, Christa, trans. John Cullen, *Medea: A Modern Retelling* (London: Virago, 1998).

Wolfe, Rachel M. E., 'Woman, Tyrant, Mother, Murderess: An Exploration of the Mythic Character of Clytemnestra in all her Forms', *Women's Studies: An Interdisciplinary Journal*, 38, 2009, pp. 692–719, available online: http://dx.doi.org/10.1080/00497870903021554.

Wygant, Amy, *Medea, Magic and Modernity in France* (Aldershot: Ashgate, 2007).

Yeo, Stanley, *Unrestrained Killings and the Law: A Comparative Analysis of the Laws of Provocation and Excessive Self-defence in India, England and Australia* (Delhi/Oxford: Oxford University Press, 1998).

Index of Names and Subjects

Abraham   41, 46, 210–11
Achille(s)   70–73, 97, 130, 136, 143, 157, 158
Aegisthus   34, 130, 138, 141, 142, 144–48,
    151–52, 205
Agamemnon   1, 4, 13, 16, 17, 30–35, 41–48, 66,
    68, 71–73, 100, 109, 130, 135–45, 151–52,
    154, 157, 158, 205–08
Ahluwalia, Kiranjit   132–33, 153, 154
Anagnorisis   69, 82, 84, 90, 106, 215
Aristotle   2, 11–13, 15, 47–48, 49–69, 73–74,
    76–80, 82–83, 92, 110, 117, 134, 159, 163,
    164, 168–69
    see also Anagnorisis, Catharsis, Hamartia
Armitage, Trevor   132
Atrée   see Atreus
Atreus   2, 41–42, 46, 137, 142, 147–48, 151
Augustine of Hippo   4, 25n5, 45, 85

Baumgartner, Aurore   108, 116
Beauvoir, Simone de   43
Bradley, Andrew C.   57
Butler, Judith   8

Calvin, Jean   4
Campbell, John   28, 36n26
Candoni, Nicolas   128
Catharsis   8, 52, 56, 69, 78–79, 82, 92, 129,
    195, 215
Cleary, Phil   109n5, 134n6
Clytemnestra   1x, 4, 7, 16, 21, 28, 31, 33, 34,
    40, 41–42, 72, 109, 130–54, 205–08
Clytemnestre   see Clytemnestra
Coercive control   108, 109, 153
Corneille, Pierre   15, 35, 36–38, 60–64, 102,
    117–29, 164, 185
Corneille, Thomas   128–29
Credulity   67, 91, 95–96, 99–101

Deianeira   79, 82, 89–96, 100, 105
Déianire   See Deianeira
Delacroix, Eugène   111
Des Grieux   29–30
Determinism   82, 167
    see also Genetic, Environmental

Dilemma   12–13, 20, 30–35, 44, 66, 127, 208,
    210–11
Diminished responsibility   18, 31, 35, 46, 52,
    66, 70, 73, 82, 87, 90, 93, 99, 106, 107,
    108–29, 131, 134, 158, 159, 161, 169–70,
    189
Domon, Hélène   118–19
Duchêne, Roger   64n36, 65

Eagleton, Terry   50–51, 79, 159, 163, 183
Egisthe   see Aegisthus
Environmental determinism   8, 19, 22, 39, 51
Eriphile   25, 27, 50, 64, 67–74, 138

Fatalism   8, 9, 25–30, 31, 36, 102, 104, 136, 167,
    198, 212–13
Forgiveness   83–84, 86, 97, 106, 117, 167
Free will   22–23, 38, 41, 68–69, 84, 135

Garner, Margaret   116
Genetic determinism   8, 13, 17, 23, 39, 41–46,
    51, 118, 137–38, 186–87, 193
Gilbert, Allan H.   51

Hall, Edith   12–13, 112
Hamartia   2, 8, 15, 20, 48, 49–80, 82, 92, 117,
    134, 155, 156–57, 159, 164, 168, 182, 195,
    208, 214–15
Hammond, Paul   31–32, 109n2
Harrison, Tony   114
Helplessness   22–48, 60, 70, 90, 97, 98–100,
    103–05, 107, 127, 138, 158, 167, 169, 172,
    189, 213
Homer   34, 208
    The Iliad   98
    The Odyssey   130
Humphreys, Emma   131–32, 153
Hutton, James   51

Ignorance   2, 4, 7, 16, 21, 46, 51, 59, 69, 74,
    77–78, 81–107, 158, 166, 185, 189
Iphigenia   31, 33, 40–42, 67–69, 71–74, 130,
    134–40, 147, 148–49, 150–52, 158, 205
Iphigénie   see Iphigenia

Jansenism   7, 9, 25n5, 26, 28, 30, 35–36, 64,
     85, 121
Jason   IX, 38, 60, 108–29 *passim*
Jesus Christ   83–84

Kundera, Milan   7
Kurzel, Justin   205

La Mesnardière, Hippolyte–Jules Pinet de
     61–62, 64, 109–10, 164–68
La Taille, Jean de   61, 115, 159–63, 167, 172, 174,
     178, 183, 209–10
Lewis, Clive S.   212

Macbeth   7, 9, 17, 55, 58, 82, 99–100, 155, 158,
     176, 178, 184, 201–05, 212–14
Manon Lescaut   29–30
Medea   IX, 1, 4, 7, 15, 17, 21, 38, 51, 60–61, 90,
     106, 108–129, 155, 189
Morrison, Toni   116

Naneix, Louis-Léonard   18n27, 19n28, 75n53,
     199
Necessity   27, 31–33, 35–39, 158, 168
Noble, Thomas Satterwite   116
Nussbaum, Martha   79–80, 110n10, 182n35
Nuttall, Anthony D.   80

Œdipe   *See* Oedipus
Oedipus   1, 4, 7, 12, 13, 15, 17, 21, 25, 30, 32, 37,
     42, 53, 55–58, 63, 79, 81–84, 86–89, 100,
     102–05, 155, 157
Œnone   5–7, 10–11, 17–20, 23–24, 60, 74–75,
     77, 78, 100, 101, 185, 187, 188n, 195, 198,
     199–201
Old Testament   83
Oreste(s)   1, 4, 12, 16, 25, 27–28, 71, 130–31,
     142, 148–49, 151–52, 167
Original Sin   7, 42, 44–45, 162
Ovid   83

Pascal, Blaise   85
Peer pressure   2, 7, 52, 184
Phaedra   14, 15, 17, 46, 55, 106–07, 112, 189
     See also Phèdre
Phèdre   1, 4–7, 10–11, 13, 14, 17–20, 23–24, 32,
     34, 39, 42, 44, 55, 73–75, 77–78, 82, 101,

107, 126, 168, 185, 186–92, 195, 199–201,
     202, 203
Poetic justice   3, 8, 9, 26, 54, 59, 62, 78, 80,
     159, 164, 166, 168, 180
Poole, Adrian   51
Predestination   7
Provocation   52, 82, 87, 90, 108–09, 111, 113,
     116, 130–54
Prévost, l'abbé   29–30

Racine, Jean   1, 3–4, 7–9, 10–11, 17–18, 20,
     23, 25–30, 32, 35, 39–42, 45, 46, 49–50,
     54–56, 60, 64–79, 80, 82, 85, 99, 101,
     107, 121, 126, 128, 134, 135–38, 164, 167,
     168–69, 178, 186–201, 212
     see also Index of Plays

Sartre, Jean-Paul   39
     see also Index of Plays
Saul (King of Israel)   155–83
Scapegoats   2, 5, 7, 13, 19, 21, 42, 46, 66, 77,
     100n37, 113, 139–41, 184–215
Schweitzer, Zoé   124n46, 126n50, 127n52
Seneca   7, 9, 36, 38, 119
     see also Index of Plays
Shakespeare Behind Bars   4
Shakespeare, William   X, 4, 8, 15, 38, 39, 44,
     54, 57, 99–101, 109, 176, 200, 201–05
     see also Index of Plays
Short, J.P. (Pat)   26–28, 36n26
Soare, Antoine   196–97
Socrates   105, 107
Stoicism   9, 36, 38–39, 102, 121

Tantale   *see* Tantalus
Tantalus   130, 152
Thornton, Sara   132, 133, 134, 153, 154
Thurber, James   204
Thyeste(s)   41–42, 63, 137, 151

Williams, Bernard   20
Wolf, Christa   113–14
Wright, Geoffrey   201, 205
Wygant, Amy   111n12, 117

Index of Plays

Aeschylus
    Agamemnon   30–33, 43–44, 47, 205–08
    The Choephori   131, 146
    The Eumenides   131
Anouilh, Jean
    Médée   111, 119
    Tu étais si gentil quand tu étais petit   109,
        146–49

Bernstein, Leonard
    West Side Story   1–2
Bèze, Théodore de
    Abraham sacrifiant   41, 210–11

Charpentier, Marc-Antoine
    Médée (opera)   128–29
Cherubini, Luigi
    Médée (opera)   129
Cocteau, Jean
    La Machine infernale   104–05
Corneille, Pierre
    Médée   38, 60–61, 117–18, 119–29, 185
    OEdipe   36–38, 102
    Polyeucte   64
Corneille, Thomas
    Médée (libretto)   128–29

Du Ryer, Pierre
    Lucrèce   24, 186
    Saül   25, 163–68, 174

Euripides
    Alcmaeon   11–13
    Bacchae   47, 82, 98
    Electra   130–31, 142
    Heracles   82, 96–97
    Hippolytos   55, 106, 107
    Medea   106, 111–16, 119, 126

Gide, André
    OEdipe   104
    Saül   177, 180–82, 183
Giraudoux, Jean
    Electre   138–41, 154
Giraudoux, Jean-Pierre

Electre   151–52
Grillparzer, Franz
    Medea   119

Ionesco, Eugène
    Macbett   201

Kennelly, Brendan
    Euripides' Medea   119, 122
Kurosawa, Akira
    Throne of Blood (film)   202

Lamartine, Alphonse de
    Saül   177–80
La Taille, Jean de
    Saül le furieux   155n1, 159–63, 173, 174, 183,
        209–10
Longepierre, Hilaire-Bernard de Requeleyne
    de
    Médée   110–11, 128

Marlow, Christopher
    Dr Faustus   59
Miller, Arthur
    Death of a Salesman   7, 184

Nadal, Augustin
    Saül   168–75

Racine, Jean
    Alexandre le Grand   25, 26
    Andromaque   9, 25, 27–28, 65–67, 71
    Athalie   41, 45–46, 82, 212
    Bérénice   25, 27, 28, 74n52, 138
    Britannicus   9, 67, 193–95, 195–97
    Esther   212
    Iphigénie   25, 27, 40, 41–42, 67–74, 135–38
    La Thébaïde   25, 30
    Mithridate   25, 27, 28
    Phèdre   4–7, 10–11, 17–20, 23–24, 26, 32,
        36, 39–40, 42, 44, 55, 60, 73, 74–79,
        82, 100, 101, 107, 184, 185, 186–93, 195,
        197–201, 203
Raine, Craig
    1953   66

Rotrou, Jean
    Hercule mourant   82, 89, 92–96

Sartre, Jean-Paul
    Les Mouches   141
Seneca
    Hercules furens   82, 96–97
    Hercules Oetaeus   82, 89, 92–93
    Medea   38n, 110–11, 116, 119, 121, 125–26
    Oedipus   89
Shakespeare, William
    A Midsummer Night's Dream   192n13
    A Winter's Tale   44, 109
    Hamlet   7, 180, 212
    King Lear   38–39, 44
    Love's Labour's Lost   35
    Macbeth   IX, 7, 9, 55–56, 59, 82, 99, 155, 158, 176–77, 184, 201–05, 212–14
    Othello   IX, 11, 82, 100, 184, 212
    Richard II   39
    Romeo and Juliet   11
Sophocles
    Ajax   97
    Electra   207

Oedipus at Colonus   81, 86–89, 105–06
Oedipus tyrannos   32, 55–56, 57–58, 82–84, 86–89
The Women of Trachis   46–47, 82, 89–92, 105–06

Tabori, George
    M   114
Teevan, Colin
    Alcmaeon in Corinth   11–13

Varoujean, Jean-Jacques
    La Ville en haut de la colline   149–51
Voltaire
    OEdipe   102–04
    Saül   175–77, 183

Williams, Tennessee
    A Streetcar Named Desire   7, 82, 184

Yourcenar, Marguerite
    Clytemnestre, ou Le Crime   143–46, 154
    Electre, ou La Chute des masques   142–43, 154